THE BIG PARTY COOKBOOK

The publisher would like to thank the following for their assistance during the photography of this book: Armadillo, Australian Mushroom Growers' Association, Barbara's House and Garden, Barbecues Galore, Catering Aids Proprietary Limited, Cebu Cane, Companion, Covered Barbecues of Australia, Cray & Seeley, Crown Corning, Dalsonware, Dansab Proprietary Limited, Decor Gifts, Deeko, Elof Hansson, Fitz and Floyd, Fred Pazotti, General Electric, Georg Jensen, Glass Artist, Grace Brothers Proprietary Limited, Hale Imports Proprietary Limited, Hygienic-Lily, Johnsons Overalls, Kabuki Shop, Kitchen Plus, Klimbim Kitchenware, Kosta Boda, Lifestyle Products Proprietary Limited, Made Where, Marimekko, Market Imports, Orrefors, Penfold Wines, Peters Gifts of Kensington, Phillips & House Group, Rinnai, Stanley Rogers Silver Cutlery, Teddy & Friends, The Bay Tree Kitchen Shop, The Wild Flower Farm, United Distillers, Vasa Agencies, Villa Italiana, Villeroy & Boch (Aust) Proprietary Limited, Weber of Adelaide, Wedgwood.

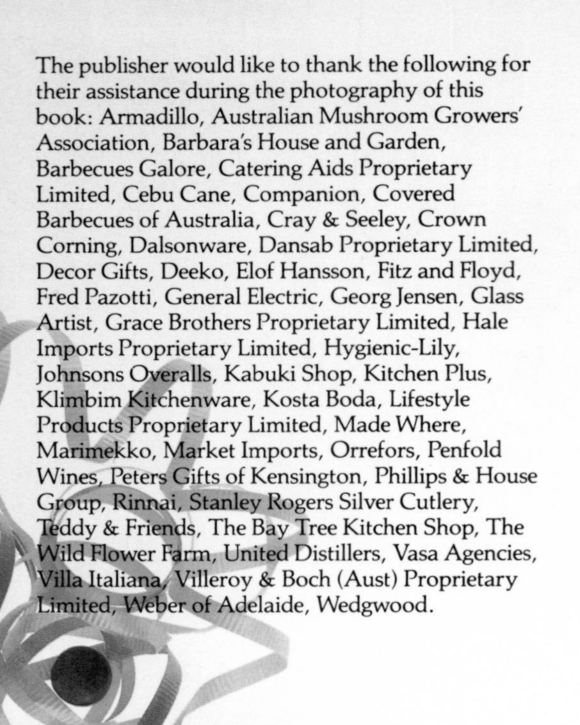

This edition specially produced for CEEPI/Dealerfield Ltd in 1989
ISBN 1-86256-409-4

Published by Bay Books
61-69 Anzac Parade,
Kensington NSW 2033

Publisher: George Barber

Photography: Ashley Barber, John Garth and Norm Nicholls
Additional photos: Alan Foley Photographic Library
Food presentation and styling: Elizabeth Carden, Karen Davidson, Kay Francis and Voula Kyprianou
BBC87
Printed in Singapore by Toppan Printing Company.

THE BIG PARTY COOKBOOK

Jane Aspinwall Digby Bignell
Fiorella de Boos Smith
Christine Heaslip Voula Kyprianou
Duske Teape-Davis
Jan Wunderlich

CAXTON

CONTENTS

Let's Have A Party	6
Time to Celebrate	14
Children of All Ages	60
Barbecue Entertaining Outdoors	100
Specially Healthy Parties	140
Brunches, Lunches and Dinner Parties	178
Elegant Afternoon Teas and Late-Night Suppers	214
The Cocktail Hour	246
Drinks for All	268
Special Occasion Menus	272
Glossary	294
Index	297

LET'S HAVE A PARTY!

Any reason for a party is a good reason. Whether you're celebrating a very special affair such as a wedding or anniversary in grand style, or simply in the mood for sharing a good time with those you care about, having a party is one of the best ways to socialise and enjoy life.

The art of entertaining well depends on planning and experience. If you're a first time party giver, you'll probably feel a few doubts about your organisational abilities. Don't fret, simply opt for an easy party outdoors such as a picnic or a barbecue, which involve a minimum of fuss and bother. Each time you entertain you'll gain more confidence until you can branch out into something more complicated. For the experienced host, you might like more of a challenge, such as a fancy cocktail party or a formal dinner dance.

This book offers you a guide to organising a wide range of parties from dazzling cocktail receptions to bright and breezy brunches. Each chapter outlines clever menus, hints, ideas and instructions that are easy to follow and fun to adapt to your own particular party style. When it all comes together we hope you discover that entertaining is not only an art form, it's a joy!

THE RIGHT MIX OF PEOPLE

What makes some parties buzz with excitement and fun while others tend to fizz out in unfulfilled expectation? Mostly, it's the blend of people that determines the life of the party. Too many talkers and not enough listeners can result in a loud and obnoxious group who are continually fighting for centre stage, while a thoughtful bunch of philosophers will most likely spend the night mumbling into their beards! Mix interests, lifestyles and age groups till you have a marvellous medley from all walks of life — then watch the conversation crackle!

If you're an inexperienced host, do yourself a favour and avoid a large gathering; invite only those friends and family you feel comfortable with. If disaster does strike (and one day, dear reader, it will), at least with a team of friendly faces around you, you will be able to grin and bear it!

WHAT SORT OF PARTY CAN YOU AFFORD?

As with most things in life, the type and size of your party usually depends on your finances. When you set down your party budget, list all the expensive items such as food, drink, decorations and flowers, invitations, equipment rentals (chairs, glassware, cutlery, lighting, etc.) and proceed to eliminate those you can. If your mother, sister or next door neighbour has a particularly splendid garden full of blooms, they may let you select a few for decorative purposes, and you'll probably be able to borrow extra seating from friends and family.

Drawing up a guest list to suit your budget can be difficult. How do you possibly *not* invite one couple when you've decided to invite others? This is always a personal dilemma but if you're tactful and graceful, you shouldn't harm too many friendships. Consider scaling down other areas of expense in order to accommodate an extra guest or two . . . often, it's the only real solution.

INVITATIONS

An informal party calls for little more than a quick telephone call or a casual mention at your next encounter. More formal occasions — weddings, engagements and christenings for example, will always call for a letter or invitation card. You can make these yourself if you have the time and creativity; your guests will be pleased with your extra thoughtfulness and find it an invitation hard to refuse. Make sure you specify all the vital information: date, time, address, type of party, attire (formal, informal, fancy dress or 'come as you are'), telephone number, reply address and an RSVP date. If you're holding the party at an unusual venue that may be unfamiliar to the guests, it's always wise to include a map or directions. Try to issue post and telephone invitations on the same day, so that no one will feel they're an afterthought. And if you do suddenly remember someone you had left off the list, don't try to make excuses; just issue a casual 'Are you free on such-and-such for a little get together I'm having?' Don't make a fuss and you'll be saved from embarrassment.

CONSIDER A THEME

Consider special effects for both formal and casual occasions: you can go all the way and ask your guests to dress up appropriately, or simply use the theme as a way of linking food, music, lighting and venue. Possible themes might be Sixties, gangster, Australiana, any nationality, colour (e.g. black and white), buffet, formal, beach, riverside picnic. If holding a fancy dress party, make sure you give your guests plenty of time to invent their costumes. Remember, a theme gives people something to focus on; it can make planning easier for you and the party much more unusual and exciting for your guests.

CHILDREN

Always be prepared for entertaining children. They usually don't want to be part of the adults' party so try to give them something amusing to do on their own. Videos and popcorn can be very useful.

If you have children of your own, ask friends to bring theirs along — this way you won't have to worry about your brood getting bored and your guests will save on babysitting costs.

Babies should be in a convenient bedroom away from the noise but near the parents, who'll probably spend all night ducking in and out to check on them.

NEIGHBOURS

People and parties inevitably mean noise — sometimes more noise than you had anticipated! Show your neighbours some consideration by observing noise pollution curfews if they apply in your neighbourhood. Ask rowdy guests to move inside the house where more noise can be absorbed; issue guests with parking suggestions if off-street sites are limited and make sure they don't encroach on your neighbours' private land. The best neighbour-taming method is to invite your immediate neighbours to join in — they may decline the invitation but appreciate it anyway.

MENU PLANNING

There's no need to spend hours in the kitchen in order to provide spectacular party fare: all you need is the right mix of food and a little care in its presentation. Visualise the food and drink you intend to serve as a painting — look for balance and harmony in colour, taste and texture. Choose exciting and different ways to garnish plates and serving dishes as this can make all the difference to the 'eye appeal' of the food, no matter how tasty it is.

Your main guidelines for menu planning should be based around the occasion itself; what's good fare for one party may be inappropriate for another. Never experiment with new dishes on the day or night of the party — always stick with tried and true successes (but not the same dish over and over to the same guests, please!) or have a test run a week before. Combine interesting flavours and colours, and watch for too much soft or too much hard food served together.

PLAN AHEAD

Do try to make things easy for yourself by doing as much preparation ahead of time as possible. All-important mood setters like lighting and music, should be thought about well in advance, leaving no room for last minute panic. Decorations such as flowers can be arranged the day before. Easy-to-prepare-and-serve foods will leave the host more relaxed and able to enjoy the occasion just as much as the guests. Many dishes can be frozen successfully, leaving only garnishes to be added. The better the planning, the greater your enjoyment will be.

A stunning party menu is achieved by careful planning and attention to detail

Glasses:- Which One For Which Drink?

The ideal glass is one that shows its contents to best advantage; coloured glassware may look pretty but it can hide what's inside and may raise doubts in the drinkers' minds as to what they are about to consume! Certain drinks like wine require specific shapes in order to appreciate the taste and bouquet, while other beverages must be handled delicately during both pouring and drinking (such as champagne), so the glassware should accommodate this need.

The diagram below illustrates basic shapes and the drinks commonly served in them. For home entertaining you should aim to have 8–12 of each of the basics and a set of extras if you wish. Greater quantities of any type are available from any hire outlets.

PROPER CLEANING

After use, your glassware should be washed separately from all other plates and utensils in warm to hot soapy water — beer glasses are an exception to this rule as soap suds will leave tiny traces of detergent which cause the beer to go flat very quickly. Always check glassware when dry for waterstains and avoid fingerprints by polishing the bowl of the glass while holding its base or stem.

HIRING

These days the options are incredible. You can hire anything from cups to camels! The advantages of hiring are obvious. Firstly, because of the range of food, music and decorations available for hire, you can give the kind of party you'd never be able to arrange all by yourself.

Most importantly, hiring can save you enormous amounts of time and trouble. You can hire staff to act as waiters and cleaners, leaving you free to enjoy the party.

A word about breakages: In virtually every instance, the hirer is responsible for damages and breakages. And, while all companies will have some form of public liability insurance (if, for example, someone trips over a marquee rope and hurts themselves) you may also like to insure yourself.

All companies will deliver and most expect cash on delivery. If you employ a catering company, they will expect a substantial deposit some time before the date of the party.

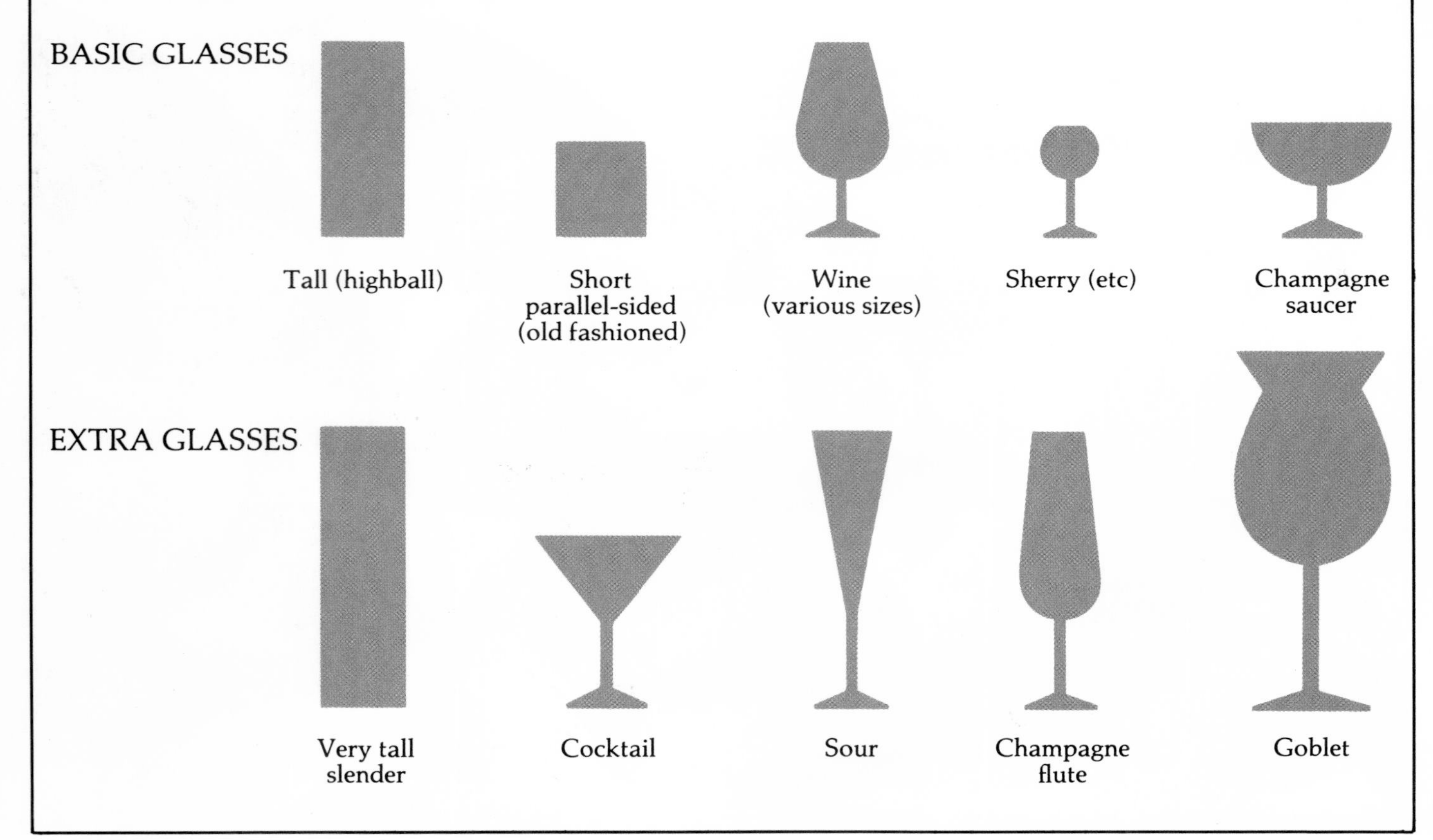

The At-a-Glance Stain Removal Guide

You'll be lucky if you escape a large party without some minor damage to your furnishings. The most common mishaps are food and drink stains. Here's a guide to quick clean ups.

SOURCE	REMOVAL METHOD
Beer	Warm water and detergent; if stain persists after second application, try a 50/50 peroxide and water solution, — use on pale coloured furnishings only
Blood (fresh)	Cold water and mild soap
Blood (dried)	Warm to hot water and soap
Chocolate	Warm water and detergent
Coffee	Warm water and detergent; if stain persists, use a mild bleach solution.
Cosmetics	Dry cleaning fluid
Fruit juice	Warm water and soap; glycerine for second application.
Grass stains	Methylated spirit; glycerine on second application.
Gravy	Hot water and soap; dry cleaning fluid on second application
Grease	Dry cleaning fluid
Ice-cream	Hot water and soap; dry cleaning fluid on second application
Mustard	Dry cleaning fluid or methylated spirit
Oils	Hot water and soap; dry cleaning fluid
Sauces (bottled)	Glycerine; peroxide and water solution on second application
Soft drinks	Hot water and detergent; dry cleaning fluid on second application.
Urine, Vomit	Hot water and detergent
Wine (red)	Salt rubbed into fresh spill followed by glycerine
Wine (white)	Warm water and mild soap; glycerine on second application.

It's worth noting that most fresh stains will yield to detergent and hot water. Take action to treat carpet stains quickly as they may become permanent if allowed to dry. If you don't discover stains until the day after the party, try using a commercial carpet cleaning powder for an extended time. Beware using solvents and spirits on synthetic fabrics and carpets as chemicals may cause damage; try a small test patch in an inconspicuous corner first.
Be sure to work the stain removing solution into the stain and blot excess remover from carpet or fabric. Use only small amounts for some chemicals can rot carpet backings if the patch is saturated. Always keep stain removal chemicals well out of reach of children — most are toxic and flammable.

The Disaster-proof Party Checklist

TIMETABLE	BASIC ORGANISATION	FOOD SHOPPING AND COOKING SCHEDULE
Two to three weeks before:	Issue invitations by mail or telephone; keep a list to tick off acceptances and regrets	Select possible recipes for menu; mark for future reference
Ten days before:	Select bar beverages and serving styles Work out seating arrangements (if needed) and table decorations Decide on house decorations Choose entertainment and assess equipment in hand Check tableware and list specific needs such as candles, place cards, vases, etc. Assess house and yard for any major or minor repairs Make a list of helpers that may be required such as florists, liquor store, window cleaners, baby sitters and equipment hire outlets. Book them if needed	Draw up food shopping list from definite menu; assemble necessary utensils, serving ware; check that all pieces are in good working order Check that all kitchen needs are supplied such as paper towels, plastic and foil food wrap, cleaning agents, wash cloths, etc. Add to shopping list if necessary
One week before:	Arrange pick up and delivery of all hired and ordered goods Telephone those who have not responded to invitations; make last minute invitations to others if necessary	Prepare any food that can be frozen without losing flavour or texture (e.g. casseroles) Polish special serving pieces if necessary Shop for non-perishable foodstuffs and other items such as decorations
Two days before:	Do major house cleaning and repair jobs; cut lawns, clean windows and doors Prepare glassware and tableware Confirm deliveries	Shop for rest of foodstuffs except seafood (wait till early on the day itself) Double check that shopping list is complete
Day before:	Lay out guest rooms if required Set up bar and rearrange furniture if necessary Set table basics such as linen and cutlery	Make any dishes that require setting in the refrigerator Bake cakes, bread or rolls (leave pastry till the party day)
Early on the day:	Check that entertainment and sound equipment is set Add flowers and last minute decorations to house and tables Check bar has adequate ice, glassware, coasters and snacks available Set out ashtrays	Prepare bases for sauces, gravies, prepare vegetables, fill bread baskets Assemble and begin preparing any dish that requires long cooking times List all dishes and accompaniments and place the list in a prominent place in the kitchen; prepare dessert if possible
One hour before:	Check that all seating and eating arrangements are in order Give yourself at least 20 minutes to get dressed	Line up all salads and vegetable dishes ready for final cooking and/or presentation Check that the first course is almost ready to be served (it should be served around 30 minutes after guests have arrived)
Party time:	Forget anything that hasn't been done already — you won't miss it! Pour yourself a drink, relax and smile!	Arrange first course on serving ware.

WEIGHTS AND MEASURES

DRY INGREDIENTS

Metric	Imperial
15 g	½ oz
30 g	1 oz
60 g	2 oz
90 g	3 oz
125 g	4 oz (¼ lb)
155 g	5 oz
185 g	6 oz
220 g	7 oz
250 g	8 oz (½ lb)
280 g	9 oz
315 g	10 oz
345 g	11 oz
375 g	12 oz (¾ lb)
410 g	13 oz
440 g	14 oz
470 g	15 oz
500 g	16 oz (1 lb)
750 g	24 oz (1½ lb)
1000 g (1 kg)	32 oz (2 lb)

CUP MEASURES

1 cup	=	250 mL
½ cup	=	125 mL
⅓ cup	=	80 mL
¼ cup	=	60 mL

LIQUIDS

Metric	Imperial
30 mL	1 fl oz
60 mL (¼ cup)	2 fl oz (¼ cup)
100 mL	3 fl oz
125 mL (½ cup)	4 fl oz (½ cup)
150 mL	5 fl oz (¼ pt)
185 mL (¾ cup)	6 fl oz (¾ cup)
250 mL (1 cup)	8 fl oz (1 cup)
300 mL (1¼ cups)	10 fl oz (½ pt)
360 mL (1½ cups)	12 fl oz (1½ cups)
420 mL (1¾ cups)	14 fl oz (1¾ cups)
500 mL (2 cups)	16 fl oz (2 cups)
625 mL (2½ cups)	20 fl oz (1 pt)

LENGTHS

Metric	Imperial
5 mm	¼ in
1 cm	½ in
2 cm	¾ in
2.5 cm	1 in
5 cm	2 in
6 cm	2½ in
8 cm	3 in
10 cm	4 in
12 cm	5 in
15 cm	6 in
18 cm	7 in
20 cm	8 in
23 cm	9 in
25 cm	10 in
28 cm	11 in
30 cm	12 in
46 cm	18 in
50 cm	20 in
61 cm	24 in
77 cm	30 in

SPOON MEASURES

1 tablespoon	=	20 mL
1 teaspoon	=	5 mL
½ teaspoon	=	2.5 mL
¼ teaspoon	=	1.25 mL

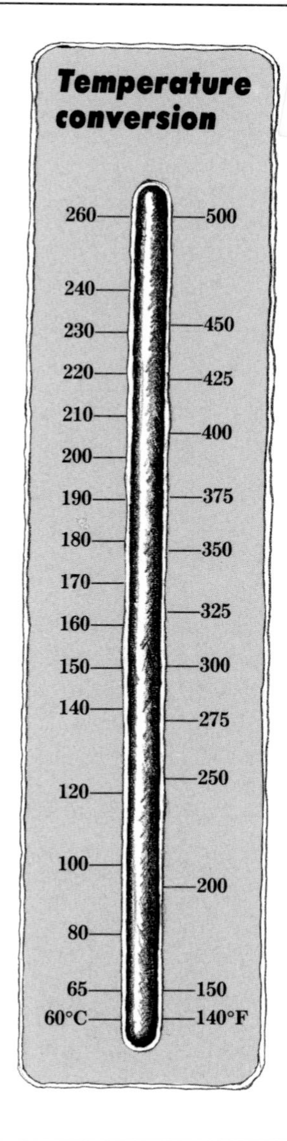

OVEN TEMPERATURE CHART	C	F	Gas Mark
Very Slow	110	225	¼
	120	250	½
Slow	140	275	1
	150	300	2
Moderate	160	325	3
	180	350	4
Moderately hot	190	375	5
	200	400	6
Hot	220	425	7
	230	450	8
Very hot	250	475	9

TIME TO CELEBRATE

Special occasions — such as birthdays anniversaries, weddings and homecomings — warrant extra-special celebrations. Now is the time for a grand affair with all the finery and trimmings.

You may find yourself with a large guest list. Don't despair — just make detailed plans, delegate to willing friends and family and try to do as much ahead of time as possible. After all, you want to enjoy the party, too!

The occasion itself will set the mood or the theme of the party. 'Landmark' birthdays for children and adults honour one special person, while traditional celebrations and religious festivals such as Christmas, tend to have customs and special foods of their own.

Whatever the occasion, make this special day one to remember by dressing up your home with fresh flowers, plants and decorations — extra attention to detail really welcomes people.

Take care with your invitations — they are your guest's first indication of the type of celebration involved. Whether you choose a quick telephone call or a printed invitation, make sure all your guests are aware of the style of party.

Red letter days call for spectacular food that tastes as good as it looks. Buffets work best for big crowds or serve bite-sized snacks and finger foods from trays. Sit-down meals for special occasions require good co-ordination and timing and a reasonably large kitchen — if you haven't got what it takes, enlist help: order extra courses from a restaurant or hire some kitchen assistance.

If you wish to use formal seating arrangements, the host and hostess usually sit at either end of the table; the guest of honour or eldest guest is seated to the hostess' right; to her left is the next VIP (the guest of honour's spouse or partner) and from there, it's customary to separate partners diagonally across the table for a good social mixture. However, seating arrangements are best when everyone feels comfortable — including you!

Canapes and antipasto make a tasty start to a special occasion

Hors d'Oeuvres

ANTIPASTO

Italians are great lovers of antipasto (literally 'before the meal') and travellers to Italy never fail to gasp on entering the best restaurants at the beautiful displays of antipasto colourfully arranged on special tables.

A good antipasto can be prepared from products bought ready from the delicatessen or the fish market, such as a platter of best quality salami or coppa, some shiny olives, a few hearts of artichokes preserved in oil, fresh oysters presented just with lemon (in Italy oysters are an expensive delicacy and only a maximum of six per person is served), prawns, crab, mussels open and served raw in their shell, mangoes decorating a plate of thinly sliced ham, smoked salmon — the list could go on.

Antipasto should be presented in small portions, to stimulate the appetite, and should always be arranged as pleasantly as possible to put the diner in a good mood, and reassure him or her as to the quality of the cooking to follow.

CANAPES

Canapes provide a bite-sized starter to any party. Remove crusts from white, wholemeal or rye bread. Toast or pan-fry bread slices. Brown both sides. Cut bread slices into 2.5 cm squares, rounds or use a small scone or biscuit cutter to cut bread into shapes. Allow toasted bread shapes to cool.

Cheese pastry shapes can be made as an alternative to bread shapes. Make a quantity of cheese pastry, roll out thinly, cut into various shapes and bake. A variety of savoury crackers can also be used.

TASTY TOPPINGS

SMOKED OYSTER

1 quantity Spicy Sardine Topping (see recipe)
105 g can smoked oysters or *mussels*
finely chopped parsley, to garnish

Butter toast as for Spicy Sardine Canapes. Top each with smoked oyster or mussel. Sprinkle with finely chopped parsley.
Makes ⅔ cup

Mixed Antipasto

CREAM CHEESE

250 g cream cheese, softened
105 g can drained, smoked oysters or
¼ cup finely chopped pecans and
pinch cayenne pepper or
¼ cup finely chopped chicken meat and
pinch dry mustard and
1 tablespoon chopped parsley
parsley, fresh herbs or *watercress, to garnish*

Combine ingredients, spread on toasts or crackers and garnish.
Makes approximately 1¼ cups

SPICY SARDINE

60 g butter
1½ teaspoons lemon juice
1½ teaspoons prepared mustard
sardines and *pimiento, to garnish*

Combine ingredients and spread toast or crackers with mixture. Top with half a sardine and a thin strip pimiento.
Makes ⅓ cup

SAVOURY BUTTERS

125 g butter, softened
1 teaspoon lemon juice
¼ teaspoon paprika
1 tablespoon anchovy paste or
30 g blue vein cheese or
½ teaspoon finely chopped chilli or
30 g minced smoked salmon
parsley, olives, watercress or *fresh herbs, to garnish*

Combine butter, lemon juice and paprika with 1 of the optional extras, beating well. Spread toast or crackers with butter. Garnish with parsley, olives, watercress or fresh herb sprig.
Makes ½ cup

OYSTER CHEESE PUFFS

125 g butter
1½ cups grated tasty cheese
2 teaspoons sherry
1 egg, separated
2 × 105 g cans smoked oysters, drained
32 × 4 cm bread rounds
1 tablespoon finely chopped parsley
paprika, to taste

Beat butter, cheese and sherry together. Add egg yolk and blend well. Whisk egg white till soft peaks form. Fold egg white into cheese mixture.

Place 1 oyster on each round of bread. Top with a teaspoonful of cheese mixture. Sprinkle with chopped parsley and paprika. Place on oven trays. Bake at 230°C (45°F) for 10 minutes and serve piping hot.
Makes 32

PRAWN AND CHEESE PASTRIES

PASTRY
1½ cups flour
pinch salt
100 g butter
½ cup grated cheese
2 tablespoons cold water

FILLING
½ cup chopped cooked prawns
1 cup grated tasty cheese
1 tablespoon chopped leek
4 eggs
½ cup cream
½ cup milk
pinch mustard powder
grated rind 1 lemon
salt and pepper, to taste

Preheat oven to 190°C (375°F). Sift flour and salt into a bowl. Rub in butter to resemble breadcrumbs. Mix in cheese and sufficient water to form a soft dough. Knead lightly on floured board. Roll out thinly and cut into 24 × 6 cm rounds to fit patty tins.

Press pastry gently into base of tins. Place small amount of chopped prawns into base of pastry. Top with portion each of cheese and leek. Blend together eggs, cream, milk, mustard, lemon rind, salt and pepper. Spoon egg mixture over prawns and cheese.

Bake pies at 190°C (375°F) for 15–20 minutes or until golden and puffy. Serve hot or cold.
Makes 24

FILO DELIGHTS

1 × 375 g packet filo pastry
200 g butter, melted

SEAFOOD FILLING
¼ cup cottage cheese
220 g can crabmeat, drained
2 shallots, chopped
salt and pepper, to taste

SPINACH CHEESE FILLING
4 leaves spinach, shredded and cooked
1 small onion, chopped
30 g feta cheese, crumbled
½ teaspoon lemon juice
pepper, to taste

CHILLI MEAT FILLING
125 g cooked minced meat
1 tablespoon chilli sauce or to taste
1 small onion, chopped

CREAM CHEESE FILLING
125 g cream cheese, softened
2 shallots (spring onions), chopped
salt and pepper, to taste

To prepare the fillings, combine ingredients adjusting seasoning as necessary.

Place pastry between 2 dry tea towels and cover with a just damp tea towel. Take 2 sheets of pastry and place 1 on top of the other. Cut pastry into 6 pieces, across the width. Brush each piece of pastry with a little butter.

Place a teaspoonful of selected filling in left-hand corner of pastry. Fold other corner of pastry up to cover filling to form a triangle shape. Fold left-hand corner up to form second triangle. Continue folding in triangles to the end of the pastry. Brush with melted butter. Repeat with remaining pastry and fillings.

Place on baking tray. Bake at 200°C (400°F) for 15–20 minutes until golden brown. Serve hot.
Note: Filo Delights can be filled in advance. Layer uncooked triangles between sheets of plastic wrap and freeze for up to 2 weeks. Place frozen into hot oven to cook and brown.
Makes approximately 50

Filo Delights (left) and Prawn and Cheese Pastries

SUMMER ROLL

60 g butter
1 large onion, sliced thinly
3 medium-sized carrots, grated
1 bunch spinach, shredded
3 small sprigs dill or *½ teaspoon dried dill*
2 avocados, chopped
1 cup mung beans or *Chinese bean sprouts*
6 readymade puff pastry sheets

Melt butter and saute onion and carrot for 10 minutes with lid on pan, stirring occasionally. Add spinach and dill. Stir well and cook further for a few minutes until spinach is soft. Allow to cool.

Add avocados and mix well. Add sprouts.

Place filling on puff pastry sheets and roll up. Decorate with strips of pastry if desired. Place filled rolls on greased tray. Glaze pastry with milk before baking. Cook at 220°C (425°F) until lightly browned.

Note: This Summer Roll filling can also be rolled with wholemeal pastry and filo pastry.

Serves 6

CREPES

1 cup flour
salt, to taste
3 eggs, beaten
⅔ cup milk
½ cup water
10 g butter, melted
extra butter, for frying

Sift flour and salt into a bowl. Make a well in centre and add the eggs. Combine milk, water and butter and gradually combine with flour. Beat mixture until smooth and allow to stand 10 minutes before cooking.

Heat small frying pan. Grease lightly with butter. Pour 2 tablespoons mixture into pan tilting to coat evenly. Cook over moderately high heat until bubbles form and burst on surface of crepe. Turn crepe to brown. Cool 30 seconds and remove to plate. Repeat process with remaining batter, greasing pan as necessary.

Note: Crepes can be served either sweet or savoury. Sweet crepes can be sprinkled with sugar and served with lemon juice and banana; apple puree and jam; maple syrup and peach slices; strawberries and cream and/or ice cream.

Savoury crepes can be served with meat sauce; minced chicken; various seafood fillings.

Makes 12 crepes

Summer Roll

ROCK MELON STUFFED WITH CHEESE

250 g blue vein cheese
250 g cream cheese
¼ cup cream
1 rock melon, halved and seeded

Thoroughly blend cheeses together. Beat in cream until fluffy. Scoop melon balls from rock melon. Spoon cheese dip into rock melon shell. Serve with savoury biscuits and melon balls skewered on toothpicks.

Serves 4

PAWPAW WITH PRAWNS

3 cups diced, cooked prawns
3 cups grated fresh coconut
2 teaspoons chopped ginger root
4 pawpaws, peeled, halved and seeded
½ cup lime juice
preserved ginger, for garnish

Combine prawns, coconut and ginger. Pile into pawpaw halves. Spoon lime juice over prawn mixture. Garnish with thin slices of preserved ginger.

Serves 8

LYCHEE COCKTAIL

250 g lychees, peeled, halved and seeded
1 cup diced pineapple
1 cup diced orange
1 tablespoon sugar
2 teaspoons lemon juice

Combine fruits and chill for 1 hour. Add sugar and lemon juice. Serve in chilled cocktail glasses.

Serves 4

Mains

SMOKED SALMON QUICHE

PASTRY

2 cups flour
salt, to taste
125 g butter
3–4 tablespoons cold water

FILLING

185 g smoked salmon
4 egg yolks, beaten
4 whole eggs, beaten
300 mL sour cream
2 tablespoons lemon juice
¾ cup cream
½ teaspoon cayenne pepper
freshly ground pepper
½ cup grated Swiss cheese

Preheat oven to 200°C (400°F). Sift flour and salt into a bowl. Rub in butter to resemble breadcrumbs. Add sufficient water to form a soft dough. Knead lightly on floured board. Roll out dough to fit 20 cm flan tin. Prick base of case with fork. Bake pastry case for 10 minutes.

Layer salmon in pastry case. Blend egg yolks, eggs, sour cream, lemon juice, cream, cayenne and black pepper. Strain and pour into pie case. Top with grated cheese.

Bake at 190°C (375°F) for 45-60 minutes or until set and browned on top. Cut into slices and serve hot or cold.
Serves 12–16

PARISIAN LOBSTER

1 × 2 kg live crayfish or *lobster*
2 onions
5 carrots
½ cup vinegar
1 bouquet garni
½ teaspoon black peppercorns
½ medium loaf unsliced white bread
1 small turnip
90 g green beans, diced
90 g shelled peas
4 button mushrooms, chopped
60 g ham, chopped
1 small gherkin, diced
30 g capers
mayonnaise
2 × 400 g cans artichoke hearts
1 mignonette lettuce, washed
25 g aspic jelly crystals
strips of eggplant (aubergine) skin
black caviar, to garnish

Ask your fishmonger to kill crayfish. To make court bouillon, slice onions and 4 carrots and place in a large boiler with vinegar, bouquet garni, peppercorns and about 3 litres water. Bring to the boil.

Add crayfish and simmer for 20–25 minutes. Allow to cool in the liquid.

Remove crayfish and lay belly side up on a chopping board. Using a pair of scissors, carefully cut away membrane covering tail flesh and peel it back. Gently remove the tail flesh whole and slice into 6 or 8 medallions, depending on size.

Remove crust from bread and cut it diagonally into 2 triangular blocks. Arrange crayfish with a triangle of bread under its chest and head to raise it, on a large serving dish. Wrap crayfish legs around the bread.

Peel remaining carrot and turnip and dice. Drop into boiling water and cook until tender. Drain well and refresh.

Drop beans and peas into boiling water and cook until tender. Drain well and refresh.

Place mushrooms, ham and gherkin in a bowl with vegetables and capers. Stir through enough mayonnaise to bind the ingredients.

Drain artichoke hearts and carefully pat dry with paper towels. Arrange lettuce around crayfish on serving plate, ensuring all bread is covered. Prepare aspic jelly by dissolving in 2½ cups water, following packet instructions.

Place medallions of crayfish on a wire rack. Using a small star cutter or other decorative shape, cut eggplant skin into shapes. Dip into aspic and place on crayfish. Place rack over a roasting pan and spoon aspic over medallions. Allow to set.

Brush crayfish shell with remaining aspic.

Arrange medallions, in overlapping slices, down the back of the crayfish. Carefully spoon some of the vegetable mixture into the artichoke hearts, garnish with caviar and arrange around crayfish. Serve remaining vegetable mixture separately.

Note: Pre-cooked crayfish can be used. Omit poaching the crayfish in court bouillon.
Serves 6–8

Parisian Lobster

CREAMY CRAYFISH CURRY

80 g butter
1 small onion, finely chopped
1 green apple, peeled, cored and chopped
12 peppercorns
⅓ cup flour
2½ teaspoons curry powder
1 bay leaf
pinch nutmeg
2½ cups milk
2 teaspoons lemon juice
½ teaspoon Worcestershire sauce
extra 60 g butter
750 g uncooked crayfish meat, chopped
¼ cup cream
2 tablespoons sherry
1 tablespoon finely chopped parsley, to garnish

OPTIONAL ADDITIONS

20 g butter
1 cup diced carrot
1 cup frozen peas
1 red for green capsicum, diced
90 g button mushrooms

In a saucepan, heat butter and saute onion, apple and peppercorns over medium heat until onion is transparent. Add flour, curry powder, bay leaf, and nutmeg and cook for 1 minute. Stir in milk, lemon juice and Worcestershire sauce. Bring slowly to boil and simmer until mixture thickens, stirring continually. Cook 1–2 minutes longer, taste and adjust seasoning.

Strain sauce through a fine sieve, pressing vegetables against sieve to extract all sauce.

Melt extra butter in frying pan. Saute lobster meat for 3 minutes. Remove from heat and set aside. Saute any optional additions and combine with curry sauce, cream and sherry. Gently heat through and fold in lobster meat. Simmer for 2 minutes. Spoon curry into serving dish. Sprinkle with chopped parsley.
Serves 6

CURRY VARIATIONS

CURRY OF PRAWNS

Replace crayfish meat with *500g shelled uncooked prawns*
Serves 6

CURRY OF CHICKEN

Replace crayfish meat with *750 g diced chicken meat* or *1.5 kg chicken pieces*
Serves 6

PARTY CRAB CREPES

16–18 crepes (see recipe)

FILLING

20 g butter
6 mushrooms, sliced
2 tablespoons finely chopped onion
225 g crabmeat, drained
20 g extra butter
⅓ cup flour
½ teaspoon dried rosemary
salt and pepper, to taste
1½ cups chicken stock
1½ cups sour cream
1 tablespoon chopped parsley
1 cup grated Swiss cheese
paprika, to taste
parsley, to garnish

To prepare filling, melt butter in frying pan. Add mushrooms and onion and saute 3 minutes. Add crabmeat, remove pan from heat.

Melt extra butter in another saucepan. Add flour, rosemary, salt and pepper and cook, stirring constantly, for 3 minutes. Gradually stir in chicken stock, bring to boil and cook for 3 minutes. Add sour cream, parsley and ½ cup Swiss cheese. Fold in crab mixture and stir until heated through.

Allow to cool slightly. Place ¼ cup filling along centre of each crepe and roll up. Arrange fold-side down in a single layer in a baking dish. Top with remaining cheese and sprinkle with paprika. Heat in oven at 180°C (350°F) for 10–15 minutes. Garnish with parsley to serve.
Serves 16–18

Party Crab Crepes (rear) and Creamy Crayfish Curry

SEAFOOD PLATTER WITH TWO SPICY SAUCES

BEER BATTER

3 cups flour
pinch salt
2 eggs, separated
2 cups beer
1 cup milk
60 g butter, melted
oil, for deep-frying

SEAFOOD PLATTER

1.5 kg fish fillets (gemfish, whiting)
250 g calamari rings
500 g uncooked prawns, shelled and deveined
250 g scallops
lemon twists and *parsley, to garnish*

MANGO SEAFOOD SAUCE

1 small mango, peeled, seeded and sliced
1 cup sour cream
¼ cup natural mayonnaise (see note)
2 teaspoons finely grated onion
1 tablespoon finely chopped coriander

LEMON MAYONNAISE

1 cup mayonnaise
2 tablespoons lemon juice
1 tablespoon finely chopped parsley
1 teaspoon finely chopped capers
freshly ground pepper

Sift flour and salt into a bowl. Make a well in the centre and add egg yolks. Stir in a little of the surrounding flour. Combine beer, milk and melted butter. Gradually add beer mixture, beating until smooth then strain. Allow mixture to stand for at least 30 minutes. Whisk egg white until stiff and fold into batter. Use at once.

Check fish fillets for bones. Heat oil for deep-frying. Dip a few pieces of the seafood at a time into the batter. Cook 6 pieces of seafood at a time until golden brown and cooked through. Drain on paper towel and serve garnished with lemon twists and parsley.

To make Mango Seafood Sauce, place mango in a food processor and puree or press through a sieve using the back of a wooden spoon. Combine with remaining ingredients and beat until smooth. Taste and adjust seasonings if desired. Serve immediately in a sauce boat.

To make Lemon Mayonnaise, combine all ingredients in a small bowl and mix until thoroughly blended. Taste and adjust seasonings if desired. Serve in a sauce boat.

Note: Natural mayonnaise has no preservatives or artificial food colourings. It can be purchased from delicatessens and supermarkets.

Serves 10

PAELLA

250 g calamari
4–6 chicken thighs
salt and pepper, to taste
½ teaspoon paprika
3 tablespoons oil
1½ cups water
1 cup dry white wine
1 bay leaf
125 g chorizo, sliced diagonally
2 green capsicum
4 tomatoes, peeled, seeded and chopped
1 onion, chopped
pinch saffron threads
¾ cup long-grain rice
500 g medium or large uncooked prawns
300 g mussels, scrubbed and cleaned

Pull out and discard intestines of calamari. Cut off tentacles and set aside. Discard 'feather' from calamari, then rinse and rub off skin. Rinse again.

Season chicken thighs with salt, pepper and paprika. Heat oil in a heavy-based frying pan. Cook chicken in oil until golden on both sides. Reduce heat. Carefully cover with water, white wine and bayleaf and simmer 15 minutes. Drain chicken and strain 2 cups of cooking liquid.

Add chorizo to pan and cook for 4 minutes, turning. Add prepared calamari, capsicum, tomato, onion and saffron. Cover and cook over a gentle heat for 10 minutes, stirring occasionally.

Sprinkle rice over vegetables and pour in 1½ cups strained cooking liquid. Bring to boil, reduce heat and simmer, covered, for 20 minutes, stirring occasionally.

Place mussels, prawns and chicken thighs in rice. Test rice and add more stock if necessary. Cover and cook over a gentle heat until rice is tender and mussels and prawns cooked. Serve from the dish.

Note: Chorizo is a Spanish sausage. If unavailable substitute a peppery salami.

Serves 4–6

Paella

FILLETS OF FISH IN SANGRIA SAUCE

12 whiting fillets
½ cup flour
salt and pepper, to taste
2 tablespoons lemon juice
60 g butter
juice ½ orange
1 tablespoon orange zest
¼ cup rose or *white wine*
2 egg yolks, beaten
cayenne pepper, to taste
¼ cup cream
1 tablespoon chopped parsley
5 g extra butter
peel from 1 orange, cut in fine strips and blanched

Coat fish fillets in combined flour, salt and pepper. Combine half the lemon juice and half the butter in frying pan. Heat till butter melts. Fry 6 fish fillets, 2 minutes on each side. Set fish fillets aside on platter. Drain juices from pan. Heat remaining lemon juice and butter and fry remaining fish fillets. When cooked, place on serving platter, cover with aluminium foil and keep warm in oven.

Combine orange juice, zest and white wine in top of double saucepan. Bring to boil, then reduce heat to simmer. Add egg yolks and cayenne, stirring until thickened. Remove pan from heat.

Stir in cream, parsley and butter. Pour sauce over fish fillets and serve garnished with orange strips.

Serves 6

CUBAN-STYLE FISH

1 × 2 kg whole snapper
2 litres fish stock
2 large ripe avocados
2 tablespoons olive oil
juice 2–3 limes or *1½ lemons*
½ small onion, grated
salt and pepper, to taste
extra limes, to garnish

Wipe fish, check for scales and clean body cavity if necessary.

Place stock in roasting tin or other pan large enough to take fish. Place over 2 burners and bring to simmering point.

Place fish in stock, cover with foil and poach 30 minutes or until fish is tender when tested. Carefully lift fish from stock, drain and place on a serving plate.

Cuban-style Fish

When snapper is cool enough to handle, remove the top layer of skin. Cover fish and refrigerate until serving time.

Halve, pit and peel the avocados. Puree and add oil, lime juice, onion and salt and pepper. Beat well, taste and adjust seasoning as necessary. Return avocado seeds to the sauce to prevent it turning black, cover and refrigerate.

When preparing dish for serving, remove avocado seeds, spread some of the sauce thickly and evenly over fish. Garnish with slices of lime and serve remaining slices separately.

Serves 4–6

1 Carefully place fish in stock to poach

2 Remove top layer of skin

3 Spread avocado sauce thickly over fish

VEGETABLE GARDEN IN A CHICKEN

1 × 1.5 kg chicken
salt and pepper, to taste
Madeira
½ cup sliced carrots
½ cup diced turnips
½ cup diced celery
white part of 1 leek
½ cup string beans 5 cm long
½ cup diced mushrooms
350 g lean veal
75 g veal kidney or *chicken liver*
½ cup cream
2 lengths muslin, 50 × 100 cm
1 large oven bag

Cut down the back of chicken and remove carcase, leaving wings and drumsticks but removing thigh bone. Season with salt, pepper and a little Madeira. Set aside.

Put chicken bones with trimmings of vegetables in a large saucepan with 1 litre water and make a stock. Place carrots, turnips, celery and leek in boiling salt water to cover for 3 minutes. Strain and refresh. Cook beans in boiling salt water for 3 minutes, strain and refresh. While vegetables are cooling, finely mince veal and kidney. In a bowl over ice, blend cream, salt and pepper. Lay chicken out on dampened muslin.

Fill centre with layers of prepared vegetables and meats. Lay leek in the middle of stuffing, lengthwise, roll muslin up like a sausage, very tightly around sides of chicken, so it resembles the original shape. Fasten at both ends with string. Place into oven bag with Madeira. Punch several holes in top of bag. Poach in strained stock for 1 hour. Remove and leave in bag for 30 minutes before unrolling muslin and serve with a chicken veloute sauce enriched with cream and Madeira on a bed of rice.

If serving this dish cold, remove muslin after cooking, lightly brush chicken with oil, and rewrap in clean muslin as before. If muslin is not changed it will dry on the chicken skin and the skin will come off when untied.
Serves 5–6

AVOCADO CHICKEN CASSEROLE

1.5 kg chicken, cut into portions
¼ cup flour
salt and pepper, to taste
60 g butter
¼ cup white wine
2 avocados
1 tablespoon lemon juice
extra 60 g butter
1¼ cups flour
1½ cups cream
¾ cup milk
100 g cooked noodles
125 g grated tasty cheese
2 tablespoons finely chopped parsley and *paprika, to garnish*

Remove skin from chicken portions. Coat chicken in combination of flour, salt and pepper.

Melt butter in frying pan and brown chicken on all sides. Add wine and cover frying pan with lid. Simmer chicken for 30 minutes.

Peel avocado. Remove seed and slice thinly. Coat avocado with lemon juice and set aside.

Melt extra butter, add flour and cook 3 minutes, stirring. Gradually cream and milk; cook, stirring until thickened. Fold half the tasty cheese into sauce.

Fold half quantity of sauce into noodles.

Arrange chicken portions in base of casserole dish. Spoon noodle mixture over chicken. Layer avocado slices over noodles. Top with remaining sauce and cheese. Sprinkle with parsley and paprika.

Bake at 180°C (350°F) for 25 minutes. Serve hot.
Serves 6

CHICKEN, TOMATO AND CAPSICUM CASSEROLE

2 kg chicken pieces
1½ teaspoons salt
1 teaspoon sugar
1 teaspoon curry powder
1 bay leaf
2 tablespoons soy sauce
2 tablespoons olive oil
1 tablespoon white wine
¾ cup flour
salt and pepper, to taste
60 g butter
2 green capsicums, sliced
3 tomatoes, peeled, sliced and seeded
2 cups chicken stock
60 g mushroom caps
1 tablespoon chopped parsley, to garnish

Remove skin from chicken pieces. Place chicken in shallow dish. Combine salt, sugar, curry powder, bay leaf, soy sauce, olive oil and wine. Pour over chicken and marinate overnight. Drain marinade from chicken. Coat chicken portions in combined flour, salt and pepper.

Melt butter in frying pan and brown chicken portions. Add capsicum and tomatoes to chicken. Pour in marinade and top with mushrooms. Cover with a lid and simmer 30–45 minutes. Remove chicken and vegetables to serving dish.

Boil pan juices to a thick consistency and pour over chicken. Sprinkle with chopped parsley to serve.
Serves 6

CHICKEN WITH PLUM AND LYCHEE SAUCE

1.5 kg chicken, cut in bite-sized pieces
1 clove garlic, crushed
1 teaspoon minced ginger
1 tablespoon soy sauce
½ cup Chinese plum sauce
¼ teaspoon chilli sauce
1 tablespoon oil
¼ cup water chestnuts
¼ cup bamboo shoots, sliced
225 g can lychees, drained
¼ cup lychee juice
2 tablespoons cornflour
1 teaspoon sesame oil

Remove skin from chicken pieces. Marinate for 2 hours with garlic, ginger, soy, plum and chilli sauces. Drain and reserve liquid. Add sesame oil to wok, heat and stir-fry chicken pieces; cover with lid and simmer 5 minutes.

Add marinade juices. Cover and cook further 5 minutes. Add water chestnuts, bamboo shoots and lychees and stir-fry 1–2 minutes. Combine lychee juice and cornflour, add to wok and heat until thickened. Stir through sesame oil and serve hot with steamed rice.
Serves 6

SHREDDED BARBECUE DUCK WITH BARBECUE SAUCE

2 kg duck
1 clove garlic, crushed
1 tablespoon sesame oil
1 tablespoon honey
1 tablespoon Hoi Sin sauce
1 tablespoon soy sauce
1 teaspoon chilli sauce

BARBECUE SAUCE

½ teaspoon finely grated ginger root
1 tablespoon light soy sauce
1 tablespoon honey
1 tablespoon dry sherry
1 tablespoon Hoi Sin sauce

Preheat oven to 190°C (375°F). Clean duck and dry with paper towel. Combine garlic, sesame oil, honey, Hoi Sin, soy and chilli sauces. Brush marinade over duck.

Place duck on rack in baking dish. Cover with aluminium foil and bake 1 hour brushing occasionally with marinade. Remove foil, and bake a further 30–40 minutes or until cooked when tested.

Allow duck to stand 15 minutes before slicing into thin strips. Joint legs and wings. Serve duck arranged in layers on platter with wings and legs at end of platter. Serve hot or cold. To make sauce, combine all ingredients in a pan, heat through and serve in a sauce boat.
Serves 6

ALMOND FRIED CHICKEN WITH SPICED GINGER SAUCE

2 kg chicken pieces
⅔ cup grated Parmesan cheese
⅓ cup dry breadcrumbs
¼ cup ground almonds
salt and pepper, to taste
2 eggs
1 tablespoon milk
⅓ cup flour
oil, for frying

SPICED GINGER SAUCE

1 tablespoon finely grated ginger root
1 teaspoon whole allspice
1 teaspoon whole peppercorns
½ teaspoon mustard seed
½ teaspoon whole cloves
⅔ cup dry white wine
3 tablespoons white wine vinegar
2 tablespoons soy sauce

Remove skin from chicken pieces. Pat dry with paper towel. Combine Parmesan, breadcrumbs, almonds, salt and pepper. Set aside. Blend together eggs and milk.

Dip chicken pieces in flour then egg mixture then almond mixture. Heat oil in frying pan. Fry chicken portions in oil, turning to brown all sides. Fry gently 10 minutes. Drain on paper towel and serve hot or cold.

To make Spiced Ginger Sauce, combine ginger and spices in a mortar and pestle and crush lightly. If you do not have a mortar and pestle, place on a sheet of aluminium foil, fold the foil over and crush with a rolling pin. Combine white wine, vinegar and soy sauce in a small saucepan. Add spices and gently heat until boiling. Boil for 8 minutes then strain. Serve sauce in a shallow bowl suitable for dipping.
Serves 6

PORK AND PINEAPPLE HOTPOT

60 g butter
1.5 kg pork fillet, diced
220 g can pineapple pieces, drained
2 green capsicums, seeded
1 cup chopped celery
220 g can champignons, drained
1 red chilli, diced
1 cup white wine
salt and pepper, to taste
1 cup chicken stock
3 tablespoons cornflour
2 tablespoons chopped parsley

Melt butter in a large saucepan, add pork and cook 10 minutes turning constantly. Add pineapple, capsicum, celery, champignons and chilli. Cook 1 minute, stirring to combine. Add wine, salt and pepper and simmer 20 minutes. In a separate bowl combine stock, cornflour and parsley. Add to casserole and cook over medium heat 10 minutes, stirring occasionally. Serve with boiled rice.
Serves 6

SLICED BEEF PLATTER WITH GREEN SAUCE

1.5 kg fillet of beef
salt and freshly ground pepper
90 g butter
¼ cup brandy
1 cup beef consomme
2 tablespoons sherry
1 tablespoon gelatine
125 g ham
1 tablespoon mayonnaise
pinch cayenne
1 egg, hard-boiled
1 stuffed green olive
1 shallot, to garnish

GREEN SAUCE

3 tablespoons finely chopped watercress
3 tablespoons finely chopped parsley
1 clove garlic, crushed
freshly ground pepper
4 capers, finely chopped
3 tablespoons olive oil
juice 1 lemon
salt, to taste

Trim fillet, remove all skin and tissue with a sharp knife. Rub meat with salt and pepper.

Melt butter in shallow pan. Saute fillet for 10 minutes or until brown on all sides. Warm brandy, ignite and pour over beef fillet. Cook until flame dies down.

Place fillet in a shallow roasting pan. Pour over pan juices. Bake at 200°C (400°F) for 15–20 minutes. Allow beef to cool. Chill in refrigerator.

Place consomme, sherry and gelatine in saucepan and bring to boil. Boil for 5 minutes. Remove ¾ cup soup and set aside. Pour remaining soup into shallow pan. Chill to set.

Puree ham till smooth. Fold in mayonnaise and cayenne. Spread cold beef with ham paste. Cut slices of egg white to form petals of a flower, arrange on beef. Slice stuffed olive to form centre of flower. Dip shallot into boiling water for 1 minute. Cut stems and leaves from green and arrange on beef.

Spoon cold gelatine glaze over beef. Chill well. Arrange beef on platter. Chop up remaining glaze and spoon around beef fillet. Serve with Green Sauce.

To make Green Sauce, combine watercress, parsley, garlic, pepper and capers in a small bowl. Add oil, drop by drop, beating constantly. Gradually add lemon juice and taste to adjust seasonings. Store in refrigerator in a screw-topped jar until ready to serve.
Serves 8

STIR-FRIED BEEF AND MUSHROOMS

5 dried Chinese mushrooms
500 g round steak, cut in slivers across the grain
2 cloves garlic, crushed
¼ teaspoon chopped ginger root
1 tablespoon soy sauce
2 tablespoons oyster sauce
1 tablespoon oil
125 g snow peas
2 stalks celery, sliced
3 leaves spinach, shredded
1 teaspoon sesame oil

Soak mushrooms in hot water for 20 minutes. Drain and discard stalks.

Combine steak, garlic, ginger, soy and oyster sauces. Marinate for 1 hour, drain and reserve liquid.

Heat oil in wok. Add beef slivers and fry till browned. Add marinade juices, fry for 3–5 minutes. Add mushrooms and cook for 2 minutes. Add snow peas and celery and fry 1 minute. Serve hot on spinach and sprinkle with sesame oil.
Serves 6

SAUCY LAMB CASSEROLE

60 g butter
1 small onion, thinly sliced
1.5 kg lamb, diced small
125 g green beans
½ tablespoon chopped fresh mixed herbs
4 carrots, sliced
1 cup diagonally sliced celery
500 g potatoes, diced
250 g mushrooms, sliced
2 tablespoons tomato paste
salt and pepper, to taste
1 tablespoon flour
2 tablespoons water
300 mL sour cream
1 tablespoon chopped parsley, to garnish

Saute butter and onion in large saucepan for 3 minutes. Add lamb and brown lightly for 10 minutes. Add beans, herbs, carrots, celery, potatoes, mushrooms, 1 cup boiling water, tomato paste, salt and pepper. Stir to combine.

Cover and cook slowly for 30 minutes.

Combine flour with water and stir into casserole. Bring to boil, stirring occasionally until thickened.

Add sour cream stirring until combined — do not boil. Serve hot sprinkled with parsley.
Serves 8

Stir-fried Beef and Mushrooms (rear) and Fillets of Fish in Sangria Sauce (p. 28)

Festive Favourites

ROAST TURKEY

5–6 kg turkey
stuffing of your choice (see recipes)

BASTE

¼ cup orange juice
60 g butter, melted

Rinse turkey and pat dry with paper towel. Fill cavity with selected stuffing and sew or skewer openings. Secure drumsticks under skin and tail. Place breast side up, on rack in roasting pan. Brush turkey with baste (orange juice and butter, combined), cover with aluminium foil and bake at 175°C (340°F) for 3 hours.

Remove foil, baste again and continue cooking a further 30 minutes–1 hour to brown. Cover and allow turkey to stand 20 minutes before carving. Serve hot or cold.
Serves 12

HERB STUFFING

185 g butter, melted
2 teaspoons salt
½ teaspoon fresh sage
½ teaspoon fresh thyme
pepper, to taste
4 cups soft bread cubes
¾ cup milk
2 stalks celery, chopped
1 small onion, chopped

In large bowl combine all ingredients, taste and adjust seasoning. Cover and refrigerate till required.

Makes sufficient stuffing for 5–6 kg turkey.

APPLE AND PRUNE STUFFING

2 cups pitted prunes
3 large cooking apples, peeled, cored and quartered
squeeze lemon juice
freshly ground pepper, to taste

Combine all ingredients, cover and refrigerate until required.

Makes sufficient for a 5–6 kg turkey.

BAKED MUSTARD HAM

3–4 kg pickled leg of pork
1 bay leaf
6 peppercorns
2 tablespoons sherry
4 tablespoons coarse-grain mustard
1 tablespoon apricot jam

Place pork in large boiler and cover with water. Add bay leaf, peppercorns and sherry. Cover with lid and bring to boil. Reduce heat and simmer for 2 hours then allow meat to cool in liquid and drain.

Combine mustard and apricot jam. Spread over surface of ham. Place pork on rack in baking pan and cover with aluminium foil. Bake in oven at 180°C (350°F) for 1 hour. Remove foil and continue baking 45 minutes. Remove from oven and allow to cool. Serve in fine slices.
Serves 10

OYSTER STUFFING

⅔ cup finely chopped chicken liver and heart
125 g butter
105 g can drained fresh oysters
2 stalks celery, chopped
1 onion, finely chopped
1 cup grated apple
½ cup water
24 slices dry bread
2 teaspoons salt
pepper, to taste
½ teaspoon sugar
2 eggs, beaten

Lightly fry chicken liver, heart and butter for 3–5 minutes. Drain and toss lightly with remaining ingredients, adjusting seasoning to taste. Cover and refrigerate until required for use.

Makes sufficient for 5–6 kg turkey.

Clockwise from top: Baked Mustard Ham, Boiled Fruit Cake, Roast Turkey

ROAST FRUIT DUCK WITH APRICOT CITRUS SAUCE

2.5 kg duck
2 cloves garlic, crushed
2 cups grated apple
12 pitted prunes
4 tablespoons breadcrumbs
1 egg
2 tablespoons brown sugar
salt and pepper, to taste

APRICOT CITRUS SAUCE

425 g can apricots, drained and chopped
½ cup white wine
juice and finely grated rind 1 orange
½ small onion, finely chopped

Preheat oven to 180°C (350°F). Wash duck and remove oil sacs from tail. Dry duck with paper towel and prick back several times with a skewer. Combine remaining ingredients and fill cavity with mixture. Secure opening with skewer.

Place duck on roasting rack in baking dish. Cook for 1 hour covered with lid or aluminium foil. Remove cover and bake additional 30–40 minutes. Cover and allow duck to stand 15 minutes before carving. Serve hot or cold.

To make sauce, combine all ingredients in pan, bring to boil then reduce heat and simmer 10 minutes. Pour into a sauce boat and serve.

Serves 6

ROAST GOOSE

6 kg goose
1 quantity Apple and Prune Stuffing (see recipe)

BASTE

3 tablespoons chicken stock
2 tablespoons Calvados or *brandy*
¼ cup apple juice
freshly ground pepper

Preheat oven to 180°C (350°F). Rinse goose. Remove oil sacs from tail, pat goose dry and prick the back several times with a skewer. Fill cavity with stuffing and secure opening with skewers. Place, breast side down, on rack in roasting pan. Brush goose with baste (stock, brandy, juice and pepper combined), and cover with foil.

Bake goose covered with aluminium foil for 3 hours. Drain away excess fat from pan twice. Turn goose breast side up and baste with remaining mixture. Roast uncovered further 30 minutes–1 hour longer. Cover and allow goose to stand 20 minutes before carving. Serve hot or cold.

Serves 12

PORK ROAST WITH CHERRY SAUCE

3–4 kg pork loin
2 tablespoons cooking oil
1 tablespoon coarse salt
6 cloves garlic
12 small bay leaves

CHERRY SAUCE

½ cup pitted cherries
¼ cup corn syrup
2 tablespoons vinegar
salt and pepper, to taste
pinch nutmeg
pinch cinnamon
pinch ground cloves

Deeply score rind of pork into 1.5 cm strips.

Place pork loin skin side down in a roasting pan and pour in 2 cups boiling water. Bake roast at 200°C (400°F) for 15 minutes. Remove pan and drain off liquid, reserving it for basting.

Add oil to pan. Rub pork skin with salt. Insert cloves and bay leaves in score marks. Roast pork, skin side up at 190°C (375°F) for 3–3½ hours. Baste with drained liquid every 3 minutes. When cooked remove from pan. Cover and allow to stand for 20 minutes before carving.

In saucepan, combine sauce ingredients, bring to boil and cook for 3 minutes until heated through.

Carve pork and serve sliced on platter with Cherry Sauce.

Serves 12

Pork Roast with Cherry Sauce

Salads

GREEN SALAD WITH DIJON MUSTARD DRESSING

3 cups torn spinach
½ head lettuce, torn
4 stalks celery, chopped
½ green capsicum, diced
1 cucumber, rinsed and sliced
2 tablespoons chopped chives
6 green olives, pitted and sliced
1 avocado, pitted, peeled and sliced

DIJON MUSTARD DRESSING

1 tablespoon vinegar
2 tablespoons vegetable oil
1 teaspoon Dijon mustard
freshly ground pepper

Wash and drain spinach and lettuce and combine with celery and capsicum. Place row of cucumber slices around edge of salad dish. Sprinkle chives over.

To make dressing, combine all ingredients in a screw-topped jar and shake well.

Toss spinach mixture with dressing, pile into centre of serving dish and garnish salad with olives and avocado slices.
Serves 6

LETTUCE AND SOUR CREAM SALAD

1 head lettuce
1 cup sour cream
1½ tablespoons sugar
1 tablespoon vinegar
1 tablespoon grated onion
2 tablespoons prepared horseradish
1 teaspoon salt
1 tablespoon finely chopped parsley
paprika, to taste

Wash and dry lettuce leaves, shred and chill in refrigerator.

Combine sour cream, sugar, vinegar, onion, horseradish, salt and parsley. Spoon mixture over lettuce, to coat lightly. Pile lettuce into salad bowl and sprinkle with paprika.
Serves 6

Green Salad (foreground), Red Cabbage Nut Slaw and Avocado and Lettuce Salad

RED CABBAGE NUT SLAW WITH TAHINI ORANGE DRESSING

3 cups shredded red cabbage
1 cup shredded green cabbage
½ cup whole toasted blanched almonds

BASE DRESSING

2 tablespoons cream
1 tablespoons tarragon vinegar
1 teaspoon prepared mustard
¼ teaspoon garlic salt

TAHINI ORANGE DRESSING

2 tablespoons tahini
2 tablespoons water
juice and finely grated rind 1 orange

Combine red and green cabbage, wash, drain and chill in refrigerator. Combine base dressing ingredients in a screw-top jar and shake well. Toss cabbage with dressing and ¼ cup almonds. Pile into salad bowl and top with remaining almonds. To serve, spoon over Tahini Orange Dressing.
Serves 6

AVOCADO AND LETTUCE SALAD WITH MUSTARD SEED DRESSING

1 lettuce
2 avocados, peeled, sliced and sprinkled with juice ½ lemon
1 small cucumber, peeled and sliced
6 shallots, trimmed
alfalfa sprouts

MUSTARD SEED DRESSING

2 tablespoons natural yoghurt
1 tablespoon vegetable oil
2 teaspoons mustard seeds
1 teaspoons grated ginger root

Wash and dry lettuce. Refrigerate 30 minutes until crisp then tear into bite-sized pieces. Place in salad bowl. Top with avocado slices. Add cucumber and garnish with shallots and alfalfa sprouts.

To make dressing, combine all ingredients mixing until smooth. Just before serving pour over salad and toss.
Serves 8–10

POTATO AND CELERY SALAD

450 g boiled new potatoes, cold and sliced
1¼ cups sliced celery
1¼ cups green peas, cooked
1 small white onion, cut in thin rings
150 mL yoghurt
1 tablespoon horseradish cream
juice 1 lemon
salt and pepper, to taste
12 capers
6 large lettuce leaves

Mix together potatoes, celery, peas and onion in a bowl. Blend yoghurt, horseradish cream, lemon juice, and seasoning and mix with vegetables. Arrange in a shallow dish, dot with capers and decorate with lettuce leaves.
Serves 6

RICE SALAD WITH PRAWNS AND MUSSELS

200 g rice
500 g freshly cooked king prawns
1 kg mussels
½ cup dry white wine
2 lemons
6 tablespoons olive oil
pepper, to taste
1 small bunch parsley, finely chopped
3 anchovy fillets, chopped

Brush mussels under running water to free shells of grit. Discard any open ones. Put them in a wide pan with wine and bring to boil. Lift them out as soon as they open. Shell approximately half of them, reserving the other half for decoration. Shell prawns.

Boil rice in salted water, drain it and run some cold water through it to separate grains. Season it with juice of half a lemon, oil, plenty of pepper, parsley and anchovy fillets. Add salt if necessary.

Just before serving, stir prawns into rice, reserving some for decoration. Arrange rice in a glass bowl and decorate it with reserved prawns, mussels in shell and lemon slices. Serve very cold.
Serves 4

HARICOT BEAN SALAD

300 g dried haricot beans
2 small onions, thinly sliced
¼ bunch parsley, chopped
1 red capsicum, seeded and chopped
1 hard-boiled egg, chopped
1 tomato, chopped
60 g black olives, pitted
juice 1 lemon
olive oil

Soak beans in water to cover for 24 hours. Drain and cook in unsalted water until tender. Allow to cool in liquid. Drain and place in a shallow dish. Cover beans with onions, parsley, capsicum, egg and tomato and top with olives. Sprikle over the lemon juice and pour over olive oil to taste. Serve chilled.
Serves 4–6

SPINACH AND EDAM SALAD

275 g spinach
175 g Edam cheese, diced
2 carrots, in matchsticks
1 red capsicum, cut in strips
2 shallots, sliced
4 radishes, sliced
75 g button mushrooms, sliced
3 tablespoons raisins
juice 1 orange
juice 1 lemon

Tear spinach leaves into pieces and combine with prepared ingredients in a salad bowl. Add raisins, mix orange and lemon juice, pour over salad and toss lightly.
Serves 4

Rice Salad with Prawns and Mussels

Turkey and Roquefort Salad

FRUIT AND NUT SALAD

1 cup chopped pineapple
2 grapefruits, segmented
2 oranges, segmented
1 large green apple, diced
1 tablespoon lemon juice
½ cup stuffed olives
½ lettuce
¼ cup toasted pine nuts
¼ cup toasted almonds
¼ cup chopped walnuts
1 tablespoon olive oil
2 tablespoons vinegar
salt and pepper, to taste
1 tablespoon chopped chives

Combine pineapple, grapefruit and orange segments and chill. Toss apple in lemon juice to prevent browning and add. Top with olives. Wash and shred lettuce, place on serving platter. Spoon mixture over lettuce and sprinkle with nuts. Combine oil, vinegar, salt, pepper, chives and pour over salad just before serving.
Serves 6

TURKEY AND ROQUEFORT SALAD WITH CRANBERRY DRESSING

1 cup shredded lettuce
3 cups diced cooked turkey
1 cup diced celery
½ cup seedless grapes
½ cup toasted pecans, chopped
45 g Roquefort cheese, crumbled

CRANBERRY DRESSING

250 g jar cranberry sauce
¼ cup dark soy sauce
1 small clove garlic, crushed
2 tablespoons lemon juice
2 tablespoons sherry
1 tablespoon vegetable oil

Combine lettuce, turkey, celery, grapes and pecans. Pile mixture into shallow serving dish. Crumble Roquefort cheese over top of salad.

To make Cranberry Dressing, combine all ingredients in a small saucepan and heat until well blended. Serve separately in a sauce boat.
Serves 6

ICED SUMMER SALAD

1 peach
1 banana
75 g strawberries
2 teaspoons sugar
225 g cream cheese
½ teaspoon ground ginger
2 tablespoons lemon juice
2 tablespoons whipped cream
¼ cup chopped hazelnuts
shredded lettuce, to serve
Vinaigrette Dressing (see recipe)

Peel peach and banana and hull strawberries. Dice fruit and sprinkle with sugar. Blend cream cheese with ginger, lemon juice, then fold in cream, fruit and nuts. Pour mixture into 4 individual moulds and freeze for 1–2 hours, until firm. Dip each mould into hot water and turn salad onto a bed of shredded lettuce. Serve immediately with dressing.
Serves 4

FRUITED CHICKEN SALAD

1½–2 cups cooked chicken meat, diced
½ cup cooked brown long-grain rice
2 grapefruits, peeled and segmented
2 carrots, in matchsticks
2 teaspoons chopped onion
1 large avocado
2 tablespoons lemon juice
1 tablespoon vinegar
1 tablespoon oil
lettuce or *Chinese cabbage*
watercress, to garnish

DRESSING

6 tablespoons mayonnaise
1 teaspoon curry powder

Place chicken, rice, grapefruits, carrots and onion in salad bowl. Season and toss well. Peel and dice avocado and cover with lemon juice. Combine vinegar and oil and add to chicken mixture with avocado and lemon juice. Toss gently. Blend dressing ingredients together. Serve salad on bed of lettuce and garnish with watercress. Serve dressing separately.
Serves 4

CHICKEN AND CHEESE SALAD WITH ITALIAN DRESSING

3 cups torn endive
½ head lettuce, torn
3 hard-boiled eggs, peeled and sliced
½ cup sliced radishes
2 tomatoes, peeled, chilled and quartered
1 cup cooked chicken strips
1 cup Swiss cheese strips
¼ cup thinly sliced ham
¼ cup thinly sliced tongue
¼ cup thinly sliced salami
½ cup Italian dressing
anchovy fillets, to garnish

Combine endive, lettuce, egg and radish slices. Halve mixture. Place half endive mixture in row on square platter. Place tomato wedges next to endive mixture in row. Combine chicken and cheese strips and arrange in a row alongside tomatoes. Put rest of endive mixture beside chicken and cheese. Complete salad platter with combined mixture of ham, tongue and salami. Coat each row lightly with salad dressing and garnish with anchovy fillets.
Serves 6

MARINATED LAMB SALAD

750 g roast lamb, trimmed of fat and cut in strips
½ cup olive oil
1 cup red wine vinegar
3 tablespoons honey
1½ teaspoons salt
pinch dry mustard
2 teaspoons dried mint
¼ teaspoon oregano
¼ teaspoon thyme
¼ teaspoon anise seed
1 cucumber, peeled and sliced
4 tomatoes, quartered
½ bunch curly endive
1 cup pitted black olives

Combine lamb with olive oil, vinegar, honey, salt, mustard, mint leaves and herbs. Refrigerate for 1 hour.

Line serving dish with cucumber, tomato quarters and curly endive. Drain lamb strips, reserving dressing. Spoon lamb strips into centre of dish. Combine dressing and olives. Pour over meat and vegetables to serve.
Serves 6

Marinated Lamb Salad

Breads

HOT FILLED LOAVES

1 long French loaf

FRENCH ONION BREAD

250 g cream cheese
1 packet French onion soup mix

CHEESE AND CHIVE BREAD

60 g butter
250 g cream cheese
2 tablespoons chopped parsley
2 tablespoons chopped chives
2 tablespoons chopped fresh herbs
freshly ground pepper

GARLIC AND HERB BREAD

3 cloves garlic, crushed
100 g butter
2 tablespoons chopped parsley
pinch mixed herbs

MUSSEL BREAD

105 g can smoked mussels, drained
250 g cream cheese
1 tablespoon chopped parsley

HAM AND BLUE CHEESE BREAD

100 g butter
1 tablespoon chopped parsley
60 g ham, finely minced
30 g blue vein cheese

Combine ingredients of the filling of your choice. Slice bread and spread slices with filling. Put the loaf back together again and wrap in aluminium foil. Bake at 200°C (400°F) for 10 minutes, open the foil wrapping and bake a further 5–10 minutes until loaf is crisp and cheese is hot. Serve immediately in bread basket.
Note: Bread sticks can be filled, wrapped in foil and frozen ready for baking.

PATAFLA

1 baguette or other long French loaf
6 tomatoes, peeled and chopped
1 onion, finely chopped
6 shallots, finely chopped
2 green capsicums, seeded and chopped
1 red capsicum, seeded and chopped
250 g black olives, pitted and chopped
3 tablespoons capers
3 gherkins, chopped
freshly ground pepper, to taste
3 tablespoons olive oil

Halve the loaf lengthways and scoop out the crumb. Place crumb in a bowl with vegetables, olives, capers and gherkins, beat mixture well, add pepper then stir in oil.

Divide tomato mixture between 2 bread halves. Reassemble and wrap firmly in foil. Refrigerate overnight. Cut into thin slices to serve.
Serves 10–12

Clockwise from top: Patafla, Savoury Scone Roll, Hot-Filled Loaves

Sweets and Afters

BRANDY ORANGE SAVARIN

2 cups flour
¼ teaspoon salt
3 teaspoons dry yeast
¾ tablespoon sugar
⅔ cup warm milk
2 eggs, beaten
125 g softened butter
¼ cup glace cherries
2 glace pineapple rings, cut into eighths

SYRUP

⅔ cup water
100 mL orange juice
1 cup sugar
1.5 cm piece vanilla bean
3 tablespoons brandy

GLAZE

½ cup sweet orange marmalade
1 tablespoon water
1 tablespoon orange liqueur (eg Curacao or Cointreau)

Sift flour and salt together in a bowl. Combine yeast, sugar and warm milk. Make well in flour. Add yeast mixture. Sprinkle over a little flour. Cover with plastic wrap. Allow to rise in a warm place for 15 minutes.

Add eggs and softened butter and mix to a smooth elastic dough. Cover mixture with plastic wrap and again leave in a warm place to double in bulk — 30 minutes.

Place mixture into well-greased 23 cm ring mould or cake tin. Allow to stand, covered with plastic wrap, until mixture rises to top of tin. Bake at 200°C (400°F) for 20 minutes.

Combine ingredients for syrup in saucepan. Stir over heat until sugar dissolves. Bring to boil, boil for 10 minutes, then strain. While Savarin is hot, pour over hot syrup. Allow Savarin to stand 30 minutes until syrup is absorbed. Turn onto serving plate.

To make glaze, combine marmalade, water and orange liqueur in saucepan. Heat for 5 minutes. Glaze Savarin with three-quarters of mixture. Decorate with glace cherries and pineapple pieces. Drizzle over remaining glaze. Serve sliced with whipped cream.

Serves 8

MOCHA CHEESECAKE

CRUST

1 packet semi-sweet chocolate biscuits, crushed
1 cup walnuts, crushed
100 g butter, melted

FILLING

450 mL cream, whipped
3 eggs, separated
250 g cream cheese
3 tablespoons sugar
1 tablespoon coffee powder combined with 1 tablespoon hot water
¼ cup chocolate liqueur
2 teaspoons gelatine
3 tablespoons hot water, extra

GARNISH

150 ml cream
chocolate curls
glace cherries

Combine biscuit crumbs, walnuts and melted butter. Press biscuit mix into base of 23 cm spring-form cake tin. Bake at 190°C (375°F) for 10 minutes then chill.

Whip cream. Cream egg yolks with cream cheese. Blend in sugar, coffee and hot water and chocolate liqueur. Dissolve gelatine in hot water over low heat. Whisk egg whites until stiff. Combine egg whites, cream, cream cheese mixture and gelatine. Blend evenly. Pour cheesecake mixture into tin.

Chill overnight in refrigerator. Remove outside of spring-form tin. Whip extra cream. Pipe rosettes of cream onto top of cheesecake. Decorate with chocolate curls and glace cherries. Return to refrigerator until ready to serve.

Serves 6–8

CHERRY AND NUT STRUDEL

12 sheets filo pastry
100 g butter, melted
1 kg pitted cherries, morello style
¾ cup dried breadcrumbs
1 cup sugar
¼ cup chopped almonds
icing sugar

Preheat oven to 200°C (400°F).

Place filo pastry between 2 dry tea towels and cover with a just damp tea towel to prevent pastry from drying out while cooking. Remove 1 sheet pastry at a time and brush with melted butter. Cover with a second sheet pastry and brush again with butter. Continue with remaining pastry, using up half the butter.

Combine cherries, breadcrumbs, sugar and almonds. Place on pastry lengthways leaving 2 cm edge. Fold long edge over filling then over sides. Brush with butter. Roll up pastry, brushing with butter to seal ends. Place seam side down onto baking tray. Bake for 30 minutes until browned. Remove from tray to serving plate. Dust with icing sugar to serve.

Serves 8

Clockwise from top; Party Cocktail Trifle (p. 51), Mocha Cheesecake and Meringue Baskets (p. 53)

BLACK FOREST CREPE CAKE

CREPE MIXTURE
pinch salt
2 cups flour
2 eggs
600 mL milk
20 g butter

FILLING
440 g can pitted black cherries
¼ cup orange-flavoured liqueur
2 tablespoons sugar
2 tablespoons cornflour

GARNISH
1 cup cream, whipped
3 tablespoons almond flakes, toasted

Sift salt and flour together; blend in eggs and milk to form a smooth batter.

Grease crepe pan with butter. Pour 1 tablespoon crepe mix into hot pan, turn pan to cover base thinly with mixture. Cook until dry on surface. Continue until 15–20 crepes have been made. Layer crepes between paper towel and allow to cool.

Place cherries, liqueur, sugar and cornflour in saucepan. Bring to boil, stirring. Allow to thicken and then cool. Mould crepes together with cherry filling. Spreading filling between each layer. Form crepes into dome shape.

Whip cream. Coat outside of crepes with cream. Pipe crown of rosettes on top of cake. Decorate sides of cake with toasted almonds. Refrigerate until serving. Serve sliced.

Note: Keeps 1–2 days in refrigerator.
Serves 10–12

AUSTRIAN CHERRY WALNUT CAKE

1 cup glace cherries
2¼ cups self-raising flour
185 g butter
⅔ cup caster sugar
3 eggs
¾ cup milk
1½ cups walnuts, finely chopped
½ cup desiccated coconut

Grease and line a 23 cm square cake tin. Preheat oven to 180°C (350°F). Halve the cherries and mix with 4 tablespoons of flour.

Beat butter until soft. Add sugar and continue beating until mixture is light and fluffy. Add eggs, one at a time, beating well between additions.

Fold in flour and milk alternately, starting and finishing with flour. Fold in cherries, walnuts and coconut.

Spoon mixture into prepared tin and bake for 50-60 minutes until cooked when tested. Remove and cool on a cake rack.
Serves 8–10

Black Forest Crepe Cake

NOUGAT WALNUT SPONGE

SPONGE
12 eggs, separated
1 cup sugar
3 cups self-raising flour
½ teaspoon bicarbonate of soda
pinch salt

FILLING
100 g nougat
¼ cup apricot conserve
60 g butter
3 tablespoons sugar
1 tablespoon boiling water
1 tablespoon milk
¼ teaspoon vanilla
1 cup crushed walnuts
220 g can peach slices, drained
¼ cup glace cherries
¼ cup water
2 teaspoons sugar
2 teaspoons gelatine

Blend egg yolks and sugar together. Sift flour, bicarbonate and salt together. Whisk egg whites till stiff. Fold egg yolks, flour mixture and egg whites together.

Grease and line the base of a 23–25 cm spring-form cake tin. Place one-third of cake mix into tin. Bake at 180°C (350°F) for 10–15 minutes or until lightly browned. Remove from tin immediately. Remove paper from base, allow to cool. Repeat with second and third layers of cake mix.

Place 1 layer on serving plate. Melt nougat in a double saucepan and spread over cake base. Spread thin layer apricot conserve over nougat. Add second layer. Cream butter and sugar till smooth and sugar is dissolved. Gradually blend in boiling water. Beat 2 minutes. Fold in walnuts. Spread walnut cream over cake layer.

Add remaining cake layer. Decorate with peach slices. Place cherries, water, sugar and gelatine in saucepan. Bring to boil; boil 2 minutes. Cool slightly, spoon over top of cake and allow to set. Serve sliced.

Note: Refrigerate no more than 3 days.
Serves 12–16

CHOCOLATE LIQUEUR ROLL

125 g cooking chocolate
2 tablespoons strong black coffee
4 eggs, separated
¾ cup caster sugar
2 tablespoons cocoa, sifted
½ cup cream, whipped
1 tablespoon Kirsch
extra ¼ cup cream, whipped
4 strawberries, cut into fans

Melt chocolate in double saucepan with the coffee. Beat egg yolks and sugar until thick. Whisk egg whites until stiff. Fold melted chocolate into egg yolks. Fold in egg whites. Spoon mixture into greased and lined Swiss roll tin. Bake at 210°C (412°F) for 10 minutes. Turn off oven. Leave cake mixture for 15 minutes in oven. Leave cake in tin, cover with damp tea towel till cool. Turn out onto a sheet of greaseproof paper dusted with cocoa. Spread with whipped cream flavoured with Kirsch. Roll up and chill. Decorate with whipped cream rosettes and strawberry fans.
Serves 8–10

SICILIAN CASSATA

700 g very fresh ricotta
⅘ cup sugar
1 cup candied lemon peel
100 g cooking chocolate
4 tablespoons rum or to taste
400 g sponge cake or *sponge fingers*

Using a large bowl and a wooden spoon, cream ricotta until very smooth, add sugar, 1 tablespoon rum, candied peel and chocolate chopped in very small pieces. Sprinkle remaining rum on sponge cake and line bottom and sides of a mould or souffle dish. Fill mould with ricotta mixture and refrigerate for at least 3 hours before serving. If you wish to unmould cassata, line mould with greaseproof paper brushed with rum.
Serves 6

PARTY COCKTAIL TRIFLE

25 g packet red jelly crystals
2 cups boiling water
1 large jam-filled Swiss roll
3 tablespoons sherry
600 mL milk
2 eggs
2 tablespoons cornflour
vanilla essence
2 tablespoons sugar
300 mL cream, whipped
2 tablespoons desiccated coconut, toasted

Combine jelly crystals and boiling water until dissolved. Pour into shallow baking tin. Allow to set in refrigerator then cut up roughly. Slice Swiss roll into 1.5 cm slices. Line base and sides of glass serving dish with cake slices. Sprinkle sherry over cake slices.

In large saucepan combine milk, eggs, cornflour, vanilla and sugar and whisk till fluffy. Bring to boil whisking until thickened. Allow to cool slightly. Pour over cake slices. Chill overnight. Top with jelly and pipe with cream to decorate. Sprinkle with toasted coconut before serving.
Serves 6–8

CARAMELISED ORANGES

¾ cup sugar
40 g butter
4 large oranges (navels)
4 tablespoons toasted slivered almonds
whipped cream, to serve (optional)

Dissolve sugar over low heat, stirring constantly, and simmer until syrup is a golden colour. Remove from heat; add butter and stir until smooth. Peel oranges, removing all pith and white membrane. Slice thinly and arrange on a serving dish in overlapping layers. Pour sauce over them and sprinkle with almonds. Serve with whipped cream, if wished.
Serves 4

Caramelised Oranges

PLUM FLAN

PASTRY

100 g butter
1⅓ cups wholemeal flour
1 egg yolk
milk, to mix

FILLING

3 egg yolks
¼ cup honey
300 mL natural yoghurt
½ teaspoon powdered cinnamon
500 g small plums, halved and stoned
½ cup blanched almonds
1 tablespoon brown sugar

Rub butter into flour, add egg yolk and enough milk for form a firm dough. Roll out and line 20 cm flan dish. Prick base a few times with fork.

Beat yolks with honey, yoghurt and cinnamon. Pour into pastry case.

Arrange plums, cut side down in yoghurt mixture. Bake at 200°C (400°F) for 35–40 minutes, until custard is set. Sprinkle with nuts and brown sugar and brown under a hot grill.
Serves 6

PEACHES IN SPUMANTE

4 perfectly matured freestone peaches
a little icing sugar
1 bottle good quality dry Italian spumante (or French champagne)

Drop peaches in boiling water for 30 seconds, remove and peel.

Halve each peach and remove stone. Sprinkle each half with a little icing sugar and let it rest for no more than 5 minutes or peach will go black. Take 4 large champagne glasses and arrange in each one 2 peach halves. Fill up the glass with Italian spumante and serve.
Serves 4

Peaches in Spumante

MERINGUE BASKETS

2 egg whites
½ cup caster sugar
¼ teaspoon cream of tartar

Whisk egg whites until stiff. Add sugar beating well for 20 minutes. Fold in cream of tartar. Fit piping bag with large rose pipe. Fill with egg white mixture and pipe meringue in small 10 cm rounds forming a basket shape on lightly oiled tray.

Bake at 110°C (225°F) until crisp but still white. Baking time can vary from 2–4 hours. Allow to cool in oven. Fill baskets with whipped cream and fruit and serve.
Makes 8

CHOCOLATE MERINGUE BASKETS
Add 2 teaspoons sieved cocoa

COFFEE MERINGUE BASKETS
Add 2 teaspoons instant coffee powder

PECAN NUT MERINGUES

3 egg whites
pinch cream of tartar
1 cup caster sugar
⅔ cup chopped pecan nuts
20 crushed salty crackers
1 teaspoon vanilla
1 teaspoon cornflour
extra pecan nuts
½ cup cream, whipped

Whisk egg whites with cream of tartar until stiff. Gradually add sugar. Beat until stiff. Fold in chopped pecans, crushed crackers and vanilla.

Lightly dust oven tray with cornflour. Pile mixture onto tray, spread out to 5 cm circles. Bake at 150°C (300°F) for 30 minutes. Transfer to serving plate. Allow to cool and decorate with nuts and whipped cream.
Serves 6–8

ALMOND SNAPS

2 cups sugar
½ cup sesame seeds
butter, for frying
4 tablespoons white vinegar
1 tablespoon water
1⅔ cups slivered almonds

Melt butter in frying pan. Toss in sesame seeds and cook till golden brown. Combine sugar, vinegar and water in saucepan and dissolve over low heat. Bring to boil about 10 minutes without stirring. Mixture should be golden brown and when a little is dropped into a glass of cold water, a ball forms.

Grease a 30 × 20 cm lamington tin and sprinkle almonds and half sesame seeds over base. Pour toffee mixture over nuts and sprinkle remaining sesame seeds over top. Leave to cool slightly before cutting into squares.
Makes 12–15

SWEET FRITTERS

2⅘ cups flour
50 g butter
1 tablespoon sugar
2 eggs
1 teaspoon vanilla essence
pinch salt
oil for deep-frying (peanut or sunflower)
icing sugar

Combine flour, butter, sugar, eggs, vanilla and salt and knead into a smooth soft dough. Shape into a ball, cover it with a kitchen towel and let it rest for an hour or so.

With a rolling pin, roll dough out very thinly. Cut into ribbons and twist in bows, butterflies, or whatever shape takes your fancy. Heat enough oil for deep-frying and drop the fritters in a few at a time until golden and a little puffed. Drain on paper towel, sprinkle with icing sugar and serve hot or cold.
Serves 4

Sweet Fritters

Something Traditional

Christmas wouldn't be Christmas
without all the trimmings

GRAN'S TRADITIONAL CHRISTMAS CAKE

500 g butter
2 cups brown sugar
10 eggs
1 cup glace cherries, chopped
½ cup mixed peel
3 cups sultanas
3½ cups currants
1½ cups raisins, chopped
½ tablespoon allspice
¼ cup rum
1 teaspoon vanilla
¼ cup milk
5 cups flour
½ tablespoon baking powder

ALMOND PASTE

1 cup ground almonds
⅓ cup icing sugar
¼ cup caster sugar
1 egg white

ICING

2 egg whites
500 g icing sugar
1 teaspoon glycerine
2 teaspoons lemon juice
food colouring (optional)

Preheat oven to 160°C (325°F). Cream butter and sugar until smooth. Add eggs one at a time and beat mixture for 5 minutes. Add fruits, spice, rum, vanilla and milk. Lastly add sifted flour and baking powder and blend.

Spoon mixture into a double-lined 23 cm round or square cake tin. Carefully bang tin twice on benchtop to release air pockets from cake mix. Bake for 5–5½ hours. Insert wooden skewer to test if cake is cooked.

Stand on cake rack and cool cake in tin ½–1 hour before inverting onto cake rack to cool. Leave lining paper on cake. When cold, wrap in greaseproof paper and aluminium foil to store. Decorate cake with almond paste and icing or with Christmas fruits and nuts.

Almond paste Blend together ground almonds and both sugars in a bowl. Stir in egg white and knead mixture to a smooth, thick paste. Dust a board with a little icing sugar and roll paste out to form a circle to fit top of cake.

Icing Beat egg whites until frothy. Add sugar gradually, beating after each addition. Lastly add glycerine and lemon juice and beat for several minutes.

Divide icing, using white icing on top and sides of cake and colouring a small amount for decoration.

Gran's Traditional Christmas Cake

CHRISTMAS PUDDING I

1½ cups raisins, chopped
½ cup blanched almonds, chopped
½ cup pitted dates, chopped
⅓ cup glace cherries, chopped
⅓ cup mixed peel
1½ cups sultanas
1⅔ cups currants
1 small apple, peeled and grated
½ cup rum or *brandy*
250 g bu
1 cup br
4 eggs
1 cup flc
pinch sa
3 teaspo
½ teaspoon bicarbonate of soda
2½ cups soft white breadcrumbs
custard, brandy butter or *cream, to serve*

Combine chopped raisins, almonds, dates and cherries in a large bowl. Add mixed peel, sultanas, currants and apple. Pour over rum, cover and allow to stand overnight.

Cream butter and sugar. Add eggs beating well. Sift flour, salt, mixed spice and bicarbonate of soda. Add breadcrumbs to flour mixture. Fold flour, butter and fruit mixtures together. Dip pudding cloth in boiling water. Squeeze out excess moisture and lay cloth flat. Sift plenty of flour over three-quarters of cloth and rub in well — this forms a seal which prevents water seeping into pudding during cooking. Spoon mixture onto centre of cloth and bring up sides of material. Secure well with string.

Bring approximately 2 litres water to boil. Lower pudding into water. Cover and boil pudding 4 hours, adding hot water as necessary. Remove pudding, drain and hang for 1 day. Reheat by boiling 2 hours. Remove from cloth. Serve with custard, brandy butter or cream.
Serves 12

BOILED FRUIT CAKE

1 cup water
1 cup brown sugar
250 g butter
1½ cups raisins, chopped
3 cups sultanas
1⅔ cups currants
1 cup glace cherries, chopped
⅓ cup mixed peel
⅓ cup glace pineapple, chopped
½ teaspoon ground cinnamon
½ teaspoon nutmeg
½ teaspoon ginger
½ teaspoon allspice
1 teaspoon bicarbonate of soda
3 eggs
2 cups self-raising flour
1 cup flour
¼ cup rum or *dry sherry*

Preheat oven to 180°C (350°F).

In large saucepan place water, brown sugar, butter, all the fruits, spices and bicarbonate of soda. Cook over low heat to melt butter and blend ingredients. Allow to cool. Add eggs and flours and mix evenly.

Place mixture in double-lined 20 cm square cake tin. (Use buttered brown paper, cutting paper 5 cm taller than tin.) Bake for 1½–2 hours.

Insert wooden skewer to test whether cake is cooked. When cooked carefully turn out on cake rack and remove paper from base and sides. Drizzle rum over warm cake.

[illegible]T-MINCE DELIGHT

[illegible]ASTRY

2⅓ cups flour
1 teaspoon cinnamon
salt, to taste
180 g butter
½ cup caster sugar
1 egg, lightly beaten

FRUIT MINCE

1½ cups mixed dried fruit
440 g can crushed pineapple and juice
1 cooking apple, peeled, cored and grated
1 cup brown sugar
1 teaspoon nutmeg
1 tablespoon cornflour blended with
1 tablespoon pineapple juice

Sift flour, cinnamon and salt into a bowl. Rub in butter to resemble breadcrumbs. Stir in sugar and egg to form dough. Knead lightly then wrap in plastic and refrigerate 1 hour. Grate half the dough over base of 30 × 20 cm lamington tin. Press down lightly and evenly with the back of a spoon. Set aside. Preheat oven to 180°C (350°F).

Place mixed fruit, pineapple and juice, apple, sugar and nutmeg in saucepan. Add cornflour paste and simmer until thickened. Cool slightly. Spread fruit mince over pastry base. Grate remaining dough over top to completely cover mince. Bake 35–40 minutes or until golden brown. Cool on wire rack. Cut into bars.

Makes 12–16

CHOCOLATE CHRISTMAS BELLS

200 g cooking chocolate, broken into pieces
8–10 Christmas decoration bells
8–10 Maraschino cherries, finely chopped

ROYAL ICING

1 egg white, whisked
1 cup icing sugar
½ teaspoon lemon juice
cochineal red food colouring

Melt chocolate in top of a double saucepan. Wash and dry bells thoroughly. Using a clean paintbrush, coat inside of bells with a portion of chocolate. Place bells on plate and freeze a few minutes. Place chopped cherries into each bell and seal with chocolate. Return to freezer for a few minutes until hardened. When hardened, unmould bell by inserting a small skewer through the bell's loop at the top.

Whisk egg white until frothy. Gradually add icing sugar, beating well. After ½ icing sugar has been added, beat in lemon juice until a firm icing is made. Colour with sufficient red food colouring. Pipe a small loop bow onto the top of each bell. Pack into Christmas box. Keep refrigerated.

Makes 8–10

FESTIVE FRUIT TARTS

2 sheets ready-rolled frozen sweet shortcrust pastry, thawed
225 g apricot jam
1 tablespoon orange juice
7 mandarin segments
10 strawberries
1 cup flaked almonds
1 green glace cherry
2 apricots
1 tablespoon pistachio nuts
50 g canned redcurrants
1 banana, sliced

Preheat oven to 200°C (400°F). On a floured board, roll out dough to 0.5 cm thick. Lightly grease and flour 6 patty or tartlet tins and line them with dough. Prick with a fork and bake blind for 20 minutes. To prepare the apricot glaze melt apricot jam and orange juice in a saucepan and sieve.

To fill the tarts as shown in the picture, clockwise from top left: arrange 7 mandarin segments in the first. Cover with apricot glaze. In the second, arrange 5 strawberries, interspersed with flaked almonds, and put a green glace cherry in the middle. Glaze lightly.

Cut an apricot in half; remove the stone. Put a strawberry in one half and arrange slices of the other half around it. Alternate the slices with pistachio nuts, and glaze. Heap the fourth tart with redcurrants and stud it with almond flakes. Glaze lightly

Cut the rest of the strawberries in half and arrange them in a rosette in the fifth tart. Centre with half a strawberry on a slice of banana. Glaze. Fill the sixth tart with banana slices garnished with redcurrants and pistachio nuts. Glaze. Serve on a dish garnished with the other apricot, halved and filled with redcurrants.

Easter Parade

Making Easter individual with homemade buns and chocolate eggs

HOT CROSS EASTER BUNS

2 cups flour
2 cups wholemeal flour
1 teaspoon salt
30 g dry yeast
1½ cups warm milk
¼ cup sugar
½ cup sultanas
60 g butter, melted
1 egg
¼ teaspoon cinnamon
¼ teaspoon nutmeg
½ teaspoon allspice

CROSS
½ cup flour
⅓ cup water

GLAZE
2 tablespoons sugar
1 tablespoon gelatine
2 tablespoons hot water

Sift flours and salt into a bowl. Cream yeast with ½ cup warm milk and 1 teaspoon sugar. Make well in centre of flour. Add milk and yeast. Sprinkle flour over top, cover bowl with plastic wrap and stand in warm place 10 minutes until mixture bubbles.

Blend together remaining milk, sultanas, butter, sugar, egg and spices. Combine flour mixture with milk and sultana mixture. Blend evenly to form dough.

Knead on floured board 10 minutes. Place dough in oiled bowl. Cover with plastic wrap. Stand in warm place 40 minutes or until dough doubles in bulk.

Punch down dough, turn onto floured surface. Knead dough till smooth. Divide dough into thirds, then cut each third into 5 equal portions. Knead each into round shape. Place buns in lightly greased 18 × 28 cm lamington tin. Cover and stand in warm place 10 minutes or until buns reach top of tin. Preheat oven to 220°C (400°F).

Combine flour and water to make crosses. Place in corner of plastic freezer bag. Snip corner from bag. Carefully pipe crosses on each bun. Bake for 15–20 minutes. Remove from oven and brush with glaze. Cool buns on cake rack.

To make glaze, place sugar, gelatine and water in small saucepan. Bring to boil. Boil 1 minute.
Makes 15 buns

MAKING CHOCOLATE EGGS

An extremely rewarding activity, making Easter eggs will require an egg mould, piping nozzles and bag, a paint brush and foil, aluminium.

chocolate (see note)

FONDANT
2 teaspoons gelatine
1 tablespoon water
1 teaspoon liquid glucose or *sweetener*
450 g icing sugar

ROYAL ICING
1 egg white, stiffly beaten
200 g icing sugar, sifted
few drops colouring (optional)

Melt chocolate in a bowl over hot water. Using a paint brush, cover the sides of your egg mould completely with melted chocolate. Chill in refrigerator 2 minutes.

Recoat mould with chocolate 3 times, so that chocolate forms a layer 2 mm thick. Chill between coats so chocolate sets.

Push top of mould gently to remove chocolate from mould and set egg halves on a piece of aluminium foil. Join egg halves with a little melted chocolate; chill in refrigerator 10 minutes to set.

To make fondant, soak gelatine in water, dissolve over heat and combine with glucose. Gradually add half the icing sugar, wrap in plastic wrap and set aside for 3 hours. Before using, add remaining icing sugar and colouring if desired. Make ornamental leaves and flowers and place on top of egg.

To make icing, fold beaten egg white into icing sugar with colouring, if desired, and beat well until stiff. Pipe decorations around and on top of egg.
Note: Quantity of chocolate depends on size of moulds and number of eggs required.

Party Punches and Fruit Cups

MIXED FRUIT CUP

1 pawpaw, peeled and seeded
2 bananas, sliced
1 litre water
1 cup sugar
1 cup orange juice
½ cup lemon juice
pulp 12 passionfruit
2 × 750mL bottles soda water
ice cubes

GARNISH

10 strawberries, sliced
1 orange, thinly sliced
mint leaves

Puree pawpaw and bananas in food processor or blender. Boil water and sugar, stirring for 8–10 minutes until sugar dissolves and thin syrup is formed. Immediately pour onto orange and lemon juices. Add pureed fruit and passionfruit. Chill until needed.

To serve, add soda water and ice cubes and garnish with strawberries, orange slices and mint leaves.
Makes 3 litres

CHILLED FRUIT PUNCH

1.5 litres cold tea
¾ cup lemon juice
2 cups fresh orange juice
1 litre pineapple juice
1 cup sugar
2.5 litres dry ginger ale
ice cubes
lemon slices
strawberries, hulled
mint leaves, bruised

Combine tea, juices, sugar and chill. Add ginger ale, ice cubes, lemon slices, strawberries and mint leaves.
Makes 30 glasses

WATERMELON PINEAPPLE PUNCH

1.5 kg piece watermelon, peeled, seeded and chopped
1¼ cups pineapple juice
1 cup lime juice
1 cup vodka
sugar, to taste
1–2 limes, thinly sliced, to garnish

Puree watermelon in blender or food processor. Force through a fine sieve, discarding any remaining pulp. Stir in pineapple and lime juices and vodka. Add sugar to taste. Chill well and serve garnished with lime slices.
Makes 1.5 litres

CITRUS CHAMPAGNE PUNCH

1 cup sugar
1¼ cups water
grated rind and juice 1 orange and *1 lemon*
1½ cups grapefruit juice
1½ cups pineapple juice
1.5 litres dry ginger ale
750 mL bottle champagne
ice cubes
orange and *lemon slices*

Dissolve sugar and water in saucepan over medium heat. Add grated rind of orange and lemon and allow to cool. Combine fruit juices and syrup and chill. Before serving, add chilled ginger ale, champagne, ice cubes and fruit slices.
Makes 20 glasses

PARTY PUNCH

2 tablespoons tea
2½ cups boiling water
grated rind and juice 3 oranges
grated rind and juice 3 lemons
1 cup sugar
1 cup water
1 cup fruit cordial
pulp 6 passionfruit
1 orange, thinly sliced
1 lemon, thinly sliced
1 lime, thinly sliced
mint sprigs
ice cubes
1 litre bottle ginger ale
1 litre bottle soda water

Make tea with boiling water; infuse for 5 minutes then strain and cool. Simmer grated orange and lemon rinds with sugar and water for 5 minutes. Strain into tea. Add cordial and passionfruit, then chill until needed. Empty into punch bowl, add remaining ingredients and serve.
Makes 3 litres

Party Punch

CHILDREN OF ALL AGES

Of all the parties an adult will ever organise, the child's party will be the most detailed, for the invited guests will need constant supervision and lively entertainment at a venue that's childproof but cheery.

Even at an early age, children compete for the most imaginative and interesting party ideas, so you may have to be a little adventurous. Visits to the zoo, cinema, park or playground score well with the young ones and keep your home free from wreckage and ruin but they do require extra adult supervision and well-planned transport arrangements. Such excursion-style parties are best kept to small numbers (say, under eight guests). Consider how many children you can comfortably handle and consult the child host about the guest list. It would never do if you neglected to invite their latest best friend!

Find out if there are any particular 'in' foods and cater for them; likewise be alert to peer trends in music and other entertainment, particularly for an over-fives party as they're starting to develop a definite social conscience! Provide, if possible, some food, drink and seating arrangements for any adults who stay to help.

Essential to a successful party formula is a selection of lively and interesting games that may be adapted to suit the party theme or location. Be sure you have at least six different activities organised as children's attention span can wane very quickly.

Try to ensure that the rules aren't too complicated and that *everyone* has a chance to win a small prize.

When foul weather threatens to dull the excitement, have on hand a suitable video — a new release cartoon or adventure film is best — or projector slides as an alternative.

Remember that children get bored very easily so don't make the party too long; two and a half to three hours is usually plenty of time for everyone to eat, drink and be merry before the squabbling sets in!

When it's time to go home, check that each child has all his or her clothes — particularly shoes and socks! — and give them a small goodie bag to take away.

Good luck!

Frosted Patty Cakes and a personally iced Victoria Sandwich will delight small guests

Anna
Jenny
Zoe
Alix

Children's Party Checklist

* Choose a location, theme and time, the more original, the better.
* Send out interesting invitations two to three weeks ahead; try to keep the guest list small.
* Choose the menu and do as much as possible ahead of time. (Check now if any guests have special dietary needs.)
* Prepare house for the intended horde — clear away all valuables and establish 'off limits' boundaries such as bedrooms, studies, etc.
* Ensure that all children can be delivered and picked up at the nominated times; have a list of contact numbers for parents in case of emergency or illness.
* Ask another adult to help out and give you support for the afternoon. You'll need it!
* Decorate party area with balloons, streamers and posters, anything that's bright and cheery.
* Give the children plenty of room to move and make a mess; preferably outdoors.
* Have on hand a good supply of prizes, at least one for every child. Extras may come in handy in case of tantrums!
* Be sure your home and yard are safe for party activities; inform your neighbours of the event so they can keep a lookout for 'escapees' and wanderers!
* Keep pets away from the party zone; they may frighten timid guests or tempt little terrors!
* Arrange a set of rainy-weather alternative games and activities.
* Assemble goodie bags as far ahead of time as possible; make a few spares for last-minute arrivals and some for brothers and sisters.

TRAFFIC LIGHTS

24 slices brown bread
60 g butter
4 processed cheese slices
4 small tomatoes, sliced
6 lettuce leaves, shredded
salt and pepper, to taste
¼ cup shredded carrot

Spread bread slices lightly with butter. Cut crusts from bread. Using a round 1.5 cm biscuit cutter, press 6 holes into 12 of the bread slices. Cut each slice of processed cheese into thirds. Using remaining 12 slices of bread, arrange layers of tomato, cheese and lettuce to form traffic light colours, then top with salt, pepper and carrot. Top with cut-out slices of bread. Cut each sandwich in half.
Makes 24

RIBBON SANDWICHES

4 slices white bread
4 slices brown bread
softened butter
3–6 different sandwich fillings (see recipe)

Remove crusts from bread. Thinly butter bread. Spread 1 of the fillings on a slice of white bread. Top with slice of brown bread. Spread with second filling. Continue layering bread, using alternate slices of white and brown bread and spreading with filling. Cut sandwich in half, then each half into 4, making ribbon layer sandwiches.
Makes 8

PINWHEELS

1 loaf unsliced white bread
softened butter
3–6 different sandwich fillings (see recipe)

Remove crusts from loaf of bread. Cut bread in half. Carefully slice each half into 8 slices lengthways. Thinly butter each slice and spread evenly with filling. Roll up each slice lengthways and secure each roll with toothpick. Continue with remaining bread and filling.
Makes 8

Pinwheel Sandwiches (left) and Pizzas

SANDWICH FILLINGS

- Meat *or* seafood paste
- Salmon
- Cream cheese mixed with finely chopped dried fruits/walnuts/chives/celery/finely grated lemon and carrot
- Finely mashed egg with mayonnaise
- Chopped lettuce and ham
- Cheese spread *or* herbed processed cheese
- Mashed sardines
- Chicken and celery mixed with mayonnaise
- Peanut butter and sultanas
- Peanut butter and honey
- Peanut butter and finely shredded lettuce
- Mashed banana, lemon juice and desiccated coconut

HOT TUNA BREAD

1 French bread stick
225 g can tuna, drained
1 small onion, chopped
1 stick celery, chopped
2 tablespoons mayonnaise
1 tablespoon chopped parsley
1 teaspoon lemon juice
pepper, to taste
3 slices processed cheese

Preheat oven to 180°C (350°F). Halve bread lengthways and scoop out bread from crust. Mix together tuna, onion, celery, mayonnaise, parsley, lemon juice and pepper. Spoon tuna mixture into bread case.

Halve cheese slices diagonally. Layer cheese over top of tuna. Cover with top of bread stick. Wrap in foil and bake for 25 minutes. Five minutes before serving, open foil so that cheese will melt and bread will crust. Serve in slices. Serves 6

OPEN-FACED SANDWICHES

16 chicken fillets, cooked
16 slices Swiss cheese
16 slices dark rye bread
Thousand Island Dressing

AVOCADO BUTTER

3 avocados, peeled and seeded
2 tablespoons lime or *lemon juice*
500 g butter, softened
¼ teaspoon ginger

Puree avocados with other ingredients for Avocado Butter and chill. Any left over will freeze well.

Spread each slice of bread with Avocado Butter, top with a slice of cheese and chicken fillet. Spoon Thousand Island Dressing over all.
Makes 16 sandwiches

PYRAMID SANDWICHES

1–2 sliced sandwich loaves
60 g butter, softened
8 slices cooked chicken
½ lettuce, shredded
4 hard-boiled eggs, chopped
¼ cup mayonnaise
¼ teaspoon salt
freshly ground pepper
2 tomatoes, peeled and sliced
1 cucumber, peeled and sliced
100 g cream cheese
½ cup chopped olives
8 rolled anchovies
watercress and *radish roses, to garnish*

RUSSIAN DRESSING

½ cup oil
¼ cup tomato sauce
⅓ cup tarragon vinegar
1 teaspoon sugar
½ teaspoon salt
½ teaspoon grated onion

To make dressing, combine all ingredients in order listed and beat until thoroughly blended.

For each sandwich, cut 5 rounds of bread varying from 2 cm to 10 cm in diameter and spread with butter. Cover largest rounds with chicken and spread with Russian dressing.

Cover next round size with lettuce and eggs mixed with mayonnaise, salt and pepper and place on chicken. Cover third round with slice of tomato and cucumber and place on egg. Spread fourth round with cream cheese mixed with olives. Top with smallest round and spear with anchovy fastened with frilled toothpick. Place both over other rounds and garnish with watercress and radish roses.
Makes 8 sandwiches

Great Game Ideas

Apple Bobbing: Best as an outdoor activity, fill large tubs or buckets with water, place whole or halved apples in the water and challenge children to retrieve the apples using teeth only. Sure to cause a few splashes but lots of fun!
Musical Statues: A variation on the musical chairs theme, each guest must dance and move about while the music is played; when it stops suddenly, each must freeze perfectly still. Those who fail to do so are eliminated until there's a final winner.
Treasure Hunt: With secret little treasures hidden throughout the house and garden, issue each guest a clue that leads them to the next clue, and the next, until eventually they uncover the booty. Small amounts of coin money are always well-received!
Eat The Chocolate: Watch how fast children consume the prize in this game! You'll need a hat, gloves, sunglasses, scarf and pair of large boots plus a jumbo-sized block of chocolate, knife, fork and plate. Place the above in the middle of a circle of children and give them a couple of dice. Each child takes turns at rolling the dice until someone lands on a six; they then leap into the middle of the circle, don all the apparel then begin to eat the chocolate using the knife and fork. Meanwhile, the other players continue to roll the dice until another six is thrown. The winner then assumes the chocolate-eating role, even if the previous winner has only just managed to fit the gloves! It's frenzied fun in a mad race for just one bite of the chocolate!
Whispers: A good standby game to help quieten a wild bunch. Line the children in single file then whisper a message to the first in line; he in turn whispers it to the next person in line and so on. The last person, when they have received the message, announces it out loud. Rarely is the message transmitted intact! This game is so simple but it has children in fits of giggles!

Scrumptious ideas for Open Sandwiches

Barbecue a children's party — hamburgers, stuffed sausages, chipolatas, frankfurts and salad

THE BURGER

The best burgers are made with the best meat. Select prime, lean beef and ask your butcher to mince it for you. Mix any seasonings in lightly; don't pound it all to a pulp. For barbecues, burgers should all be the same size so you can serve everyone together. A good size is that of an egg ring — about 2 cm thick and 7 cm across which will take 10–15 minutes to cook. Use egg and fresh breadcrumbs for binding and add seasonings to suit. Spicy burgers are tasty but children often prefer the standard flavourings.

For parties you can prepare all the patties in advance with waxed paper in between and store, covered, in the refrigerator. Then barbecue and serve with separate bowls of sliced tomato, beetroot, lettuce, pickles, sauces, mustards, mayonnaise, grated cheese and whatever else you fancy. This way your guests make their own burgers and everyone is happy.

THE HAMBURGER

1 kg prime beef, minced
1 cup fresh breadcrumbs
2–3 eggs, depending on size
1–2 small onions, finely chopped
2 tablespoons fresh herbs such as basil, rosemary, thyme and oregano, mixed to taste
Digby's Special Sauce (see recipe)

Combine all ingredients. Roll into 10 equal balls then flatten into patties about the size of an egg ring (about 2–3 cm thick and 7–8 cm across). Barbecue over a medium to hot fire 10–15 minutes, turning about halfway through. Just before the end of cooking time, brush with Digby's Special Sauce and serve with bread rolls or buns and everything else you need to make a great hamburger.
Makes 10

DIGBY'S SPECIAL SAUCE

600 mL bottle tomato sauce
1 white onion, finely chopped
1 garlic clove, crushed
¼ cup lemon juice
pepper, to taste
¼ cup brown sugar
½ cup Worcestershire sauce
½ cup chilli sauce, to taste
Tabasco sauce, to taste
1 teaspoon French mustard
1 small can tomato paste (optional) or *2 ripe tomatoes*, blended with
1 cup water
½ teaspoon oregano

Combine all ingredients and simmer in a covered saucepan for about 1 hour, stirring occasionally. Do not boil. When making this sauce remember that the ingredients can be altered to suit your own taste. Serve with almost anything that is cooked on the barbecue.
Makes about 4 cups

BACON-WRAPPED BEEF AND APPLE BURGERS

750 g minced lean beef
⅓ cup breadcrumbs
¼ cup finely chopped onion
1½ teaspoons Worcestershire sauce
pepper, to taste
2 apples, grated
6 bacon rashers

Combine beef, breadcrumbs, onion, Worcestershire sauce, pepper and apple in a bowl. Form mixture into 6 patties. Wrap a bacon rasher round each burger securing with toothpick. Grill burgers for 10 minutes, turning once to brown each side. Serve on hamburger bun with salad and sauce.
Serves 6

BEEFBURGER SUPREME

500 g minced beef
200 g grated carrot
200 g grated zucchini
200 g grated apples
400 g grated potato
1 cup breadcrumbs
2 tablespoons flour
¼ cup finely chopped parsley
1 teaspoon dried mixed herbs

Combine all ingredients and form 10 hamburger patties. Grill for 10 minutes. Turn once to brown each side. Serve on bun or 2 pita breads. Add favourite toppings and sauce.
Makes 10

The Hamburger

BARBECUED CHICKEN

Children enjoy the taste of chicken and find finger-foods easier to handle at parties. Chicken is ideal for the barbecue, fast to cook, and can be marinated in many ways for extra succulence.

The important factor to remember with eating chicken outdoors is that it should be kept cool — but not frozen — right up to the time of cooking and eating to prevent bacterial growth, and that it should be cooked very thoroughly on the barbecue to avoid the risk of salmonella poisoning. If you are cooking large pieces of chicken over a high flame, the problem is that the outside can burn and turn to charcoal long before the meat in the middle is even warmed through. Side-step this hazard by placing the chicken pieces where they will cook more gently or alternatively cut them into smaller portions.

SAUSAGES

Sausages have long been a barbecue favourite with children and adults alike. These days a wide range of traditional, continental and spicy sausages, such as curry, tomato and garlic, are available from butchers, speciality shops and delicatessen counters — teenagers may prefer to experiment with these.

The perfect barbecued sausage should be parboiled first. This way it will be cooked on the inside and browned on the outside. Some shops will stock parboiled sausages for you. Otherwise, parboil them yourself by covering with water, bringing slowly to the boil and simmering 5 minutes. Drain, cool and store sausages overnight to let them settle and get cold. Parboiling cuts down the fat, the flaring and the cooking time. Don't be afraid to cut sausages to check if they are done. If you don't use parboiled sausages, make sure you prick them before barbecuing.

When catering, count on 2–3 sausages per person remembering that cold sausages always make a great midnight snack. Serve sausages with traditional tomato sauce, mustards, Digby's Special Sauce *(see recipe)* and with thick slices of bread or crunchy breadrolls.

BANGERS 'N BUNS

sausages, plain or *flavoured, parboiled*
crispy fresh breadrolls or *a tank loaf cut into thick slices*

Barbecue parboiled sausages over medium heat 10–15 minutes controlling temperature and turning to brown evenly all round. Serve with bread or rolls, buttered if you like, sauce and mustards to taste. Barbecue time depends on the thickness of the sausages and whether or not they are parboiled. Parboiled sausages will barbecue in about 10–15 minutes, but cut into them to make sure they are cooked.

Barbecued Chicken

WEISSWURST KEBABS

weisswurst
dried fruits such as
apricots, dates and apple

This white, herb sausage is delicious whole or cut in chunks, barbecued over a medium heat and served with German mustard.

To make kebabs, skin sausage and cut into 3–4 cm thick slices. Thread on skewers alternating with dried fruits for colour. Barbecue for 15 minutes turning occasionally.

COCKTAIL BANANA KEBABS

6 cocktail frankfurts
2 bananas, peeled
3 bacon rashers
6 × 2.5 cm pieces pineapple
6 button mushrooms

Thread cocktail frankfurts onto skewers. Cut each banana into thirds. Add piece banana to skewer. Cut bacon rashers in half. Roll each half and secure onto skewer. Finish with piece of pineapple then mushroom.

Place under preheated grill and cook until all sides are browned. Serve hot.

VARIATION

Bananas can be replaced with dried fruits such as apples, dates, apricots etc.
Serves 6

STUFFED SAUSAGES

good quality sausages, beef
or *pork, parboiled*

FILLINGS

fresh oysters
asparagus spears
smoked oysters
banana slices
melted Parmesan cheese

Barbecue sausages over medium fire until cooked. Make a cut along the sausage, leaving about 1 cm uncut at each end. Insert selected fillings plus any others you wish to try.

CHIPOLATAS

Chipolatas need to be cooked gently, so parboil first then barbecue over a medium heat, turning frequently. Serve whole or sliced on skewers with mustards and sauces. They are a great favourite at sausage sizzles and children's parties served hot or cooked in advance and served cold. Barbecue time about 10 minutes.

SAUSAGES IN BLANKETS

8 thin sausages
2 sheets frozen ready-rolled
puff pastry, thawed
1 egg, beaten
¼ cup sesame seeds

Partially cook sausages in frying pan. Remove from frying pan and cool. Cut each pastry sheet into 4 triangles. Place 1 sausage on widest end of triangle and roll up. Repeat with remaining sausages and pastry. Brush each with beaten egg. Place onto lightly greased baking tray and sprinkle with sesame seeds. Bake at 200°C (400°F) for 15–20 minutes until pastry puffs and browns. Serve hot or cold.
Note: Continental frankfurts can be substituted for sausages.
Serves 8

SPICE THAT SAUSAGE SIZZLE WITH VARIETY

Many savoury sausages are now available and are excellent for barbecuing. Try some of the following:

- Beef and Blackbean
- Beef and Tomato
- Blackbean and Honey
- Boerwors
- Bratwurst
- Chicken
- Chicken and Tarragon
- Chorizo
- Colonial Beef
- Curry
- Garlic
- Italian Spicy
- Italian Tomato
- Kransky
- Lamb Provencale
- London Pork
- Merguez
- Mexicana
- Minted Lamb
- Peppercorn
- Pork and Veal
- Satay Beef
- Tomato and Onion
- Turkey and Chives
- Turkey and Sage

Weisswurst Kebabs, Cocktail Banana Kebabs and Stuffed Sausages

FRILLY CHEESE FRANKFURTS

500 g potatoes, peeled and chopped
30 g butter
¼ cup milk
pepper, to taste
¼ cup finely chopped onion
¼ cup chopped green capsicum
6 frankfurts
¾ cup grated Cheddar cheese

Boil potatoes until tender then drain. Mash potatoes with butter, milk and pepper. Add onion and capsicum, slit frankfurts lengthways. Place cut side up in baking dish. Pipe each frankfurt with potato and sprinkle with Cheddar cheese. Bake at 185°C (360°F) for 20 minutes and serve hot.
Serves 6

CHEESY SAUSAGE ROLLS

2 cups flour
125 g butter, cut in pieces
½ cup grated tasty cheese
2 tablespoons water
250 g sausage mince
1 onion, finely chopped
milk, to glaze
2 tablespoons grated Parmesan

Sift flour and salt into a bowl. Add butter, cheese and water to flour and mix to form dough. Knead lightly on a floured surface and roll dough into long strip. Fold in 3. Seal ends and give pastry a half turn. Repeat rolling and turning 3 times. (If weather is hot, rest pastry for 20 minutes between rollings.) Roll out pastry to a long strip 6 mm thick.

Combine sausage mince and onion. Place meat along pastry in long strip. Brush edges of pastry with water. Fold pastry over meat and seal edges together. Cut roll into 12 pieces.

Place on ungreased baking tray. Preheat oven to 220°C (425°F). Mark slits on each piece and glaze with milk. Sprinkle lightly with Parmesan cheese. Bake for 10 minutes. Reduce heat to 200°C (400°F) for further 5–10 minutes. Cool on cake rack. Serve hot or cold.
Makes 12

SAUSAGE AND BACON PLAIT

1 packet frozen ready-rolled puff pastry, thawed
1 egg, beaten
1 tablespoon sesame seeds

FILLING

500 g minced pork
250 g bacon, chopped
1 onion, chopped
1 tablespoon chopped parsley
salt and pepper, to taste
¼ teaspoon mixed herbs

Roll out pastry to 25 cm square on a lightly floured surface. Combine filling ingredients and place along centre of pastry. Cut pastry on each side of filling into diagonal strips 1.5 cm wide. Brush with beaten egg.

Place strips from each side alternately over the sausage mixture to form plait. Place plait onto lightly greased baking tray, glaze with egg, sprinkle with sesame seeds and bake at 200°C (400°F) for 30–40 minutes or until cooked. Serve hot.
Serves 6

SAY CHEESE PIES

2 cups flour
pinch cayenne pepper
90 g butter
1 cup grated tasty cheese
2–3 tablespoons iced water
milk, to glaze

FILLING

1 large onion, sliced
30 g butter
2 hard-boiled eggs, peeled and chopped
180 g Cheddar cheese, diced
1 tablespoon chopped parsley
½ teaspoon nutmeg
pepper, to taste

Sift flour and cayenne into a bowl. Rub through butter till mixture resembles fine breadcrumbs. Add cheese and water to form dough.

Knead lightly on floured board. Roll out dough to 6 mm thickness. Cut into 16 rounds to fit patty tins. Press 8 rounds into base of patty tins. Prick base lightly. Set aside. Preheat oven to 220°C (425°F).

Saute onion in butter until transparent, drain. Combine onion with remaining filling ingredients and divide filling between pastry-lined patty tins. Damp edges of pastry, cover with remaining pastry rounds. Seal edges together. Make small hole in centre of top of each pie. Brush with milk. Bake for 30 minutes then remove from tins to rack. Serve hot or cold.
Makes 8

Mini Pizza

MINI PIZZA

2 mini-sized pieces of pita bread
1 avocado, thinly sliced
1 tomato, thinly sliced
1 zucchini, thinly sliced
1 onion, finely chopped
1 tablespoon finely chopped capsicum
1 tablespoon chopped parsley
2 tablespoons tomato paste
1 cup grated cheese or *½ cup fresh Parmesan* and *½ cup Cheddar cheese*
few chopped olives, to garnish (optional)

Mix all ingredients except cheese in a bowl. Spread evenly over pita bread, making sure it is covered right up to the edge. Top with sliced avocado and then grated cheese.

Bake in preheated oven at 220°C (425°F), until cheese has melted and is bubbling brown, or grill until done. Serves 2

CHICKEN LEGS IN A BLANKET

4 tablespoons Parmesan cheese
½ cup grated tasty cheese
1 teaspoon oregano
12 chicken drumsticks, skinned and excess fat removed
60 g butter, melted
12 sheets filo pastry

Mix cheese and oregano together. Brush drumsticks with butter and coat with cheese mixture. Brush a sheet of filo with butter, keeping remainder of filo covered with a damp cloth. Place drumstick on pastry and roll up like a parcel. Brush each parcel with butter and arrange in a shallow greased ovenproof dish. Bake at 190°C (375°F) for 35 minutes until tender.
Serves 12

SESAME DRUMSTICKS

8 chicken drumsticks
¼ cup seasoned flour
1 egg, beaten
3 tablespoons sesame seeds
¼ cup toasted breadcrumbs
60 g butter, melted

Wipe drumsticks, dip in seasoned flour, then beaten egg and coat in combined sesame seeds and breadcrumbs.

Place drumsticks on greased baking tray and bake at 180°C (350°F) for 30 minutes. Brush drumsticks with butter. Continue cooking a further 15–20 minutes or until golden brown. Serve hot or cold.
Makes 8

BATTER-FRIED CHICKEN

6 chicken drumsticks
1 cup flour
1½ teaspoons paprika
1 egg
⅔ cup milk
20 g butter, melted
oil, for frying

Remove skin from chicken drumsticks. Pat drumsticks dry with paper towel. Sift flour and paprika into a bowl. Make a well in the centre. Add the egg and stir. Blend in milk and butter, beating till smooth. Heat oil in frying pan. Dip drumsticks in batter then fry in hot oil. Cook gently, turning to brown and cook through. Drain and serve hot with french fries.
Serves 6

Chicken Legs in a Blanket

MEATBALL BOATS

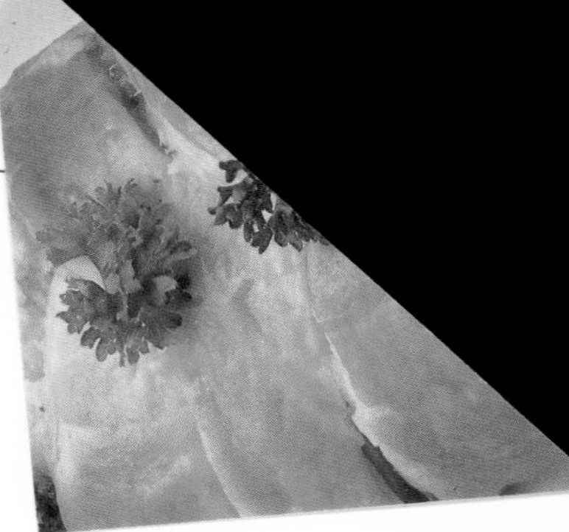

500 g minced meat
1 cup grated tasty cheese
2 tablespoons tomato sauce
pepper, to taste
½ cup desiccated coconut
15 cheese slices
30 thin slices cucumber

Combine minced meat, cheese, tomato sauce and pepper. Form mixture into 30 meatballs. Toss in coconut until well coated. Place on greased oven tray and bake at 200°C (400°F) for 15 minutes.

Cut each cheese slice into 2 triangles. Place 1 cheese slice and 1 cucumber slice together. Secure through top and bottom with toothpick to form the mast and sail. Attach to the meatball. Serve meatballs hot or cold.
Makes 30

TUNA AND NOODLE BAKE

¾ cup macaroni, cooked
220 g can tuna, drained
⅓ cup mayonnaise
½ cup chopped celery
salt and pepper, to taste
130 g can condensed cream of celery soup
⅓ cup milk
100 g grated tasty cheese
¼ cup breadcrumbs
1 tablespoon chopped parsley, to garnish

Combine macaroni, tuna, mayonnaise, celery, salt and pepper. Blend together soup and milk over heat, stirring until heated through, but do not boil. Add half the cheese, stir until melted.

Fold soup mixture with macaroni and noodle mixture. Place into 2 litre casserole dish. Sprinkle with remaining cheese and breadcrumbs. Bake at 180°C (350°F) for 20 minutes. When cooked, sprinkle with parsley to serve.
Serves 6

ase Come To A Part
Party

SAVOURY EGG BOATS

6 hard-boiled eggs
210 g can tuna, drained
½ cup finely chopped celery
¼ cup mayonnaise
pepper, to taste
¼ teaspoon dry mustard
3 slices bread
finely chopped parsley, to garnish

Peel and halve eggs lengthways. Remove yolk from white and mash yolk finely. Combine mashed yolks with tuna, celery, mayonnaise, pepper and mustard and pile into egg white halves. Cut crusts off bread. Cut each piece of toast into 4 triangles. Insert 1 triangle on top of each stuffed egg boat to resemble a sail. Garnish with chopped parsley. Refrigerate until serving time.
Makes 12

FRIED RICE

1½ cups uncooked rice
2 eggs
1 tablespoon sherry
2 tablespoons oil
12 shallots, cut into 1 cm diagonal pieces
125 g Char Sui, diced (see recipe)
½ cup diced smoked ham (optional)
1 tablespoon soy sauce
shallot curls, to garnish

Boil rice and separate the grains of rice with chopsticks or a fork. Lightly beat eggs and sherry.

Heat oil in a wok. Add shallots, Char Sui and ham and stir-fry 30 seconds. Add rice and stir-fry until heated through and each grain is coated with oil.

Pour in egg mixture. Continue stir-frying until egg is nearly set.

Add soy sauce and stir until well-combined. Serve immediately, garnished with shallot curls.
Serves 4

BUSH BABY SALAD

2 cups alfalfa sprouts
2 celery stalks, cut into 6 cm lengths
½ cup raisins
120 g cherry tomatoes, halved
4 carrots, peeled and cut into matchsticks
1 cup corn kernels

Spread alfalfa sprouts over a large serving plate. Cut celery into 6 cm lengths and arrange attractively on the alfalfa with the remaining ingredients.
Serves 6

Clockwise from top: Sausage and Bacon Plait (p. 72), Bush Baby Salad, Sesame Drumsticks (p. 75), Savoury Egg Boats

WATERMELON SALAD

½ watermelon
1–2 rock melons
3 cups cooked rice
440 g can whole corn kernels
500 g black grapes, peeled and seeded
500 g white grapes, peeled and seeded
mint or basil leaves, to garnish

Remove watermelon seeds. Scoop all flesh out of melons using a melon baller. Combine ingredients and pile into watermelon shell. Cover with foil or plastic wrap and chill. Serve garnished with mint or basil leaves. Vinaigrette Dressing *(see recipe)* can be poured over salad if desired.
Serves 6–8

Watermelon Salad

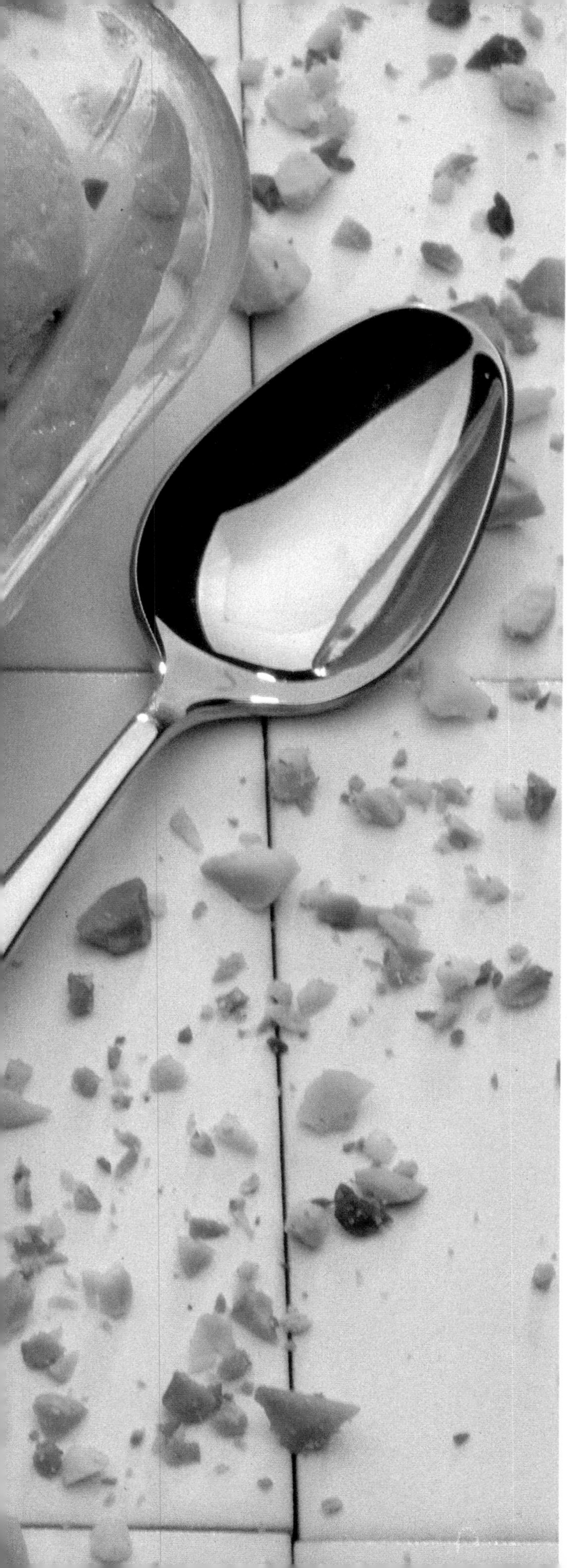

Sweet

Sugar and spice and all things nice

AVOCADO ICE CREAM

2 large avocados
3 cups cream
6 tablespoons honey
2 teaspoons vanilla essence
3 egg whites, stiffly beaten
3 bananas (if unavailable, add 1 extra avocado)

Blend avocado, cream, honey, vanilla and banana in small batches in blender until thick. Pour into ice cream tray or container.

Beat egg whites and fold into ice cream carefully with a metal spoon; freeze.

Gently stir ice cream when it is starting to freeze around the edges. Repeat twice more and then allow ice cream to freeze.

Remove from freezer about 20 minutes before serving. Serve with fresh sliced strawberries and kiwi fruit.

Note: The key to a good consistency is ensuring that the mixture is beaten initially until thick and that the ice cream is mixed as it freezes to prevent ice crystals forming.

Makes about 2 litres

AVOCADO ICE CREAM SPLIT

1 avocado, sliced lengthways into 4 pieces
4 scoops Avocado Ice Cream (see recipe)
4–6 tablespoons pure maple syrup
2 tablespoons crushed nuts
fresh strawberries, kiwi fruit or *cherries*

Place sliced avocado along sides of long shallow glass dish. Fill centre with ice cream scoops. Spoon over maple syrup and sprinkle with nuts. Garnish with strawberries, cherries or kiwi fruit.

Serves 2

Avocado Ice Cream Split

TAMARILLO ICE CREAM

1 cup sugar
1 cup water
4 tamarillos
450 mL cream
3 egg yolks, beaten

Boil sugar and water for 8–10 minutes until thin syrup is formed. Add tamarillos and simmer over low heat until just tender. Allow to cool, remove fruit, peel and discard skin. Puree fruit and strain, discarding seeds.

Bring cream to boil, add egg yolks and cook over low heat, stirring constantly until mixture coats back of a wooden spoon. Cool and combine with tamarillo puree and syrup. Pour into ice trays and freeze until nearly firm. Stir mixture then freeze until firm.
Makes 3 cups

TUTTI-FRUTTI ICE CREAM CAKE

2 litres vanilla ice cream
1 cup mixed glace fruits and *nuts*
1 punnet strawberries, hulled
2 tablespoons sherry
½ cup sugar
strawberry essence
2 drops red food colouring
225 g can red peach slices, drained
whipped cream, to serve

Divide ice cream into thirds. Mix glace fruits and nuts into 1 portion. Place in 3 litre mould and freeze. Slice strawberries and soak in sherry and sugar. Spoon them over frozen ice cream and refrigerate.

Flavour second portion of ice cream with strawberry essence and add food colouring. Spoon over strawberry layer and freeze until firm. Add layer peach slices and remaining vanilla ice cream on top. Freeze for 24 hours. Unmould and decorate with whipped cream.
Serves 10

MELON DESSERT

1 can fruit salad with syrup
2 bananas, sliced or diced
1 cup watermelon, scooped into balls
1 cup rock melon, scooped into balls
ice cream or *whipped cream (optional)*

Mix fruits and syrup together and chill. Serve plain or with ice cream or whipped fresh cream.
Note: Melon desserts look most attractive served in a glass bowl.
Serves 4–6

ORANGE BOMBS

12 large oranges
2 litres vanilla ice cream
¾ cup orange juice concentrate, well chilled
finely grated rind 1 orange
few drops orange food colouring
orange leaves or blossom, to garnish (optional)

Cut top third from each orange. Using a small knife, loosen orange flesh from just inside skin. Carefully scoop down into the oranges and remove as much flesh and membrane as possible. Reserve orange flesh for fruit juice.

Remove ice cream from freezer and allow to soften slightly. Place in large mixing bowl and, using a metal spoon, stir in remaining ingredients. If ice cream starts to soften too much, return to freezer for a few minutes.

Place orange shells on baking trays. Spoon ice cream into shells until almost full (the filling will expand when frozen). Place in freezer for 2 hours then remove and wrap in plastic wrap. Return to freezer then place bombs in refrigerator for 30 minutes before serving. The ice cream filling will soften slightly and the orange shells will collect a frosty 'bloom'. Serve topped with orange leaves or blossom if in season.
Makes 12

GRAPE KEBABS

green and purple grapes
skewers

Insert skewers through alternating green and purple grapes and freeze. A superb treat for very hot days though unsuitable for very young children.

FROZEN FRUIT POPSICLES

2 cups strawberries, washed
½ cup concentrated apple juice
½ cup unsweetened pineapple juice

Place strawberries in a food processor or blender and process until smooth. Add remaining ingredients and process a further 30 seconds. Transfer mixture into a jug and pour into ice block moulds. Place in freezer and freeze for at least 6 hours.
Makes 12

FRUITY FLAN

PASTRY
3½ cups biscuit crumbs
½ cup ground hazelnuts
1 teaspoon grated orange rind
125 g butter, melted

FILLING
8 egg yolks
1 cup sugar
5 tablespoons flour
1 tablespoon cornflour
600 mL milk, scalded
1 tablespoon orange liqueur

TOPPING
1 honeydew melon, scooped into balls
300 g muscat grapes
½ rock melon, scooped into balls
2 guavas, sliced
½ kiwano (horn melon)
1 strawberry

GLAZE
½ cup apricot jam
1 tablespoon orange liqueur

To make pastry, combine dry ingredients with butter. Press mixture into base and sides of 25 cm flan dish. Bake at 180°C (350°F) for 10 minutes, remove and cool.

To make filling, combine yolks, sugar, flour and cornflour together in a bowl to form a smooth paste. Blend in scalded milk, return to saucepan and heat gently until thickened. Do not boil. Remove from heat and stir in liqueur. Allow to cool slightly, stirring occasionally. Pour filling into prepared pastry case and allow to set. Arrange the fruit pieces decoratively over cooled filling.

To make glaze, warm apricot jam gently and stir in liqueur. Quickly brush hot glaze over fruit and allow to set.

Serve well chilled.
Serves 6–8

APRICOT AND PAWPAW FLAN

225 g frozen ready-rolled sweet shortcrust pastry, thawed

FILLING
225 mL milk
1 tablespoon cornflour
2 tablespoons sugar
1 egg yolk, beaten
5 drops vanilla essence
1 pawpaw, sliced
12 canned apricots, halved

GLAZE
3 tablespoons canned apricot syrup
3 tablespoons apricot jam
3 tablespoons sugar
1 tablespoon cornflour

TO SERVE
3 tablespoons whipped cream
5 green glace cherries

Roll out shortcrust and line a greased 20 cm flan case. Bake blind, and cool.

To make filling, mix a little milk with cornflour and sugar. Heat remaining milk in a saucepan. Combine and cook until thick. Remove from heat, stir in egg yolk and vanilla essence. Add a quarter chopped pawpaw to filling. Pour into flan case. Arrange apricot halves and sliced pawpaw on top.

To make glaze, boil apricot syrup, jam and sugar. Add cornflour mixed with water. Boil for 2 minutes until glaze clears. Pour over fruit while warm and chill. Decorate with stars of whipped cream, using a piping bag, and green glace cherries.
Serves 6–8

Fruity Flan

Basic Fancy Cake Mix

BASIC FANCY CAKE MIXTURE

60 g butter
¼ cup caster sugar
1 large egg, beaten
½ cup self-raising flour

Preheat oven to 180°C (350°F).

Cream together butter and sugar until light and fluffy. Gradually stir in egg and, using a metal spoon, fold in flour.

To bake individual cakes, spoon mixture into 8 small paper cases and bake for 15–20 minutes until golden brown and well risen. Alternatively spoon mixture into greased and lined 15 cm square cake tin and bake for 20–25 minutes. Cool cake on rack before icing.

Basic Icings

BASIC BUTTERCREAM

125 g butter
1⅓ cups icing sugar
milk, to mix
flavouring of your choice

Cream butter with fork until soft. Beat in icing sugar, a little at a time.

Add sufficient warm milk to soften the mixture. Add flavouring of your choice, such as a few drops of vanilla or almond essence, grated orange or lemon rind and a little juice, coffee essence, cocoa, melted chocolate, chopped nuts.

Makes enough to coat sides and either fill or top a 20 cm cake

MOCK CREAM

40 g butter
⅓ cup caster sugar
2 tablespoons hot water
2 tablespoons hot milk
vanilla essence, to taste

Cream butter and sugar until light and fluffy. Add water a teaspoon at a time, beating well. Add milk and vanilla. Beat well.
Makes approximately 1 cup

Selection of cakes

BASIC FROSTED ICING

2 cups loaf sugar
⅔ cup water
2 egg whites

Place loaf sugar and water in a pan and leave to stand for a while. Since this icing sets as soon as it is made, have the cake ready for icing.

Whisk egg whites until very stiff.

Gently heat sugar until it has dissolved. Place a sugar thermometer in pan and bring syrup to the boil. When temperature reaches 115°C (240°F) remove from heat.

Allow bubbles to subside and pour syrup over egg whites, beating vigorously all the time. Beat until icing is thick and fluffy and forms peaks. Spread it quickly over cake.

Makes enough to coat a 20 cm cake

Toppings, Flavourings and Fillings

COFFEE CAKES
Fold 1 tablespoon coffee essence into basic mixture before baking in paper cases. Spread cakes with coffee-flavoured icing and decorate with walnut halves.

FEATHER CAKES
Spread cooled cakes with frosted icing. Brush 4 parallel lines of orange food colouring over the icing while it is still hot and immediately make 4 parallel lines with tip of skewer at right-angles to coloured lines.

CHERRY CAKES
Spread cooled cakes with frosted icing and top with glace cherries.

QUEEN CAKES
Blend 2 tablespoons currants into basic cake mixture before baking.

ORANGE CAKES
Cut round in top of each cake and remove 'lids'. Pipe a rosette of Orange Buttercream *(see recipe)* in centre and replace lids.

LEMON CAKES
Fill cakes with lemon buttercream instead of orange buttercream.

CHOCOLATE CASES
Melt ½ cup chocolate and, using a wet brush, spread a little over inside of 8 paper cases. Leave to set before brushing with a second coat. When second coat has set, crumble a few cake trimmings into chocolate cases and sprinkle each with a little sherry. Pipe whipped cream over top and decorate with mandarin segments.

CAULIFLOWER CAKES
Bake basic mixture in square cake tin. Cut cake into circles 5 cm in diameter. Knead green food colouring into marzipan and, using a rolling pin sprinkled with a little icing sugar, roll out very thinly. Using a 5 cm pastry cutter, cut marzipan into 36 circles. Spread a little buttercream around sides of cakes and wrap 4 marzipan circles around each. Pipe rosettes of buttercream over top to represent cauliflower florets.

VICTORIA SANDWICH

Delicious as a simple sponge or decorated as a birthday cake, this is a very useful basic recipe.

125 g butter
½ cup caster sugar
2 eggs
1 cup self-raising flour
3 tablespoons jam
icing sugar

Preheat oven to 175°C (340°F). Cream butter and sugar until soft. Whisk eggs, beat into sugar mixture. Fold in flour. Spoon mixture into 2 greased and lined 15 cm sponge tins. Bake for 20 minutes. Remove cakes from tins and cool on cake rack.

Spread jam onto first cake and sandwich to second. Sprinkle top with icing sugar or ice and decorate as a birthday cake.

SERVING SUGGESTIONS
Try decorating your cake with some of the following: flowers, small toys, marzipan miniature fruits, smarties, jaffas or other sweets, hundreds and thousands, glace fruits, silver balls, whipped cream, sliced fresh fruit, candles and anything else that appeals to your imagination. Athletic boys or girls may like a cricket cake: use green icing for grass, desiccated coconut for the pitch, candles for stumps, a jaffa for a ball and small dolls to represent players. Girls may like heart-shaped cakes with plenty of fancy icing decorations. Try using different shaped tins — there is plenty of variety available.
Makes 2

Something special — dainty Jelly Cakes and a Cricketer's Cake

NURSERY CAKE

1 quantity Victoria Sandwich (see recipe)
¼ cup raspberry jam

ICING

125 g icing sugar
1–2 tablespoons boiling water
1 drop red food colouring
50 cm lace, 5 cm in width
1 plastic baby doll
silver balls

Prepare cake and bake in 30 × 20 cm lamington tin. Allow to cool. Halve cake; spread raspberry jam over 1 layer and sandwich cake together.

Combine icing sugar, water and food colouring. Blend till smooth. Cover top of cake with icing. Place baby doll onto top of cake in reclining position.

Thicken icing with extra icing sugar. Fill piping bag with small rosette tube attachment.

Pipe rosettes from waist of doll down to base of cake to resemble blanket. Secure lace around sides of cake attaching with icing rosette and decorate with silver balls.

RAINBOW CAKE

250 g butter
1 teaspoon vanilla
1 cup sugar
4 eggs
2½ cups self-raising flour
1 cup flour
¾ cup milk
1 drop red food colouring
60 g chocolate, melted

FILLING

⅓ cup raspberry jam
300 mL cream, whipped

VANILLA ICING

125 g white chocolate
2 cups icing sugar
⅔ cup milk
250 g butter
1 teaspoon vanilla

Preheat oven to 200°C (400°F). Cream butter, vanilla and sugar. Add eggs, one at a time and beat well. Sift flours and fold in alternately with milk. Divide mixture evenly into three. Leave one third plain, colour one third pink with red food colouring, and add melted chocolate to remaining one third.

Spoon mixtures separately into 3 greased and lined 20 cm cake tins. Bake for 20–25 minutes. Cool on cake rack. When cold, remove paper lining, sandwich layers together with raspberry jam and whipped cream, and ice with vanilla icing.

Melt chocolate in top of double saucepan. Blend together icing sugar, milk, butter and vanilla, fold in melted chocolate. Allow to set and decorate as desired.

SWEETHEART CAKE

2 tablespoons fine breadcrumbs
4 eggs
½ cup caster sugar
3 tablespoons flour
1 tablespoon cornflour
½ tablespoon ground almonds
20 g butter, melted
red food colouring

TOPPING

1 tablespoon cornflour
300 mL milk
½ cup caster sugar
1 tablespoon vanilla sugar
½ teaspoon vanilla essence
250 g butter
2 tablespoons raspberry jam
2 tablespoons chopped nuts
crystallised violets
sugar balls
moulded sugar flowers

Preheat oven to 190°C (375°F). Grease a heart-shaped 20 cm tin. Sprinkle with fine breadcrumbs. Whisk eggs and sugar until thick and creamy. Sift flour and cornflour and add almonds. Fold flour mixture into eggs, with melted butter and 1 drop red food colouring.

Spoon mixture into cake tin. Bake for 35–45 minutes. When cooked, remove cake and cool on cake rack. Invert cake on rack to cool completely. To make topping, blend cornflour with 2 tablespoons milk, add sugar, vanilla sugar and vanilla essence. Heat remaining milk and add to cornflour mixture. Bring to boil, stirring until thickened. Allow to cool. Cream butter and add gradually to cooled sauce.

Carefully halve cake. Spread with raspberry jam and sandwich together. Completely cover cake with buttercream sauce spreading smoothly. Pipe rosettes around top of cake and decorate with chopped nuts, crystallised violets, sugar balls and flowers. Refrigerate until serving time.

MANGO-FILLED ROLL

½ cup caster sugar
3 eggs, separated
¾ cup flour
2 teaspoons baking powder
2 tablespoons hot milk
2 tablespoons caster sugar combined with
1 teaspoon cinnamon

FILLING

1 cup mashed mango
1 cup thickened cream
1 tablespoon icing sugar, sifted

Preheat oven to 220°C (425°F). Grease and line Swiss roll tin with greaseproof paper. Sift flour and baking powder in a bowl. Beat egg whites until stiff. Gradually beat in sugar until mixture becomes thick and glossy. Beat in yolks one at a time. Fold in sifted, dry ingredients and hot milk. Pour mixture into tin and smooth surface. Bake for 10 minutes.

Turn cake out onto a sheet of greaseproof paper sprinkled with caster sugar mixture. Roll cake up and allow to cool. Whip cream till thick. Fold in mango and sugar and chill. Unroll cake and spread with cream.

Roll up and chill before serving.

Mango-filled Roll

MOCHA MALLOW CAKE

20 marshmallows
⅔ cup cocoa
½ cup hot water
2 cups self-raising flour
1 teaspoon salt
165 g butter
2 teaspoons vanilla
1 cup sugar
3 eggs
¾ cup sour cream
1 quantity Mock Cream (see recipe)

MOCHA ICING

125 g icing sugar
1 teaspoon coffee powder
30 g butter
1–2 tablespoons milk
1 small packet Smarties
1 chocolate Flake

Preheat oven to 190°C (375°F). In top of double saucepan combine marshmallows, cocoa and water. Bring pan to boil and heat until marshmallows are melted. Set aside to cool.

Sift flour and salt and set aside. Cream butter and vanilla, add sugar and blend till smooth. Add eggs to cooled cocoa mixture. Fold in flour, butter mixture and sour cream. Blend evenly. Place in 2 × 23 cm greased and lined cake tins. Bake for 35 minutes then cool on cake rack.

Sandwich together with Mock Cream. Combine icing sugar, coffee powder, butter and milk till smooth. Ice cake and decorate with Smarties and chocolate Flake.

PATTY CAKE PARADE

1 quantity Victoria Sandwich batter (see recipe)

GLACE ICING

1½ cups pure icing sugar, sifted
5 g butter
1–2 tablespoons boiling water
few drops food colourings of your choice

Line 2 patty cake trays with paper cups and fill two-thirds full with spoonfuls of Victoria Sandwich mixture. Bake at 180°C (350°F) for 15–20 minutes or until cakes are well risen and golden brown. Turn out onto a wire rack to cool before icing.

To make icing, combine icing sugar and butter in a bowl and beat; gradually add enough boiling water to mix. Add colourings, leaving 1 bowl of icing white. Ice cakes and decorate imaginatively: use white icing to pipe names of party guests or rosettes onto iced cakes; garnish with hundreds and thousands, chocolate vermicelli, silver balls, glace cherries, jellybabies, Smarties or other favourite sweets. Let your imagination create a colourful variety where every cake is different — they look wonderful massed together on large trays or serving platters.

Note: To achieve a smooth finish on your icing, use a round bladed knife and dip from time to time in hot water. Uniced cakes can be made in advance and frozen.
Makes 24

JACK-IN-THE-BOX CAKES

125 g butter
¾ cup caster sugar
2 cups self-raising flour
2 eggs, beaten
½ cup milk
vanilla essence, to taste

VANILLA ICING

125 g white chocolate
2 cups icing sugar
⅔ cup milk
250 g butter
1 teaspoon vanilla

ROYAL ICING

1 egg white
1½ cups sifted icing sugar
1 teaspoon clear honey

DECORATIONS

5 metres × 5 cm ribbon
9 toy people (clowns, dolls etc) no larger than 5 cm in height

Preheat oven to 180°C (350°F). Cream butter and sugar till fluffy. Fold in flour, eggs, milk and vanilla. Blend till smooth.

Pour mixture into greased and lined 22 cm square cake tin. Bake cake for 25–30 minutes then remove paper and cool on cake rack. Cut cake into 9 equal squares and coat each square with icing. Melt chocolate in top of double saucepan. Blend together icing sugar, milk, butter and vanilla. Fold in melted chocolate. Allow to set before decorating.

Place 1 toy onto top of each square. Cut ribbon into 9 equal lengths leaving enough ribbon for bows. Carefully secure 1 piece ribbon around each cake. With extra ribbon, make bows and attach with icing to front of each cake.

Whisk egg white lightly. Fold in icing sugar and honey to form a fairly stiff icing. Pipe Royal Icing around top of each cake to form border. To make Royal Icing, combine all ingredients and beat until smooth.

VARIATIONS

CHOCOLATE ICING

Use dark cooking chocolate instead of white.

STRAWBERRY ICING

Add 2 drops red food colouring and ¼ teaspoon strawberry essence.

CHOCOLATE CAKE

Add ½ teaspoon bicarbonate of soda, 4 tablespoons cocoa and an extra 1 tablespoon milk.

ORANGE CAKE

2 teaspoons grated orange rind. Decrease milk by 3 tablespoons and add 3 tablespoons orange juice.
Makes 9 cakes

CHOCOLATE BUTTERFLY CAKES

125 g butter
½ cup caster sugar
2 eggs, beaten
¾ cup self-raising flour
¼ cup cocoa
1 tablespoon warm water
chocolate vermicelli, to sprinkle

MOCK CREAM

40 g butter
⅓ cup caster sugar
2 tablespoons hot water
2 tablespoons hot milk
vanilla, to taste

Preheat oven to 190°C (375°F). Cream butter and sugar till smooth. Beat in eggs. Fold in sifted flour and cocoa alternately with water. Beat mixture 2 minutes. Spoon mixture into 20 paper-lined patty tins. Bake for 15 minutes. Cool on a cake rack.

Cut tops off cakes and halve. To make mock cream, beat butter and sugar until light and fluffy. Add water a teaspoon at a time, beating well. Add milk and vanilla and beat well. Spoon 1–2 teaspoonfuls of mock cream on top of each cake and press in the tops to form wings. Sprinkle each butterfly with chocolate vermicelli.
Makes 20

JELLY CAKES

1 quantity Victoria Sandwich (see recipe)
2 × 25 g packets raspberry jelly crystals
2 cups boiling water
2 cups desiccated coconut
300 mL thickened cream, whipped

Make Victoria Sandwich according to directions. Lightly grease 2 patty tins. Place 1–2 tablespoons of cake mixture into patty tins and bake in the top half of the oven at 180°C (350°F) for 15–20 minutes or until well risen and golden brown. Turn out onto a cake rack to cool.

Dissolve jelly in boiling water and pour into a heatproof dish deep enough to cover a cake. Place in refrigerator and allow to partially set. The jelly should resemble the consistency of egg white. Sprinkle coconut on a large sheet of greaseproof paper. Dip each cake in jelly then roll in coconut to coat. If a thicker coating is desired, repeat process.

Place jelly cakes in a single layer on a tray and refrigerate until set. One or 2 hours before serving, cut a little off the top of each cake. Place a small spoonful of cream on each cake and replace their tops before serving.
Makes approximately 30

APRICOT CHEESECAKE

425 g canned apricots in syrup
1 packet orange jelly
450 g cottage cheese
1 tablespoon caster sugar
150 mL whipped cream
100 g crushed ginger biscuits
1 tablespoon brown sugar
50 g butter, melted

DECORATION

2 tablespoons apricot jam
425 g canned apricots in syrup
1 tablespoon flaked almonds

Make up the syrup from the canned apricots to 300 mL with water. Bring to boil, add jelly and stir to dissolve; cool. Sieve apricots and cheese and stir in cooled jelly and sugar. Fold in cream.

Line the base of a 20 cm cake tin with non-stick paper. Pour in mixture and chill to set. Freeze until needed.

Combine biscuits, brown sugar and butter, sprinkle over set mixture and press down with a spoon. Melt jam with 1 tablespoon of apricot syrup, sieve and cool.

Turn out cheesecake and decorate with apricots. Brush with jam glaze and sprinkle with almonds.

Note: Cheesecakes freeze particularly well. Freeze it until you need it — and decorate just before serving with fruit, cream or a glaze.

THE GINGERBREAD LOG CABIN

1 kg thick honey
1 cup water
5 cups rye flour
3½ cups wholemeal flour
1 cup chopped mixed peel
1 teaspoon ginger
1 teaspoon cinnamon
½ teaspoon nutmeg
1 teaspoon bicarbonate of soda

ICING

2 egg whites
3 cups icing sugar
1 tablespoon lemon juice

DECORATION

glace cherries
blanched almonds
sweets
plastic toy trees and *people*

Bring honey and water to boil in a saucepan, stirring continuously. Leave to cool.

Sift flours and add mixed peel, spices and bicarbonate. Make well in centre and add honey mixture. Blend mixture into a soft dough. Refrigerate dough wrapped in plastic wrap overnight.

Divide dough into 6 equal portions. If dough is too stiff set aside in a warm place for 15 minutes until easy to handle.

To make roof, roll out 2 portions to 6 mm thickness and 20 cm square. Set aside on lightly greased tray and prick with a fork.

To make walls, use 3 portions of dough and roll into sausage shapes about 1 cm in diameter.

The 4 walls require a total of:

28 logs 20 cm long
4 logs 19 cm long
2 logs 16.5 cm long
2 logs 12.5 cm long
2 logs 10 cm long

To make each end wall, place on lightly greased tray side by side:

7 × 20 cm logs
1 × 19 cm log
1 × 16.5 cm log
1 × 14 cm log
1 × 12.5 cm log
1 × 10 cm log

To make remaining 2 walls, place on a greased tray side by side:

7 × 20 cm logs
1 × 19 cm log

Preheat oven to 200°C (400°F). Bake roof 12–18 minutes then cool on cake rack. Leaving 2 mm gap between each log, bake each wall 12–18 minutes. During baking, the gaps close to form the wall. Allow to cool on rack.

From 1 wall cut out:

1 door 2.5 × 6.5 cm
1 window 4 × 2.5 cm

With remaining dough, make:

4 logs 2.5 cm long and 1.2 cm thick

On baking tray place 2 logs next to each other and 2 logs on top to make double layer — this forms the chimney.

Knead remaining uncooked dough. Roll into flat 6 mm thick square 22 × 22 cm. This will form the base of the house. Prick with fork. Place on tray with chimney logs and bake 12–18 minutes. Cool on cake rack.

Whisk egg whites and fold in icing sugar to form smooth paste. Add lemon juice.

Place base on board. Using icing, join 4 walls together at corners on top of base. Allow to dry completely at each stage of construction. Join roof to house with icing.

Thin 3 tablespoons of icing with a few drops of water. Gently drizzle icing over roof to resemble snow. Attach chimney to roof.

Divide window cut out in half. Place each half on either side of window to resemble shutters and attach with icing. Decorate house and garden with icing, cherries, nuts, sweets and plastic toys. Allow to set completely.

1 Make 2 walls and 2 end walls

2 Join walls together

3 Join roof to house with icing

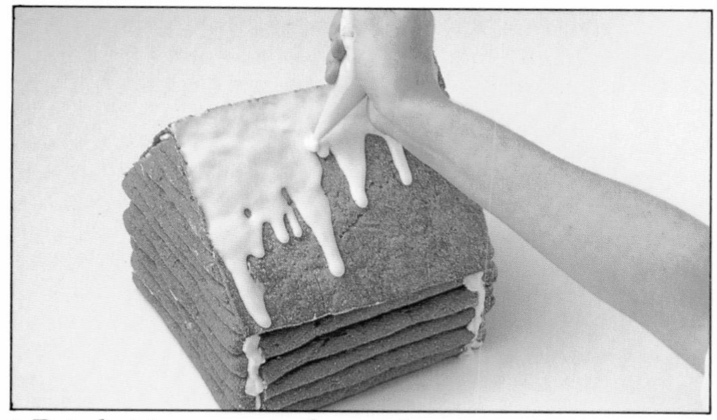

4 Drizzle icing over roof to make snow

The Gingerbread Log Cabin

SCOTCH SHORTBREAD

125 g butter
1⅛ cups flour
¾ cup cornflour
¼ cup caster sugar
1 egg, beaten
1 tablespoon cream
sugar, for dusting

Preheat oven to 180°C (350°F). Grease baking sheet. Rub butter into flour, until mixture resembles breadcrumbs. Add cornflour, sugar, egg and cream and mix to a stiff dough.

Roll dough out on a floured board to 1.75 cm thick, and cut into rounds with a 6 cm pastry cutter.

Arrange rounds on baking sheet. Prick each with a fork and bake 30 minutes. Dust with a little sugar and leave to cool.

Makes 15

PIKELETS

1 cup wholemeal flour
2 teaspoons baking powder
½ cup milk
vanilla, to taste
2 egg whites
butter, for frying

Combine sifted flour and baking powder. Stir in milk and vanilla. Beat until smooth. Add egg whites and beat well.

Place tablespoons of mixture in sizzling buttered hot pan. Cook and turn over. Cook until both sides are golden brown.

Serve with favourite toppings e.g. maple syrup or cottage cheese.

Makes approximately 15

Scotch Shortbread

ALPHABET BISCUITS

125 g butter
½ cup caster sugar
2 cups flour
¼ teaspoon baking powder
2 egg yolks
1 teaspoon vanilla essence
1 teaspoon grated lemon rind
pinch salt
hundreds and thousands
chocolate vermicelli
¼ cup chopped glace cherries

ICING
1 cup icing sugar
2–3 tablespoons lemon juice

Preheat oven to 200°F (400°F). Cream butter and sugar. Fold in flour, baking powder, egg yolks, vanilla essence, lemon rind and salt to form a stiff dough. Wrap dough in plastic wrap and refrigerate 1 hour.

Roll out dough to 30 cm square. Cut into 26 × 1.5 cm blocks. Roll into sausage shapes 1.5 cm in diameter, form into the 26 alphabet letters and flatten slightly. Place on greased baking tray and bake for 8–10 minutes. Allow to cool on tray 2 minutes before removing to cake rack.

Stir icing sugar with lemon juice to give a thick icing. Ice letters while still warm. Decorate with hundreds and thousands, chocolate vermicelli or glace cherries. Allow to cool and set.
Makes 26

CHOCOLATE CHIP BISCUITS

125 g butter
¼ cup sugar
½ cup brown sugar
1 egg
1 cup flour
½ teaspoon salt
½ teaspoon bicarbonate of soda
rind 1 orange, grated
¾ cup chocolate chips or *chopped chocolate drops*
¾–1 cup chopped walnuts

Preheat oven to 190°C (375°F). Grease baking sheet.

Cream butter, sugar and brown sugar together until light and fluffy. Add egg and beat thoroughly.

Sift, flour, salt and bicarbonate of soda into mixture and beat. Stir in orange rind, chocolate chips or pieces, and nuts.

Drop teaspoonfuls of mixture on baking sheet and bake for about 10 minutes until golden brown. Cool and serve.
Makes 48

CINNAMON BISCUITS

125 g butter
¾ cup caster sugar
pinch salt
2 teaspoons cinnamon
1 egg
2¼ cups flour
⅓ cup milk
¾ cup flaked almonds
1 tablespoon icing sugar

Preheat oven to 220°C (425°F). Grease baking sheet.

In a warmed mixing bowl, cream butter with a wooden spoon. Add ½ cup caster sugar, reserving the rest, and beat with butter until light and fluffy. Stir in salt and half the cinnamon.

Beat egg into butter mixture. Sift flour and fold in gradually to form a smooth, thick paste.

Dissolve rest of sugar and cinnamon in milk. Spread this over paste. Scatter with flaked almonds and dust with icing sugar. Cut into squares and set on a baking sheet.

Bake for about 20 minutes until biscuits are slightly browned. Cool and serve.
Makes 20

WALNUT FUDGIES

125 g butter
1¼ cups brown sugar
2 eggs
1¼ cups flour, sifted
3–4 tablespoons cocoa
few drops vanilla essence
1 cup chopped walnuts
2 tablespoons icing sugar

Preheat oven to 180°C (350°F). Grease a baking sheet.

In a large bowl, cream butter and sugar until light and fluffy. Add eggs, one at a time and beat.

Sift flour and cocoa and fold in using metal spoon. Add vanilla and chopped nuts. Continue to mix until thoroughly blended.

Drop teaspoonfuls of mixture on baking sheet. Dust with icing sugar. Bake for about 12 minutes. Cool on wire rack and serve.
Makes 48

Walnut Fudgies (top), Chocolate Chip Biscuits (centre) and Cinnamon Biscuits (bottom)

TOFFEE APPLES

10 red apples

TOFFEE

250 g butter
1 cup sugar
3 tablespoons water
¼ teaspoon salt
1 teaspoon vanilla

Remove stalks from apples and push a wooden skewer into each one.

Place toffee ingredients in saucepan and heat until sugar dissolves, stirring occasionally. Bring to boil. Boil rapidly, without stirring, until the toffee reaches 145°C (280°F) or until a spoonful of mixture, when dropped in cold water, separates into threads which are hard but not brittle. Carefully dip apples into toffee one at a time. Cover apple completely. Plunge into ice water for 5 seconds. Stand on well-oiled greaseproof paper until set.

Makes 10

RAINBOW POPCORN

6 cups popped corn
1 cup sugar
½ cup water
¼ cup light corn syrup
1 teaspoon vinegar
2 teaspoons selected essence
¼ teaspoon selected food colouring
20 g butter

ESSENCES	FOOD COLOURINGS
Strawberry	*Red*
Almond	*Green*
Orange Blossom	*Orange*
Pineapple	*Yellow*
Butterscotch	*Brown*
Raspberry	*Purple*
Cinnamon	*Red*
Lemon	*Yellow*

Divide popped corn into 3 separate bowls and keep warm. In saucepan, combine sugar, water, corn syrup and vinegar. Heat until sugar dissolves. Bring mixture to boil without stirring. Boil until mixture heats to 135°C (275°F). Remove saucepan from heat and add essence and food colour. Quickly pour syrup into warm bowl. Add warm popped corn to syrup. Quickly stir to coat corn. Dot corn with butter. Turn corn onto waxed paper and separate kernels. Cool thoroughly. Repeat process with various essences and flavours. Store in airtight container.

Makes 6 cups

Toffee Apples, Rainbow Popcorn and Alphabet Biscuits (p. 94) are sure to please

POPCORN BALLS

3½ cups uncooked popping corn
140 g butter
1½ cups molasses
¼ cup water
½ cup sugar
1 tablespoon vinegar
½ teaspoon salt
1 tablespoon vanilla

OPTIONAL ADDITIONS

1 cup desiccated coconut
1 cup raisins
1 cup salted peanuts
1 cup puffed wheat

Place popping corn and 60 g butter in large saucepan. Cover with lid. Allow butter to melt, then shake pan, holding lid on, over heat to pop corn. Continue shaking until popping stops. Turn corn into warm large bowl. Stir in any optional additions at this point.

In saucepan combine molasses, water, sugar, vinegar and salt. Cook over medium heat, stirring occasionally, until mixture heats to 135°C (275°F) or a small amount dropped into ice water separates into hard but not brittle threads.

Remove from heat and add 80 g butter and vanilla. Gradually pour hot syrup into the centre of the popped corn. Quickly stir corn and syrup to coat.

With buttered hands, gather and press corn into firm balls. Push wooden skewer into ball. Allow to cool. Wrap each ball in a square piece of cellophane, drawing the paper around the ball and twisting on top.

Makes 15

ALMOND CHOCOLATE FUDGE

360 g cooking chocolate
440 g can condensed milk
2 teaspoons vanilla
1 cup chopped roasted almonds

Melt chocolate in top of double saucepan. Blend in condensed milk, stirring until combined. Remove from heat. Add vanilla and beat until smooth. Fold in almonds. Pour mixture into greased square cake tin. Chill in refrigerator until set. When firm, cut into 2.5 cm squares.

Makes 40 squares

Children's Drinks

PASSIONFRUIT PUNCH

½ cup sugar
½ cup water
1 cup orange juice
1 cup lemon juice
1 cup passionfruit pulp
ice cubes
750 mL bottle ginger ale or
passiona
orange and lemon slices for
garnish

Bring sugar and water to boil, stirring constantly. Continue to cook for 5 minutes then allow to cool. Add orange and lemon juices and passionfruit. Chill until needed. To serve, place a quantity of ice cubes in punch bowl, pour syrup over ice, pour in ginger ale and garnish with orange and lemon slices.
Makes 1.5 litres

STRAWBERRY SODA WHIZZ

2 cups pineapple juice
2 cups ginger ale
2 cups soda water
500 g frozen strawberries
1 cup lemon juice

Combine pineapple juice, ginger ale and soda water. Add strawberries (which will thaw in punch) and lemon juice. Serve chilled with cocktail umbrellas and coloured straws in tall glasses.
Makes 1.5 litres

LEMONADE

½ cup lemon juice
¼ cup apple juice
concentrate
orange essence, to taste
ice blocks
soda or *mineral water*

Combine lemon juice, apple juice concentrate and orange essence. To 2 tablespoons of mixture, add ice blocks and soda water to fill a glass.
Serves 5–6

EMERALD SMOOTHIE

½ avocado, chopped
1 teaspoon honey
1¼ cups milk
2 scoops natural vanilla ice
cream
cinnamon, to garnish

Blend all ingredients in blender and serve sprinkled with cinnamon
Serves 2

ICE CREAM MANGO WHIP

2 mangoes, peeled, seeded
and chopped
1 cup milk
2 tablespoons honey
3 drops almond essence
2 cups vanilla or
strawberry ice cream

Combine first 4 ingredients and process until smooth. Add ice cream and process for 10 seconds. Serve immediately with straws and spoons.
Serves 4–6

TROPICAL SUPERWHIP

1 avocado, chopped
1 banana, chopped
¼ cup chopped pawpaw
2 teaspoons honey
2 teaspoons desiccated
coconut
6 fresh mint leaves
600 mL orange juice or *milk*

Blend all ingredients and serve in very tall glasses, with a slice of kiwi fruit on the side of the glass. Decorate with a cocktail umbrella or fancy straw.
Serves 4

Clockwise from top: Passionfruit Punch, Ice Cream Mango Whip, Emerald Smoothie

BARBECUE ENTERTAINING OUTDOORS

Barbecues make great parties. They are the easy way to feed large numbers of people with a minimum of fuss. With a little organisation much of the food can be prepared in advance leaving everyone relaxed and free to mingle and enjoy the fun. Cooking is part of the fun.

WHAT KIND OF PARTY?

Barbecues are flexible. Bring a little imagination to choosing food and decorations and you can create completely different atmospheres. A buffet barbecue can be gourmet and glamorous or as casual as Sunday brunch with family and friends.

Children adore barbecues. Make their menu simple and fast. Foods like hamburgers, sausages and frankfurts are ideal. Hungry young mouths don't like to wait around too long! To keep them busy, ask them to make up their own kebabs choosing their meat, vegetables and fruits. They will have fun and the food will be nutritious.

CHOOSING A MENU

Whatever the food, the main interest of the occasion usually centres on the barbecue itself. Part of the fun is watching the cook and the food, smelling the mouthwatering aromas and waiting — but not too long.

The secret of success is to be able to serve everyone hot food at the same time. To do this, shop carefully for your prawns or trout or same-sized chicken pieces. Or, cut food into same-sized portions before cooking. It is also important to be able to offer guests their steak cooked just the way they like it. If you have a fillet of beef, for example, you can offer rare, medium and well done steaks to your guests simply by carving from the thicker end (for rare) and the thinner (for well done).

Virtually every type of meat and seafood is suitable for barbecuing — pork, lamb, beef, chicken, fish, shellfish. Bastes add flavour during cooking, and sauces provide the right touch to the table. Make sure you label sauces — not everyone likes chilli. And don't forget vegetables and fruits. Vegetables should be cooked very briefly on the barbecue. Potatoes are terrific wrapped in foil and placed among the coals, but they can be cooked ahead of time and simply reheated on the barbecue. A good idea with onions is to blanch them briefly first in boiling water.

Complement the cooking with an array of interesting salads and breads prepared beforehand. And if the cooking is going to take a while, hand around some simple appetiser to ward off hunger pangs. Choose titbits which you can prepare well ahead of time.

For dessert, offer flambe fruit or fruit kebabs from the barbecue or favourite cold desserts prepared ahead of time.

THE IMPORTANCE OF PREPARATION

One of the most delightful things about a barbecue party is that it lets the host relax as much as the guests . . . that is, if the party has been well prepared.

Decide if you want to do all the cooking yourself or if you want to let guests — so long as there aren't too many — cook for themselves. Cooking is part of the fun. If you decide to let your guests help with the cooking, set up a raw food buffet next to the barbecue so everyone can help themselves. Salads, breads and accompaniments should be at a separate table to avoid congestion near the cooking area.

Barbecue plans should include the possibility of bad weather. Rain doesn't have to spoil a barbecue. Either cook the food outside on a portable barbecue in a sheltered spot or move everything indoors and use your oven.

Make a checklist of everything you require, from food, to crockery and decorations. Make sure you have lots of plates (not just one per person) and utensils as people tend to put them down and forget them.

Prepare those dishes which can be made ahead — such as desserts, starters and salads — long before the guests arrive, the day before if possible. You'll then be calm and relaxed when the door bell rings.

It is a good idea to collect everything to be taken out to the barbecue on a food trolley. You'll save time and energy that way.

Plan the order in which you'll cook the food so that there's a constant supply of beautiful hot food. Some foods like sausages can be kept warm at the side of the grill, others, like fillet steak, must be served the minute they are cooked.

From bottom left clockwise: Tandoori Chicken (p. 112), Sate Prawns (p. 109), Barbecue Whole Fillet (p. 117) Barbecue Fish (p. 111),

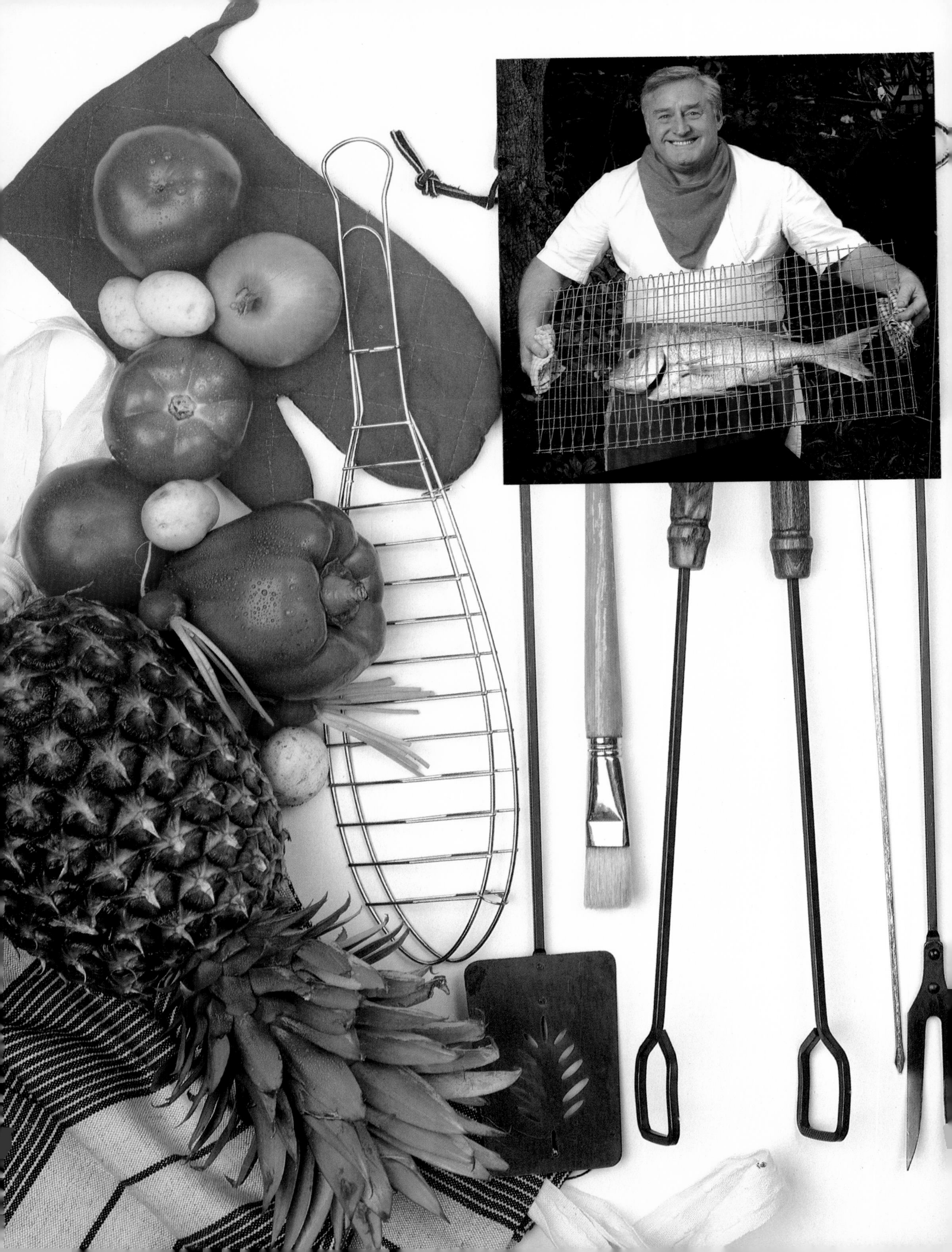

BARBECUE EQUIPMENT

Like the range of barbecues available, the accessories and equipment you buy really depend on your needs. If you just want to cook sausages and chops for the family, don't bother with expensive meat thermometers or rotisseries. If you plan to entertain a lot and barbecue a variety of exotic foods, there are many accessories designed to help you with the task. There's no need to rush out and buy everything. Take a long hard look in your kitchen cupboards first. There are usually tongs or pots and pans which can be retired to start a new life as barbecue equipment. Keep all your barbecue equipment together — then you always have it when you need it.

BASIC ESSENTIALS

Ensure that all equipment is sturdy and will stand up to rough treatment. All handles should be insulated and long enough to keep the cook's hands clear of the cooking surface. A list of basics should include:
Long handled tongs, essential for adjusting hot coals and turning food
Long handled fork, useful for turning food or pricking sausages
Long handled spatula, for turning foods that tend to fall apart such as hamburgers and fish
Stiff metal brush, for scrubbing the grill
Butcher's knife, for trimming meat
Parer knife, for fruit and vegetables
Basting brush, for dabbing bastes and sauces over food, small 5 cm wide paint brushes are suitable
Skewers, essential for kebabs. Flat, metal skewers with an insulated handle are best. If using bamboo sate sticks, soak them in water beforehand. The hairpin style skewer is also useful and you can make it yourself. Bend stainless steel wire into hairpin-shaped skewers about 20 cm long and 1.5 cm wide. (You can make them while you watch television.)
In the basket
A wire basket lets you handle large foods which have to be turned. Whole fish can simply be clamped into the basket — not too tight — and turned as required to cook evenly right through. Prepare baskets by lightly greasing with oil or spraying with a non-stick spray coating.
Barbecue wire baskets, for holding large pieces of food like whole fish. You can buy these or make them yourself using galvanised steel mesh
Heavy duty aluminium foil, so useful for wrapping potatoes, vegetables or bread
Frypan, a long-handled cast iron pan can be used in place of a hotplate for cooking onions, eggs and spectacular flambes
Pots, small saucepans especially are useful for heating sauces on the side of the barbecue
Crockery and cutlery, sturdy, non-breakable varieties with bright colours to brighten the party atmosphere
Oven mitt or cloth, essential to prevent burnt fingers. Make sure mitts are comfortable.
Apron, sturdy is best to guard against splatters
Aerosol vegetable spray, for greasing.

EXTRA ACCESSORIES

There is an enormous range of attachments, accessories and gadgets designed for the modern barbecue. Few are essential, but many prove very handy for specialised cooking, particularly if you like entertaining. They are often expensive, so make sure you will be able to make good use of them.
Rotisserie, absolutely spectacular, especially when you have guests. They can be simple hand-operated types or more expensive battery charged models. When buying, make sure it fits your particular barbecue. Look for a sturdy spit that will not bend and a heavy-duty motor that will keep on turning.
Kebab turner, several varieties. The simplest kind is just a metal box with a series of notches cut into the top of each long side to hold the skewers. Alternatively, you can purchase a motorised version which automatically turns the skewers as well.
Meat thermometer, a long probe with a temperature dial at one end which is inserted into the meat or poultry before cooking. As the meat cooks, the dial indicates the internal temperature. A meat thermometer ensures there are no nasty surprises when serving — especially if you have a large piece of meat on the spit. Often it is easy to assume the meat is ready because of the external appearance, when in fact it is still uncooked inside. The thermometer eliminates error. Meat thermometers are particularly useful for spit roasting and when using a covered barbecue. They are absolutely essential if you are barbecuing a whole pig or lamb.
Wok holders, the newly developed barbecue wok holder has brought the delights and diversity of Asian foods to outdoor eating, greatly increasing the cook's repertoire. Make sure you use the right shaped wok — one with a curved base.
Gas lighters, essential for owners of gas barbecues. It is often impractical to light gas burners with matches. Modern lighters deliver a good strong spark that will light the burner even in a breeze.
Electric starters, used for lighting charcoal.
A fire extinguisher or fire blanket, either of these would be a sensible purchase. Both will quickly extinguish a fire in an emergency.

Basic essentials for a trouble-free barbecue

Starters

CHICKEN LIVERS AND MUSHROOMS IN BACON

fresh chicken livers
lean bacon rashers, rinds removed
field mushrooms

Cut bacon into 8 cm lengths. Slice mushrooms into pieces same size as livers. Arrange liver and mushroom on each piece of bacon, roll up and secure on small skewer. Allow about 3 rolls per skewer. Barbecue 15 minutes over a medium fire making sure that the flames do not catch the bacon. Delicious with or without a sauce.

SPICED BEEF MEATBALLS

500 g extra lean mince
1 small onion, very finely chopped
2 eggs
fresh breadcrumbs
pinch garlic powder, to taste
Madras curry powder or *Tandoori Paste, to taste* (see recipe Tandoori Chicken)

Mix mince, onion, eggs and breadcrumbs together so that meat will not fall apart. Add garlic and curry and mix in thoroughly. Roll into 2.5 cm diameter meatballs, place on skewers and barbecue 10 minutes taking care not to burn. Serve with a spicy sauce of your choice.
Makes approximately 20

CHICKEN LIVERS INDIAN

16 fresh chicken livers
2 bananas (almost ripe)
Madras curry powder
6 lean bacon rashers, rinds removed

Cut livers in half or smaller if they are large. Slice banana into 1–2 cm thick slices sprinkling curry powder on both sides. Cut bacon into 3 cm lengths. Wrap a piece each of liver and banana in bacon and pin with a small skewer. Barbecue gently until cooked, about 10–15 minutes, turning frequently.
Makes 32

HAM AND ASPARAGUS ROLLS

8 slices leg ham, halved
16 green asparagus spears
cracked pepper

Place 1 asparagus spear on each half of leg ham. Roll up and pin with mini forks or toothpicks. Season with cracked pepper and serve.
Makes 16

From top clockwise: Chicken Livers Indian, Spiced Beef Meatballs, Ham and Asparagus Rolls, Mushroom and Caviar

MUSHROOM AND CAVIAR

medium-sized mushroom caps
butter
pate
red and black caviar

Wipe mushroom caps clean. Place a small dob of butter in each cap and then fill with pate. Top with red or black caviar for garnish and just heat through on barbecue to warm.

Scallops and Lychees in Bacon served with a salad

SCALLOPS AND LYCHEES IN BACON

fresh scallops with roe attached
canned lychees
bacon rashers, rinds removed

Buy fresh scallops and use canned lychees for convenience. Cut bacon into 7.5 cm lengths and lychees in half. On each strip of bacon, place half a lychee and a whole scallop. Roll up and thread on small skewers. Allow about 2 rolls per skewer. Barbecue over a good hot fire turning occasionally and taking care that the flame does not touch the food. Serve with lemon juice and pepper. Barbecue time about 10 minutes.

ALTERNATIVE FRUITS

Dried apricots, dried apples or dried dates (fresh dates are too soft), halved.

MINI CLUBS OF CHICKEN

2 kg chicken wings

MARINADE

½ cup soy sauce
2 cloves garlic, crushed
1 × 250 g jar sate sauce
½ cup water

Wash and dry wings. Cut off wing tips at joint (and save to make stock). Holding small end, pare around bone with sharp knife to cut meat free. Cut, scrape and push meat down over end of bone until they look like little clubs. Combine marinade ingredients and marinate wings overnight. Drain, reserving marinade to baste while barbecuing — about 10 minutes over medium heat.
Serves 8

Outdoor entertaining: Chicken Livers Indian (p. 104), Barbecued Whole Fillet (p. 117), Barbecued Turkey Breast (p. 115), salad, sauces, bread and fresh grapes

SEAFOOD KEBABS

large scallops with roe attached
small to medium-sized uncooked prawns

Shell and devein prawns and remove tails. Thread scallops and prawns alternately on lightly greased skewers and barbecue 10 minutes over a good hot fire, turning occasionally. When nearly cooked, dab kebabs with a seafood sauce *(see recipes)*.

PRAWNS WITH CREAMY SATE SAUCE

½ cup peanut butter
1 clove garlic, crushed
2 tablespoons light soy sauce
finely grated rind and juice 1 lemon
1 teaspoon dried prawn paste
1–2 red chillies, seeded and finely chopped
½ cup cream
1 kg uncooked prawns, shelled, deveined, with tails on

Combine all ingredients except cream and prawns, in a small saucepan. Stir over gentle heat until well blended. Remove from heat and gradually stir in cream.

Soak 20 bamboo skewers in boiling water for 10 minutes (this will prevent them burning when barbecuing). Thread prawns onto skewers and cook over hot coals basting frequently with sauce. Serve with any remaining sauce.
Serves 10

KING PRAWN KEBABS

uncooked king prawns or *king prawn cutlets with tails on, graded same size*

Shell and devein prawns leaving the tail on. Thread prawns on skewers (about 6 prawns per skewer) and barbecue over a good hot fire turning frequently. The cooking time will depend on the size of prawns you use. When they are just about ready, brush prawns with sauce of your choice *(see recipes)*. Arrange on platter and serve.

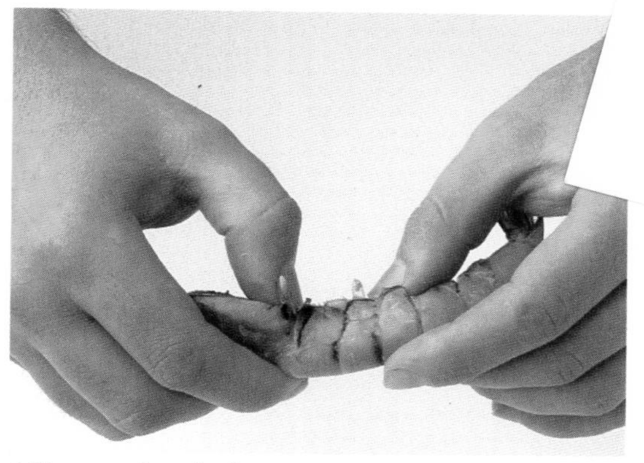

1 Remove head of prawn

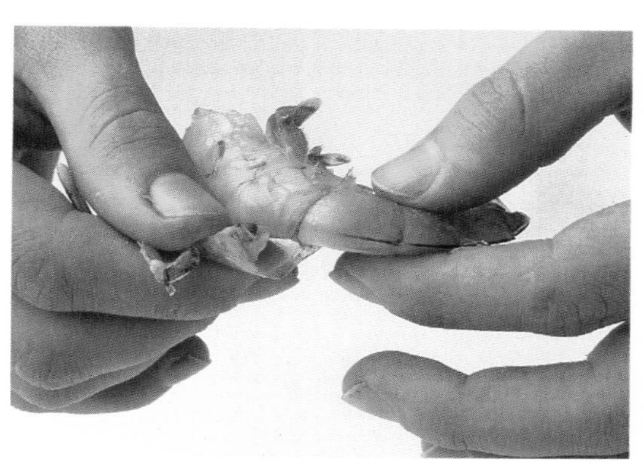

2 Remove legs and shell

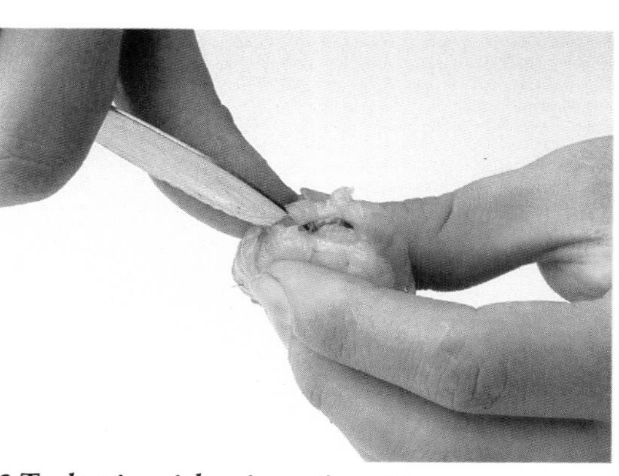

3 To devein, nick vein section at top

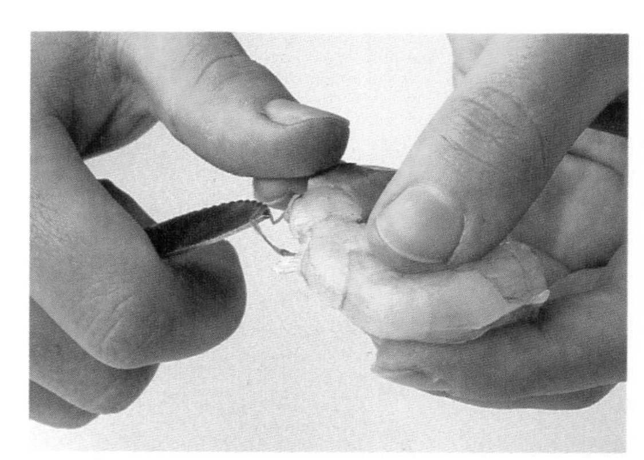

4 Make a small cut to expose vein just above tail. Pull vein through

RAYFISH TAILS

uncooked crayfish tails,
graded same size
butter
salt and pepper
lemon wedges

Make a full-length, deep cut along underside of crayfish and insert thin slices of butter. Place tails in wire barbecue basket and cook whole, shell down for about three quarters of the cooking time. This means they will tend to cook in their own juice. Allow about 30–40 minutes for 500 g tails over a medium to hot fire. Take care not to burn the shell by damping the charcoal to control heat. On a gas barbecue, move food to the cooler sides to control temperature or turn the burners down. When tails are nearly cooked, brush with melted butter and lemon juice.

Chop into portions — you should get about 6–8 portions per tail — and serve with lemon wedges and salt and pepper to taste. Hollandaise Sauce *(see recipe)* goes well with crayfish. Barbecue time about 30–40 minutes.

Crayfish tails served with a salad

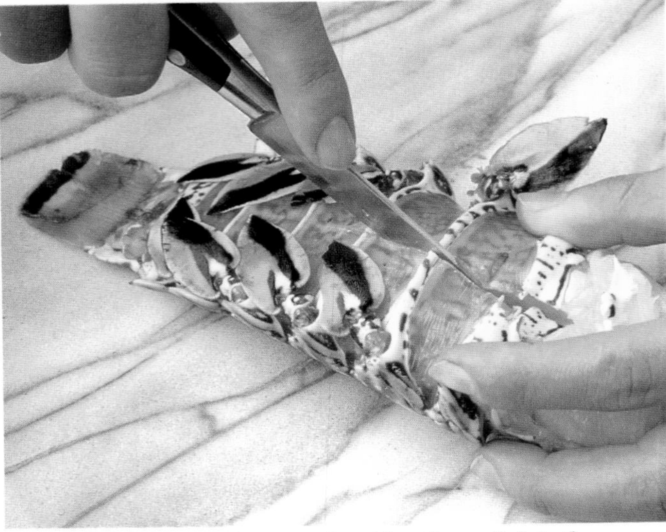

1 ***Make deep cut along underside of crayfish tail***

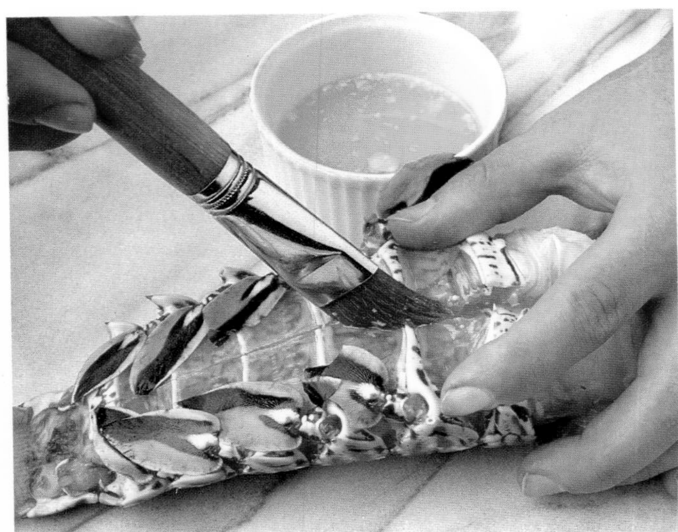

2 ***Insert thin slices butter or dab melted butter***

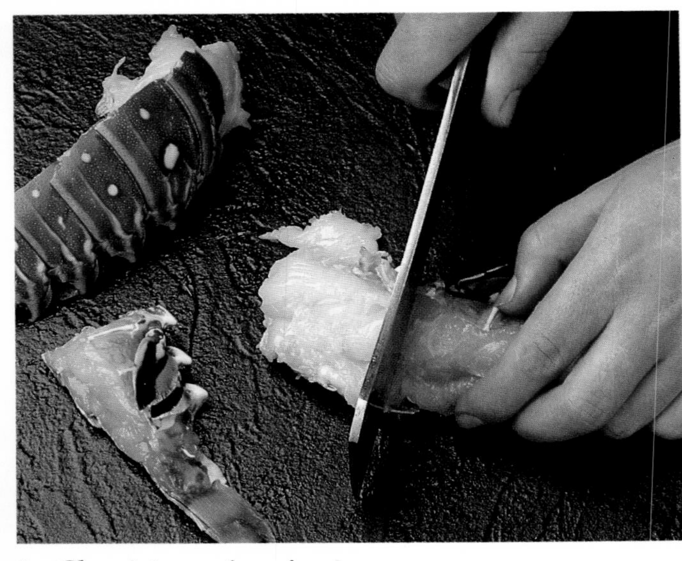

3 ***Chop into serving pieces***

PREPARING A WHOLE FISH

To prepare a whole fish for cooking, wipe it over with a damp cloth and check for scales near the head and fins. If further scaling is necessary, use a teaspoon and scrape lightly but firmly from the tail to the head on both sides. This is best done under running water because the scales then collect in the sink and can easily be discarded.

Trim fins and neaten the tail with a pair of kitchen scissors if you like. The eyes can be removed but may be better left in because when they turn white you know the fish is cooked. If you find them unsightly cover them with a garnish before serving.

Open the cavity of the fish and sprinkle about 2 teaspoons of salt into it. Take a wad of kitchen paper and clean well down the backbone to remove any blood spots. Rinse well with cold water. Pat the fish dry, cover and refrigerate until used.

Barbecued Trout

BARBECUED WHOLE SMOKED FISH

whole smoked gemfish, blue cod or *tailor*

Place whole fish in greased wire barbecue basket and clamp. Barbecue over a medium fire, skin down, for about three-quarters of the cooking time. Turn and cook other side. Serve with lemon wedges or Avocado Sauce *(see recipe)*. Barbecue time about 20 minutes per kilo.

BARBECUED FISH

2 × 1.5–2 kg whole cleaned fish (whiting, bream or *mullet)*
2 lemons
salt and freshly ground pepper, to taste
3 onions, sliced in rings
250 g mushrooms, sliced
4 tomatoes, sliced
80 g butter
lemon wedges, to serve

Remove scales and wipe fish with a damp cloth. Peel rind from 1 lemon, cut into julienne strips and simmer for a few minutes; drain and cool. Sqeeze lemons and brush lemon juice over both fish. Season with salt and pepper. Place fish on 2 large pieces of aluminium foil, shiny side down. Spread onion rings over both fish, then cover with mushrooms and tomatoes. Season with pepper and dot butter over fish. Drizzle over any remaining lemon juice and sprinkle with rind. Wrap fish in foil, forming a seal on 1 side.

Cook fish over glowing coals for 25–40 minutes or until cooked when tested. (Cooking time will depend on heat of fire and thickness of fish.) Serve fish with the vegetables and cooking juices. Garnish with lemon wedges.

Serves 10–12

BARBECUED TROUT

whole trout, graded same size (allow 1 per person)

Prepare wire barbecue baskets by greasing with vegetable oil or spraying. Clean trout and pat dry. Place in basket and barbecue over a medium fire turning frequently and taking care not to scorch skin during cooking. Barbecue time is about 15 minutes per 500 g.

Finely sliced almonds, placed in trout cavity before cooking, provide a tasty variation.

Serve with Bearnaise or Hollandaise Sauce *(see recipes)* or with lemon wedges and salt and pepper to taste.

GRILLED TROUT

8 trout, same size
8 bacon rashers, rinds removed
2 eggs
1 tablespoon cream
1 teaspoon chopped fresh parsley
1 clove garlic, crushed
½ teaspoon allspice
oil

Beat eggs with cream, parsley, garlic and allspice. Coat trout, inside and out, with this mixture. Place a bacon rasher in each trout and barbecue about 15 minutes until fish flakes with a fork. Serve with a light seafood sauce *(see recipes)*.

Serves 8

TANDOORI CHICKEN

2 × 1 kg chicken or *chicken pieces*
Tandoori Paste to taste (see recipe following)
1 kg natural yoghurt
250 g fruit yoghurt, such as apricot

TANDOORI PASTE

1 large onion
4 cloves garlic, peeled
½ teaspoon ginger
½ teaspoon coriander
½ teaspoon cumin
chilli powder, to taste (no more than ½ teaspoon)
2 teaspoons salt
1 tablespoon vinegar
juice 1 lemon

Prepare a yoghurt marinade by mixing together natural and fruit yoghurts and the Tandoori Paste you have made or bought. Try the taste test to make sure you have the spicy marinade mixed to suit your palate.

To make Tandoori Paste, grind onion and garlic together to a paste, add ginger, coriander, cumin ,chilli and salt. Mix thoroughly then stir in vinegar and lemon juice.

Cut chicken into portions, immerse in Tandoori mix and marinate for at least 1 hour prior to cooking — the longer the better. Drain and arrange pieces on barbecue grill over a medium fire. Keep wings to the outside as they do not take as long to cook. Barbecue time is about 30 minutes.

If you prefer you can barbecue half chickens this way or spit-roast whole Tandoori chickens, although the cooking times will be longer. A spit-roasted chicken will take about 1–1½ hours to cook.
Serves 8

Tandoori Chicken with pickle, chutney and pappadams

Tarragon Tempters

TARRAGON TEMPTERS

chicken drumsticks (allow 2 per person)
melted butter
lemon juice
dried tarragon
paprika, to taste

Brush drumsticks with melted butter and arrange on grill over a good hot fire. Barbecue about 5 minutes, turn and sprinkle with lemon juice and dust with tarragon and paprika. Repeat turning, sprinkling and dusting until drumsticks are cooked, 20–25 minutes (juice runs clear when cooked). Serve with small paper napkins wrapped around bone.

CHICKEN WITH ONION AND CAPSICUM

fresh chicken fillets, without skin
white onions
red and green capsicums
Tropical Sauce or *Peppercorn Butter* (see recipes)

Cut chicken breasts into 3–4 cm pieces, quarter onions and cut capsicums into pieces same size as chicken. Thread alternately on skewers for colour (allow 2 skewers per person) and cook over a medium fire about 15 minutes. Just before removing from barbecue, brush with Tropical Sauce or Peppercorn Butter. Serve with more sauce for dipping, or extra Peppercorn Butter.

Chicken Kebabs

CHICKEN WITH PINEAPPLE AND ORANGE

fresh chicken breast fillets, cut into 3 cm pieces
fresh pineapple pieces, cut in 3 cm triangles (pineapple should be a little on the unripe side)
orange or *mandarin segments, about same size as pineapple pieces*
Tropical Sauce (see recipe)

Thread chicken, pineapple and orange segments alternately on skewers, allowing about 3 pieces of each per skewer. Barbecue about 15 minutes over a medium fire. Brush with Tropical Sauce when almost cooked. Barbecue 1 minute more and serve accompanied with more sauce for dipping.

CHICKEN KEBABS

Chicken kebabs are best made with skinned breast meat, cooked over a medium fire and basted just before serving. Spicy chicken kebabs can be marinated before barbecuing for additional flavour. It is important that pieces are cut the same size and the heat is controlled during cooking time.

CHICKEN AND MUSHROOM KEBABS

fresh chicken breast fillets cut into 3–4 cm portions
fresh field mushrooms cut into same-sized pieces
melted butter
dried tarragon

Allow about 4 pieces each of chicken and mushroom per skewer. Thread mushroom and chicken pieces on skewers alternately then barbecue over a medium fire for about 15 minutes. Just before serving brush with butter and tarragon.

SATE CHICKEN

fresh chicken fillets
Sate Sauce, freshly made (see recipe) *or bought*

Cut chicken fillets into slightly smaller pieces than for kebabs — about 2 cm square. Thread on skewers and cook over medium fire about 10–15 minutes, basting and turning continually. Brush with Sate Sauce and serve hot.

TURKEY BARBECUE KEBABS

turkey breast fillets, skinned and boned
dried fruits: apricots, dates, or fresh capsicum, white onions and cherry tomatoes
250 g jar cranberry sauce
dash chilli sauce (optional)

Cut turkey fillets into 3–4 cm cubes and thread on skewers alternately with selected dried fruits, onion quarters, capsicum slices and cherry tomatoes. Allow 2 skewers per person. Barbecue over medium to hot fire 15 minutes. When nearly cooked, brush with cranberry sauce mixed with a dash of chilli sauce and serve.

BARBECUED TURKEY BREAST

1.5 kg turkey breast fillet, skinned and boned
250 g jar cranberry sauce
generous dash chilli sauce to taste

You can buy whole buffet breast of turkey or whole fillet of turkey breast. Bone as you would a chicken breast by cutting straight down each side of breast bone. This produces 2 full fillets of turkey. Remove wings and use separately. The leftover bones make great stock.

Place fillet in lightly greased wire basket and barbecue 30–40 minutes over a medium to hot fire. Control heat carefully. Serve sliced into 2 cm thick portions with bought cranberry and chilli sauces mixed to your taste.
Serves 8

DUCK HALVES IN BASKETS

1.5 kg duck, defrosted if frozen

Wash and dry duck and halve following method for chicken. Arrange in greased wire basket and barbecue over medium fire until tender, about 1 hour.

Start cooking skin side down to crisp. After 10 minutes turn occasionally. Two-thirds of barbecue time should be skin up. Just before serving brush with your favourite sauce if you wish, though this is not necessary. Serve in baskets with sweet mango chutney or more of your favourite sauce.
Serves 4–6

Sate Chicken

GARLIC
MUSTARD

BARBECUED WHOLE FILLET

2 kg whole tenderloin

Trim membranes, tendons and any excess fat. Barbecue whole over a good hot fire for about 30 minutes, turning frequently as this will allow the fillet to baste in its own juice. When cooked, carve into 1–2 cm thick slices starting at the thinner end — which will be well done. As you continue carving you will notice that the thicker portion of the fillet will be rarer — so off 1 fillet you can present well-done, medium, rare and blue beef.

Serve with horseradish sauce and your choice of mustards. Slices of whole fillet look very attractive on thin slices of French bread.

Serves 8

Prime Rib Roast, Barbecued Whole Fillet and Barbecued Beef Kebabs

FILLET OF BEEF WITH BEARNAISE SAUCE

2 kg whole tenderloin
Bearnaise Sauce (see recipe)

Prepare tenderloin by trimming off membranes, tendons and any excess fat. Barbecue about 30 minutes over good hot fire turning frequently. Warm Bearnaise Sauce in pot at side of barbecue. Carve beef starting at thinner end of fillet following technique described in Barbecued Whole Fillet *(see recipe)* and serve with warmed Bearnaise Sauce and fresh, crisp salads.

Serves 8

Fillet of Beef with Bearnaise Sauce sliced to serve

BARBECUED FILLET OF BEEF WITH HORSERADISH CREAM SAUCE

1.5 kg fillet beef
4–6 rashers bacon, rinds removed

MARINADE

1 carrot, roughly chopped
1 onion, roughly chopped
1 cup port
½ cup oil
few peppercorns
1 teaspoon whole allspice
1 clove garlic, crushed

HORSERADISH CREAM SAUCE

1 cup thickened cream, whipped and chilled
1 tablespoon horseradish cream
1 shallot, finely chopped
1 tablespoon finely chopped parsley

Trim fillet of excess fat and all sinew. Place on a board and wrap bacon around in a spiral fashion. Secure with toothpicks. Combine all marinade ingredients and place with fillet in a strong plastic bag. Secure bag opening and ensure fillet is covered with marinade. Refrigerate overnight turning bag from time to time. Remove fillet from marinade and pat dry with paper towel.

Cook fillet over moderately hot barbecue coals for about 10–12 minutes for a medium rare steak or 15–20 minutes for a medium steak. Test with a skewer then remove from barbecue and stand meat for 10 minutes before carving. Carve thin slices across the grain. Arrange on a platter and serve with Horseradish Cream Sauce.

To make sauce, combine all ingredients, stir until blended and serve in a bowl.

Serves 10

PRIME RIB ROAST

2 kg prime rib roast

Ask your butcher to cut rib roast into individual prime rib cutlets, or cut them yourself. Barbecue over good hot fire for 30 minutes (well-done), 20 minutes (medium), and 10 minutes (rare) turning once. Place the 'rare' cutlets on grill later than those to be well-done. Just before end of cooking time, brush cutlets with sauce if you want.

Ribs can be served with style standing or as individual cutlets with horseradish and a range of mustards or a warmed sauce such as Bearnaise *(see recipe)*.

Serves 8

BARBECUED BEEF KEBABS

rump steak
white onions
red and green capsicums

Cut rump steak into 3–4 cm cubes. If using small white onions, parboil 5 minutes. Cut larger white onions and capsicums into 3–4 cm slices. Alternately thread meat cubes and onion and capsicum slices on skewers and barbecue over a good hot fire turning occasionally to avoid burning for 5 minutes (rare), 10 minutes (medium) or 15 minutes (well-done). Place rare kebabs on barbecue 10 minutes after those to be well-done. Just before the end of cooking time, brush with sauce or simply serve with horseradish and mustards. Mushrooms are also tasty with barbecued kebabs.

SATE BEEF

rump steak
sate sauce, home-made or *bought*
cucumber, peeled and chopped into chunky portions

Cut rump steak into 1.5–2 cm cubes (this is smaller than for Beef Kebabs as the cooking time is shorter). Thread on skewers, about 4–6 cubes per skewer — and cook over a good hot fire for no more than 10 minutes. Control heat. While barbecuing, dab with sate sauce and turn continually. Serve with rest of sauce and chunky portions of cucumber.

CARPETBAG STEAK

2 kg piece rump steak, cut 4 cm thick
2 dozen oysters, fresh or bottled
freshly ground pepper
Anchovy Butter (see recipe)

Dust steak with freshly ground pepper and allow to sit for 10 minutes. Cut a pocket in steak with a sharp knife, insert oysters and seal with small skewer or toothpick. Barbecue steak 10 minutes over hot coals, turn, top with pat of anchovy butter and barbecue 10 minutes more. Carve on serving plate.

Serves 8

Carpetbag Steak

SATE LAMB

1 large leg of lamb, boned
Sate Sauce (see recipe)

Sate lamb is delicious, so allow about 3 skewers per person. Cut lamb into 2 cm cubes — these are slightly smaller than for kebabs. Thread about 6 pieces on each skewer and cook over a good hot fire for 10–15 minutes basting continually with Sate Sauce and turning. Serve with bowl of warmed Sate Sauce and fresh fruit such as watermelon or pawpaw slices.
Serves 8

KAFTA SANDWICHES

1 kg lean lamb, finely minced
½ cup finely chopped parsley
⅓ cup finely chopped mint
1 onion, grated
salt and pepper, to taste
½ teaspoon cinnamon
½ teaspoon allspice
2 eggs
oil, for brushing

TO SERVE

flat bread
Hummus
Tabbouli

Place meat, herbs, onion, seasonings and eggs in a bowl. Mix well and knead for a few minutes. Lightly brush skewers with oil.

Divide mixture into 8 portions. Depending on size of skewers, mould 2 portions of mixture onto each skewer, forming 2 individual finger-shaped kaftas. Cook over hot coals or under a preheated very hot grill until browned on outside but still slightly pink inside.

To serve, spread a piece of flat bread with hummus and top with tabbouli. Place skewer in the centre of bread and, if desired, sprinkle with chilli. Roll up bread tightly and, holding it firmly, pull out skewers. Serve warm.

If not serving as a sandwich, serve hot with yoghurt and a salad.

Note: Many Lebanese shops sell kafta sandwiches; they make an ideal lunch. Charcoal or wood gives the best flavour to the meat, although a very well preheated grill can be used.
Makes 8

MINTED LAMB KEBABS

1 large leg of lamb, boned
dried apples
250 g jar mint jelly

Cut leg into 2–3 cm cubes and thread on skewers alternately with apples beginning and ending with lamb. Barbecue over a good hot fire, controlling the temperature and turning occasionally. When cooked, dab with melted mint jelly and serve hot.
Serves 8

MINTY LAMB BURGERS

2.5–3 kg boned leg of lamb
2 onions, finely chopped
1–2 cloves garlic, crushed
2 tablespoons chopped mint
1 teaspoon paprika
salt and freshly ground pepper, to taste
3 eggs, beaten

TO SERVE

250 g butter
2–3 tablespoons chopped mint

Trim all skin and visible fat off lamb then cut into pieces. Mince, using a food processor or mincer. Avoid processing the lamb too finely.

Place mince in a bowl with onions, garlic, mint, paprika, salt, pepper and eggs and mix well. Cover and refrigerate.

Beat butter until soft. Add mint and beat again. Taste for mint flavour and add freshly ground pepper. Spoon butter onto a sheet of foil and roll into a log shape. Refrigerate until serving time.

Divide lamb mixture into 20 parts. With wet hands, shape each into a burger shape. Cook over glowing coals for 5–10 minutes until done. Serve burgers topped with a thin slice of mint butter.
Serves 10–12

Minty Lamb Burgers

CROWN OPENER

Pineapple Pork Kebabs

BARBECUED PORK KEBABS

3 kg leg of pork, boned
dried fruits such as
apricots, dates, apples
Plum and Chilli Sauce (see recipe)

Slice off just enough pork to make your kebabs. Keep remainder for roasting or freezing.

Cut pork into 3–4 cm cubes and thread on skewers alternating with dried fruits for colour. Begin and end with pork pieces. Barbecue about 15–20 minutes over a good hot fire turning occasionally and controlling temperature. When nearly cooked, brush with Plum and Chilli Sauce and serve.
Serves 8

PINEAPPLE PORK KEBABS

3 kg leg of pork, boned
fresh pineapple, cut in 2 cm thick slices
Tropical Sauce (see recipe)

Cut pork into 3–4 cm cubes and pineapple into 3 cm triangles. Thread pork and pineapple pieces alternately on skewers beginning and ending with pork. Barbecue about 15–20 minutes over a good hot fire controlling temperature and turning occasionally. When nearly cooked, brush with Tropical Sauce and serve.
Serves 8

SATE PORK

3 kg leg of pork, boned
Sate Sauce (see recipe)

Cut boned leg pork into 2–3 cm cubes, slightly smaller than kebab-sized pieces. Thread about 6 pork pieces on each sate stick or skewer and barbecue over a good hot fire about 15 minutes turning occasionally and controlling temperature. Brush with Sate Sauce throughout cooking time and serve with more sauce.
Serves 8

Accompaniments

HAMBURGER SAUCE

125 g butter, melted
½ cup oil
½ cup tomato sauce
1 teaspoon dry mustard
dash Worcestershire sauce
1 onion, grated
juice ½ lemon

Shake all ingredients well in a covered jar. Place in a pot near barbecue to warm slightly. Baste steaks or hamburgers with sauce before serving.
Makes 1½ cups

BARBECUE SAUCE

1 onion, chopped
3 tablespoons oil
1 tablespoon Worcestershire sauce
½ cup tomato sauce

Combine all ingredients in a saucepan, bring to boil, cover and simmer 10 minutes, stirring occasionally. Allow to cool. Brush over meat before and during cooking. Suitable for rump, fillet, T-bone or any other tender steak.
Makes 1 cup

SATE SAUCE

½ cup sultanas
½ cup raisins
1 cup peanuts
40 g ginger root
3 cloves garlic, crushed
1 tablespoon chilli sauce or more
1 cup white vinegar
½ cup sugar
5 tablespoons peanut butter
2 cups water

Finely chop sultanas, raisins, peanuts and ginger and place in a saucepan with the rest of ingredients. Heat, stirring until sugar is dissolved. Simmer about 30 minutes, stirring occasionally. Suitable for poultry, beef and lamb.
Makes 4 cups

PEANUT SAUCE

300 g shelled raw peanuts
3 fresh chillies or 3 teaspoons chilli sauce
3 cloves garlic
1 onion, chopped
100 mL peanu
½ cup water
1 tablespoon s
1 tablespoon b
2 tablespoons lemon juice

Combine nuts, chillies, garlic, onion and 50 mL oil and blend to a smooth paste, adding water when necessary. Heat remaining oil in frypan. Add peanut paste and stir well for about 3 minutes. Pour in rest of water and cook until sauce is thick and smooth. Stir in soy sauce, sugar and lemon juice. Taste to achieve desired flavour. Use with almost anything cooked on the barbecue.
Makes 3 cups

CURRY SAUCE

4 tablespoons oil
2 large onions, chopped
2 cloves garlic, crushed
2 tablespoons Madras curry powder
2 tablespoons flour
4 cups coconut milk, canned or fresh

Heat oil, add onions and garlic and saute until tender. Add curry powder and flour and cook over gentle heat about 2 minutes stirring continuously. Gradually add coconut milk and simmer until sauce thickens. A little fresh cream can be used to soften the flavour if wished. Use with almost anything cooked on the barbecue.
Makes 1 litre

APRICOT AND CHILLI SAUCE

550–600 g can apricot jam
chilli sauce, to taste
fresh cream (optional)

Heat jam in saucepan but do not boil. Add desired amount of chilli sauce. Fresh cream will soften strength of chilli if required. Serve with turkey.
Makes about 2 cups

PLUM AND CHILLI SAUCE

550–600 g can plum jam
chilli sauce, to taste
fresh cream (optional)

Heat plum jam in saucepan but do not boil. Add chilli sauce to desired strength. Use fresh cream to soften strength of chilli. Serve with pork and turkey.
Makes about 2 cups

RED CURRANT SAUCE

1 teaspoon salt
1 teaspoon freshly ground pepper
1 tablespoon dry mustard
2 tablespoons brown sugar
1 cup vinegar
2 eggs
½ cup tomato sauce
1 cup red currant jelly

Combine salt, pepper, mustard and sugar. Stir in vinegar and simmer over low heat. Beat eggs lightly and add stirring constantly. When sauce has thickened add tomato sauce and red currant jelly, stirring continuously. Do not allow sauce to boil. This sauce is excellent with turkey, pork or grilled ham steaks.
Makes about 2 cups

AVOCADO SAUCE

3 ripe avocados
1 medium-sized onion, finely chopped
1 garlic clove, crushed
3 tablespoons lemon juice
1 tablespoon Worcestershire sauce
2 dashes Tabasco sauce, to taste
salt and pepper, to taste

Combine all ingredients and blend until smooth. Excellent with seafood and poultry.
Makes about 2 cups

SWEET AND SOUR SAUCE

1 cup brown sugar
½ cup white wine vinegar
¼ cup orange juice
¼ cup lemon juice
1 tablespoon capsicum, finely chopped
2 teaspoons cornflour mixed with *a little water*

Combine sugar, vinegar, juices and capsicum and simmer 5 minutes. Blend cornflour with a little water and stir in. Serve with pork, prawns or fish.
Makes about 2 cups

Take advantage of commercial sauces or whip up your own. From top clockwise: Mint Jelly, Bearnaise Sauce, Cranberry Sauce, Simple Seafood Butter and Barbecue Sauces

TROPICAL SAUCE

1 cup salad oil
1 cup pineapple juice
1–2 tablespoons light soy sauce
2 tablespoons honey
1 teaspoon ginger
1 cup pineapple juice

Prepare sauce by combining all ingredients and heating through. Do not boil. Serve with pork and poultry.
Makes 3 cups

SIMPLE SEAFOOD BUTTER SAUCE

125 g butter
good squeeze lemon juice
1 teaspoon chopped parsley
1 teaspoon chopped tarragon
1 teaspoon Worcestershire sauce
ground pepper, to taste
pinch salt (optional)

Melt butter and add remaining ingredients. Do not allow butter to brown. Use as a baste with all seafoods.
Makes ½ cup

SPIKED SEAFOOD SAUCE

150 mL slightly whipped cream
2 tablespoons horseradish
1 tablespoon finely chopped chives
dash Tabasco sauce

Whip cream slightly. Stir in horseradish until well-blended. Add chives and a dash of Tabasco. Use with all seafoods.
Makes ⅔ cup

HOLLANDAISE SAUCE

3 egg yolks
1 tablespoon tarragon vinegar
dash Tabasco sauce
125 g butter, melted

Combine yolks, vinegar and Tabasco and beat well. Add melted butter (very hot, but not burnt) in a steady stream and continue blending. Can be served with anything on the barbecue.
Makes ⅔ cup

BEARNAISE SAUCE

⅔ cup dry white wine
2 sprigs tarragon
2 tablespoons chopped shallots
2 peppercorns
2 tablespoons tarragon vinegar
3 egg yolks
1 tablespoon water
250 g butter, melted
salt and pepper, to taste

Combine wine, tarragon, shallots, peppercorns and vinegar. Boil until reduced by half. Combine egg yolks and water and beat well. Add wine mixture and beat again. Pour in hot melted butter in steady stream. Season to taste. Can be served with anything on the barbecue.
Makes 2 cups

SAVOURY BUTTERS

Make up several savoury butters and store them in the freezer until you need them. Don't forget to label the packages! Make as much or as little as you require and add herbs and spices to taste.

ANCHOVY BUTTER
Cream butter and add finely mashed anchovy fillets. Delicious with fish and veal.

BASIL BUTTER
Pound plenty of fresh basil in a mortar and pestle. Cream into butter. Delicious with vegetables, excellent with fish and veal, superb on rice or pasta.

BERCY BUTTER
Cream butter with finely chopped shallots or chives. Great on steaks, chops, crayfish, prawns, vegetables and hot crisp bread.

CHILLI BUTTER
Cream butter with Tabasco sauce and add a little chilli powder, but taste it as you mix. Very good with hamburgers and roast pork.

DILL BUTTER
Chop dill very finely and add to creamed butter. Best to use only fresh dill for this to get the maximum flavour. A great dressing for fish and vegetable dishes.

GARLIC BUTTER
Cream butter with fresh, crushed garlic and finely chopped parsley. Good on any meats that have been barbecued, lovely on baked potatoes and, naturally, great with hot bread rolls.

GREEN BUTTER
Pound parsley and chives in a mortar and pestle until liquid. Add to creamed butter until desired colour is achieved. Good with fish, roast lamb and oysters roasted in their shells.

HERB BUTTER
Cream butter with a mixture of herbs. Fines Herbes from France can be bought in most delicatessens. Tarragon and chervil are especially good. If using dried herbs, steep briefly in a minute amount of boiling water to bring out the full flavour before creaming into butter. Fantastic with grilled poultry.

HORSERADISH BUTTER
To 125 g butter add 1 tablespoon French mustard and 1 tablespoon of horseradish. Beat until light and fluffy. Excellent with grilled meats or fish and adds a zip to corn on the cob.

OREGANO BUTTER
Soak dried oregano first in a very small amount of boiling water. Add to creamed butter. First rate with tomatoes, corn on the cob and lamb or veal.

PARSLEY LEMON BUTTER
Cream butter with very finely chopped parsley and lemon juice. Serve with grilled fish, vegetables, steaks, chops or liver.

PEPPERCORN BUTTER
Cream butter with freshly ground black pepper to taste and serve with poultry and meats.

ROSEMARY BUTTER
Chop fresh rosemary very finely then add to creamed butter with a sprinkle of lemon juice. Especially nice with lamb but good on any meat.

Savoury butters can be frozen and sliced to serve

Breads

DAMPER

4 cups self-raising flour
1 teaspoon salt
30 g butter
1 cup milk
½ cup water

Sift together flour and salt into a large mixing bowl. Using fingertips gently rub butter to resemble fine breadcrumbs. Make a well in the centre and gradually add combined milk and water mixing with knife to form a soft, slightly sticky dough. Turn dough onto a lightly floured board and knead to form a smooth round shape.

Lightly grease a baking tray or heatproof dish. Place dough on tray and bake at 200°C (400°F) for 25 minutes, then reduce heat to 180°C (350°F) and bake a further 15–20 minutes until the damper sounds hollow when tapped. Serve sliced with butter or jam.
Makes 1 loaf

FRUIT AND TEA DAMPER

½ cup chopped dried apricots
½ cup chopped raisins
¾ cup dried dates, pitted and chopped
2 cups warm tea
finely grated rind 1 orange
60 g butter, softened
1 teaspoon allspice
2 tablespoons sugar
1 quantity damper (see recipe)

Combine fruits in a small bowl, cover with tea and set aside for 30 minutes to soak. Drain very well then combine with butter, allspice and sugar. Pat damper dough out to form a circle approximately 30 cm in diameter. Place fruit in the centre. Fold edges of circle towards centre (the circle should now be a square) and pinch edges together to encase filling.

Carefully place fruit damper on a greased baking tray and brush lightly with a little beaten egg. Bake at 200°C (400°F) for 25 minutes, then reduce heat to 180°C (350°F) and bake a further 15–20 minutes, or until well risen. Cool slightly before serving, otherwise the filling will be too hot.
Makes 1 loaf

Damper (rear) and Fruit and Tea Damper

HOT HERBED BREAD

1 Italian or *Greek loaf*
125 g butter
1 clove garlic, crushed
2 teaspoons finely chopped parsley
1 teaspoon finely chopped oregano
1 teaspoon finely chopped dill
2 tablespoons grated Parmesan cheese

Cut bread diagonally into 2 cm slices without cutting through base. Combine butter, garlic and herbs and mix well. Spread on both sides of bread and sprinkle cheese over top. Lay on a piece of foil. Bring ends of foil up without closing in top to allow cheese to melt. Bake in hot oven 200°C (400°F) for 10 minutes.

PARSLEY LOAF

1 French or *Vienna loaf*
100 g butter
½ cup finely chopped parsley
2 tablespoons grated cheese
1 teaspoon lemon juice

Slice bread 2 cm thick without cutting through base. Thoroughly mix remaining ingredients together and spread on both sides of bread. Wrap loaf in foil and heat through on barbecue for 20–30 minutes.

Vegetables and Salads

VEGETABLE KEBABS

vegetables in season

Select a colourful variety of vegetables in season (tomatoes, onions, capsicums, broccoli, cauliflower, mushrooms), cut into equal-sized portions and thread alternately on skewers. Barbecue over medium heat, controlling the temperature and turning occasionally until tender.

Serve with your favourite sauce. Barbecue time depends on the vegetables. Remember you want them to be hot and crunchy rather than falling off the skewer.

COLESLAW

1 kg cabbage, finely shredded
½ cup grated carrot
½ cup crushed pineapple, drained

DRESSING

1½ cups sour cream
2 egg yolks
2 tablespoons lemon juice
2 teaspoons prepared mustard
1 teaspoon horseradish cream
¼ teaspoon paprika
¼ teaspoon pepper
salt, to taste

Combine sour cream and egg yolks until well blended. Mix in remaining dressing ingredients and season to taste. Combine vegetables and fruit, add dressing and toss until well coated. Chill before serving.
Serves 8

Vegetable Kebabs

ZUCCHINI AND GREEN BEAN SALAD

250 g zucchini, sliced 1 cm thick
250 g green beans, sliced
1 glove garlic, peeled
1 bay leaf
½ teaspoon salt
1 onion, sliced
1 red capsicum, sliced

MONTICELLO DRESSING

⅔ cup olive oil
1 teaspoon sesame oil, to taste
⅓ cup tarragon or *white wine vinegar*
1 clove garlic, crushed
salt and freshly ground pepper, to taste

Blanch zucchini and beans in small amount of water with garlic, bay leaf and salt for 5 minutes. Drain and refresh under cold water. Shake dry and combine with onion and capsicum. Shake dressing ingredients together in a jar, sprinkle over salad and toss. Serve immediately.
Serves 6

MUSHROOM AND ENDIVE SALAD

250 g mushrooms, thinly sliced
1 white onion, thinly sliced
1 cucumber, thinly sliced
1 green capsicum, thinly sliced
4 sticks celery, sliced
3 tomatoes, cut into wedges
1 bunch endive, washed and torn
1 lettuce, washed and torn

DRESSING

3 tablespoons oil
1 tablespoon vinegar
1 teaspoon French mustard
1 clove garlic, crushed
salt and pepper, to taste

Prepare all vegetables and combine in salad bowl. Shake dressing ingredients together in a jar, sprinkle over salad and toss. Serve immediately.
Serves 6

SPRINGTIME SALAD

3 cups cauliflorets
1 avocado
lemon juice
1 cup asparagus pieces
1 lettuce
¼ cup chopped shallots
2 tablespoons olive oil
4 tablespoons tarragon vinegar
1 teaspoon chopped parsley
salt and pepper
¼ teaspoon mustard
sesame seeds

Steam cauliflorets until tender but crisp. Refresh under cold water, pat dry. Halve avocado, remove seed and peel. Cube, sprinkle with lemon juice to prevent browning. Cover asparagus with boiling salt water, cook 5 minutes, refresh under cold water and pat dry. Wash and shred lettuce. Combine florets, avocado, asparagus, lettuce and shallots. Chill. Combine oil, vinegar parsley, salt, pepper and mustard. Pour over salad, toss and serve garnished with toasted sesame seeds.
Serves 4–6

SPINACH AND BACON WITH AVOCADO

oil, for frying
3 rashers lean bacon, finely diced
1 clove garlic, crushed
½ cup pine nuts
1 onion, sliced in rings
1 avocado, peeled, seeded and sliced
juice ½ lemon
1 bunch English spinach, washed and drained
Vinaigrette Dressing (see recipe)

Saute bacon with garlic. Add pine nuts and toss until golden. Drain and allow to cool. Separate onion rings and coat avocado with lemon juice. Place spinach leaves in salad bowl, add remaining ingredients and toss with dressing just before serving.
Serves 6

Spinach and Bacon with Avocado

SPINACH AND BACON SALAD

1 bunch spinach
365 g tin champignons, drained
3 rashers bacon, crisply fried

DRESSING

½ cup oil
¼ cup white vinegar
1 clove garlic, crushed
salt and freshly ground pepper, to taste

Wash spinach, remove stems and tear leaves into bite-sized pieces. Shake dressing ingredients together in a jar, sprinkle over spinach and chill. Just before serving, fold through champignons, crumble bacon and sprinkle over top.
Serves 6

Springtime Salad

TOMATO CITRUS SALAD

1 kg tomatoes, cored, peeled and thickly sliced
1 teaspoon caster sugar
salt and freshly ground pepper, to taste
4 oranges
⅓ cup French Dressing (see recipe)
1 tablespoon snipped chives, to garnish

Sprinkle tomatoes with sugar and season. Carefully remove the rind from 1 orange and cut into julienne strips. Blanch the strips in boiling water for 3–4 minutes, then drain and refresh with cold water. Set aside. Peel the oranges, removing all the pith, then cut them into segments.

Arrange the tomato slices and orange segments on a serving dish and sprinkle over the French Dressing. Garnish with the strips of rind and snipped chives and serve well-chilled.

Serves 6–8

TOMATO AND ONION SALAD

6 tomatoes, cored and peeled
1 large purple onion, thinly sliced
⅓ cup Creamy Vinaigrette Dressing (see recipe)
2 tablespoons chopped parsley
1 tablespoon snipped chives, to garnish

Thinly slice the tomatoes and arrange on a flat plate. Push the onion into rings and arrange over the tomatoes.

Whisk the dressing and parsley together and pour it over the tomatoes. Cover and chill until serving time. Serve sprinkled with the chives.

Serves 4–6

Tomato and Onion Salad (rear) and Tomato Citrus Salad

SAVOURY RICE SALAD

375 g rice, cooked
1 red capsicum, finely diced
1 green capsicum, finely diced
2 sticks celery, sliced
6 shallots, finely chopped
6 water chestnuts, sliced
½ cup toasted almond flakes, to garnish

DRESSING

1 cup oil
½ cup white wine vinegar
2 cloves garlic, crushed
2 cm piece ginger root, peeled and grated
1 teaspoon cumin
salt and freshly ground pepper, to taste

Combine cooked rice, capsicums, celery, shallots and water chestnuts. Shake together dressing ingredients in a jar, pour over and toss thoroughly. Cover and chill. Just before serving, toss again and garnish with toasted almond flakes.

Serves 8

TABOULI

1 cup fine burghul
3 shallots, finely chopped
100 g parsley leaves (1 good-sized bunch)
½ cup finely chopped mint
juice 2–3 lemons
3 tablespoons olive oil
salt and pepper, to taste
1 lettuce
3 tomatoes, seeded and chopped

Place burghul in a bowl and cover with cold water. Leave to soak for 30 minutes. Drain thoroughly and press out excess water. Spread burghul on a clean, dry tea towel and leave to dry. Place burghul in a bowl with shallots and mix well. Chop parsley very finely and add to bowl. Add mint, lemon juice, oil and seasonings. Mix lightly but thoroughly.

Wash and dry lettuce leaves. Place on plates or in individual serving dishes. Just before serving, lightly fold through tomatoes into tabouli and place a generous spoonful of the mixture in lettuce cups. Serve with flat bread.

Note: Always add the tomato at the very last moment.

There are several different methods of spelling tabouli, among them tabbouleh, tabbuli and tabbuil. The quantities of mint, parsley, burghul, lemon juice and oil can be adjusted according to preference but opinion always seems to favour plenty of parsley.

Serves 4

Desserts

FRUIT KEBABS

3 bananas, thickly sliced
2 apples, cut into chunks
1 pineapple, diced
2 grapefruit, segmented
1 punnet strawberries, halved

MARINADE

1 cup orange juice
¼ cup honey
2 tablespoons Cointreau
1 tablespoon brown sugar
1 tablespoon finely chopped mint

Mix marinade ingredients together and heat gently to dissolve honey and sugar. Pour over prepared fruit and leave at room temperature 30 minutes. Thread fruit on skewers alternately for colour and barbecue about 5 minutes until heated through. Turn and baste frequently.
Note: Barbecue Fruit Kebabs can be made with any fruits in season. Just keep colours and flavours in mind as you make your selection.
Serves 8

BARBECUED BANANAS

firm, green-tipped bananas

Barbecue bananas 15 minutes over medium heat turning frequently until skin turns black and flesh is tender.

Fruit Kebabs

Pineapple Sorbet

FRUIT SALAD IN COINTREAU

1 mango, peeled and chopped
¼–½ cup Cointreau
6 red plums, stoned and chopped
6 strawberries, quartered
3 apricots, stoned and chopped
pulp 3 passionfruit
1 lime, peeled and chopped
1 banana, peeled and sliced
1 kiwi fruit, peeled and sliced
1 apple, cored and diced
1 rock melon, seeded and scooped out with melon baller
1 guava, chopped

Marinate mango in small bowl with Cointreau for several hours, then puree. Prepare remaining fruit and combine with puree. Chill thoroughly and serve.
Serves 6

PINEAPPLE SORBET

1 medium-sized pineapple
2 limes
400 mL water
¾ cup caster sugar
mint sprigs, to garnish

Cut pineapple in half lengthways; leave leaves intact. Using grapefruit knife, remove flesh, leaving shells whole for serving. Place pineapple shells in refrigerator until needed. Peel limes, removing white pith, cut in quarters. Puree lime and pineapple fruits.

Simmer water and sugar for 8–10 minutes until sugar is dissolved and thin syrup forms. Allow to cool then add to pineapple mixture. Pour into freezer trays and freeze until set. Puree again. Pour back into freezer trays, cover with foil and allow to refreeze.

When ready to serve, dip bottom of trays in hot water, tip out sorbet and cut into large dice. Pile sorbet into pineapple shells and serve. Garnish with mint sprigs.
Serves 6

FLAMBE FRUIT

3 mandarins, peeled and segmented
4 pears, cut into slices same size as mandarin segments
1 cup overproof rum
⅘ cup brown sugar
4 bananas, peeled and sliced
2 punnets medium-sized strawberries, hulled

Place mandarin segments and pear slices in a large cast iron pan (or on a large steel tray if you prefer). Add about ½ cup rum and fold in sugar thoroughly. Heat over barbecue then add banana slices. When juice starts to bubble add strawberries and stir gently. Remove pan from fire, warm rum, pour over fruit and ignite, stirring until flame dies down. Serve on a large platter with bamboo forks. Barbecue time about 5–10 minutes.
Serves 8

Flambe Fruit

PRODUCE OF AUSTRALIA
750ml

SPECIALLY HEALTHY PARTIES

This chapter offers recipes grouped under 4 broad headings: low kilojoule, low cholesterol, low salt and diabetic.

Most of us these days have a clear idea of what low-kilojoule recipes involve — avoid fatty meats, the more fattening types of dairy food, additives like oil and sugar, and anything at all in large quantities!

Cholesterol is found in foods of animal origin such as butter, cheese, milk, eggs, fatty red and white meats, offal and seafood. For those with a particular problem metabolising cholesterol, a low cholesterol diet recommends polyunsaturated oil and margarine, small quantities of grilled red and white meat trimmed of all fat and a stronger emphasis on fruits, vegetables and pulses.

A low-salt diet for those with heart or blood pressure problems, renal diseases and liver complaints, removes *all* table salt (sodium chloride) from cooking and from the dinner table. It also removes food preserved in or made with salt — cheese, salted butter and margarine, ham, bacon, most types of sausage, olives and sauces such as Worcestershire and Tabasco. In extreme cases, foods high in natural sodium which are normally good for you, must also be removed from the diet on a doctor's advice. These foods include some fresh fruits and vegetables, seafood, brown rice and dried fruits. It is worth noting that the National Heart Foundation recommends that every Australian reduce table-salt intake in the interests of future good health, particularly as the original purpose of salt — to preserve food — has largely been superseded by refrigerators.

Diabetic recipes have been carefully worked out and diabetics should have a very clear notion of what they eat during one 24-hour period. The following recipes in our diabetic section have been kindly lent to us by the Dietetic Department of the Royal Alexandra Hospital for Children, Camperdown NSW.

Finally, vegetarians will find delicious and interesting party foods in this and every other chapter of this book.

Guests with particular dietary problems usually take it upon themselves to inform their hosts of their condition. Don't be afraid to ask them for a recipe so that you can prepare a special meal for them. Likewise, you should alert guests to any unusual ingredients in certain dishes so there won't be any nasty surprises or allergic reactions later on.

If it's not possible to ask each guest what they prefer to eat, it's easiest to have a buffet-style party which features both red and white meats, perhaps a little seafood and plenty of interesting salads and vegetable dishes — you're sure to please almost everyone.

Tempt your guests with a selection of tangy fruits

Low Kilojoule

TOMATO GRANITA

8 tomatoes, peeled, seeded and chopped
2 shallots, chopped
1 stick celery, chopped
1 clove garlic, crushed
1 cucumber, peeled and diced small
1 teaspoon chopped mint

Strain tomatoes to remove excess liquid and all seeds. Combine tomatoes, shallots, celery and garlic. Pour mixture into freezer trays and freeze.

Remove from freezer 10 minutes before serving to soften ice a little. Break up tomato ice with a fork and stir in cucumber and mint. Serve in individual glass dishes.
Serves 4

PIQUANT FRUIT COCKTAIL

1 pawpaw, peeled and diced
1 cucumber, seeded and diced
1 red capsicum, seeded and chopped

SAUCE

1 tablespoon soy sauce
1 tablespoon fresh lime juice
½ cup thick coconut cream
1 fresh red chilli, halved and seeded

Shake sauce ingredients in a screwtop jar and leave for 1 hour. Remove chilli. Mix pawpaw, cucumber and capsicum together, pile into 4 individual serving dishes and pour sauce over. Alternatively, arrange fruits separately in individual serving dishes. Serve well chilled. Sauce may be served separately.
Serves 4

COTTAGE CHEESE AND PINEAPPLE DIP

500 g low-fat cottage cheese
½ cup Salad Dressing (see recipe)
½ small fresh pineapple, peeled, cored and chopped
2 tablespoons chopped chives

Combine cottage cheese and Salad Dressing and beat well. Add pineapple and chives. Cover and chill. Serve with raw sticks of vegetables for dipping.
Serves 10–12

STEAMED MUSSELS

3 kg mussels
2 quantities Tomato Dressing (see recipe)
½ cup white wine
few stalks parsley
1 tablespoon cornflour
3 tablespoons chopped parsley

Scrub mussels and remove beard. Discard any mussels with open or broken shells.

Place Tomato Dressing, wine and parsley in a pan. Bring to boil, reduce heat and simmer 3–5 minutes. Add mussels, cover and steam for 3–5 minutes until shells open. Remove mussels as they open.

Twist off top shell of mussels. Discard any that have not opened. Divide mussels between 10–12 entree plates, set aside and keep warm.

Simmer cooking liquid until reduced by half. Stir cornflour into 2 tablespoons water and pour into cooking liquid; simmer until sauce thickens slightly. Pour sauce over mussels and serve hot sprinkled with parsley.
Serves 10–12 as an entree

Tomato Granita

MUSSELS AND SNOW PEAS

1 kg mussels
250 g snow peas, trimmed
10–12 fresh lychees, peeled
4 slices ginger root, finely sliced
½ cup Tomato Dressing (see recipe)

Scrub mussels and pull out beard. Discard any mussels with broken or open shells. Bring 1 cup water to boil, add mussels, cover and steam for 3–5 minutes until they open. Remove mussels from shells and place in a bowl. Cover and set aside.

Cover snow peas with boiling water and leave for 1 minute. Drain and cool with water. Add snow peas to mussels. Halve lychees and remove stones. Place with mussels. Sprinkle ginger over.

Pour dressing over mussel mixture and stir to coat all ingredients. Cover and chill for 30 minutes. Drain off any excess dressing. Serve on individual plates.
Serves 10–12

FISH WITH HERBED YOGHURT DRESSING

16 fish fillets
few parsley stalks
few celery leaves
1 teaspoon black peppercorns
bouquet garni
½ cup dry white wine
2 cups water
double quantity Herbed Yoghurt Dressing (see recipe)

Check fish fillets for bones and set aside. Combine parsley, celery, peppercorns, bouquet garni, wine and water in frying pan. Bring to boil, reduce heat and simmer for 5 minutes.

Pour dressing into a heatproof container and stand in a bowl of very hot water. Stir occasionally so dressing heats through.

Simmer fish fillets in cooking liquid for 3–5 minutes until cooked when tested (cooking time depends on thickness of fillets). Drain fish and arrange on a serving plate. Spoon dressing over and serve.
Serves 10–12

GINGERED SCALLOPS

2 tablespoons soy sauce
1 tablespoon honey
1 teaspoon chopped ginger root
1 clove garlic, crushed
1 cup water
500 g Tasmanian scallops, deveined
1 mignonette lettuce
1 red capsicum, seeded and sliced
½ cup sliced bean sprouts
1 avocado, seeded and sliced
2 shallots, chopped
1 tablespoon oil
1 lemon or *½ grapefruit*
2 tablespoons chopped chives
1 small honeydew melon, chilled

In a saucepan, bring to boil soy, honey, ginger, garlic and water; lower heat, add scallops and simmer 3 minutes only. Remove scallops with a slotted spoon, allow to cool then slice thinly and refrigerate until ready to serve.

In a salad bowl, toss lettuce, capsicum, bean sprouts, avocado, shallots, oil and lemon juice. Arrange salad on individual plates, add scallops (moistened with lemon juice) and sprinkle with chopped herbs. Serve with peeled melon wedges.
Serves 4

Piquant Fruit Cocktail (p. 142)

BAKED SNAPPER

2 × 2 kg whole snapper, scaled and cleaned
2 lemons
freshly ground pepper, to taste
6 shallots, finely chopped
1 stalk celery, finely chopped
2 teaspoons polyunsaturated oil
4 cups wholemeal fresh breadcrumbs
grated rind 1 orange
juice 2 oranges
salt (optional)
few sprigs fennel
extra 2 lemons

Grate rind of 1 lemon and set aside. Squeeze lemons and brush juice over skin and inside cavity of both fish. Season cavity with pepper and set aside for 30 minutes.

Heat oil and fry shallots and celery 3 minutes. Drain off any oil. Combine breadcrumbs with vegetables, lemon and orange rind and enough orange juice to bind ingredients. Taste and adjust seasoning. Stuff fish with filling and secure with skewers. Place sprigs of fennel on top.

Place fish in greased baking dishes, cover with greased foil and bake at 180°C (350°F) for 40–60 minutes until cooked when tested.

Remove foil and fennel and arrange fish on serving platters. Garnish with extra fennel and lemon wedges. Serve with steamed seasonal vegetables and salad.
Serves 10–12

Baked Snapper (rear) and French Roast Chicken

FRENCH ROAST CHICKEN

2 × 1.4 kg chickens
10 g polyunsaturated margarine
2 tablespoons water
250 g button mushrooms, chopped
4 tablespoons chopped parsley
5 cups fresh wholemeal breadcrumbs
salt (optional)
freshly ground pepper, to taste
juice 2 lemons
1 litre Chicken Stock (see recipe)

Rinse and wipe chickens, discard fat found in body cavity, neck and giblets.

In a frying pan simmer margarine, water and mushrooms for 5 minutes. Allow excess liquid to evaporate and set aside to cool.

Combine mushrooms, parsley, breadcrumbs, salt and pepper. Divide stuffing between both chickens. Truss chickens for roasting and preheat oven to 190°C (375°F).

Boil chicken stock in 2 roasting dishes on top of stove. Put a rack in each dish and arrange chickens, on their sides, on the racks. Brush chickens with lemon juice and cover with foil.

Roast for 20 minutes. Turn chickens onto their other side, brush with more lemon juice, cover with foil again and roast a further 20 minutes.

Turn chickens onto their backs, brush with lemon juice and roast, covered, for a further 20 minutes. Remove foil and continue roasting, basting occasionally, until cooked through. Turn oven off and let chickens stand for 5 minutes before carving.
Serves 10–12

LAMB AND VEGETABLE KEBABS

2 kg boned leg of lamb
1½ cups Tomato Dressing (see recipe)
300 g button mushrooms
3 green capsicums, seeded

Trim lamb of all visible fat. Cut meat into 3 cm cubes and place in a bowl with Tomato Dressing; leave to marinate a minimum of 4 hours. Soak wooden skewers in water to cover for at least 30 minutes. Remove meat from the marinade and reserve liquid. Trim mushroom stalks and cut capsicums into pieces the same size as the lamb. Thread lamb, mushrooms and capsicums alternately onto drained skewers.

Grill kebabs 12–15 minutes until cooked as liked. During cooking, turn kebabs and brush with reserved liquid.
Serves 10–12

BEEF AND BROCCOLI WITH SOY SAUCE DRESSING

750 g broccoli, cut into florets and blanched
500 g lean roast beef, sliced thinly
1 red capsicum, seeded and sliced
125 g mushrooms, sliced
1 cup bean sprouts
230 g can water chestnuts, drained and halved
freshly ground pepper, to taste
¼ cup white wine vinegar
¼ cup soy sauce
1 teaspoon grated ginger root
1 tablespoon vegetable oil

In a large salad bowl combine broccoli, beef, capsicum, mushrooms, bean sprouts and water chestnuts. Season well with pepper. Combine remaining ingredients and pour over salad just before serving.
Serves 6

BEETROOT SALAD

4–5 beetroot
½ cup Herbed Yoghurt Dressing (see recipe)
½ cup Salad Dressing (see recipe)
2 tablespoons chopped parsley

Wash beetroot and trim stalks to 2 cm in length. Place in a pan with water to cover, bring to boil, reduce heat and simmer, covered, for 30–45 minutes until tender. Drain and cool.

Wearing rubber gloves, slip off skin and trim off stalks and root end of beetroot. Cut beetroot into strips about 5 cm long.

Mix dressings together and combine with beetroot. Cover and chill before serving sprinkled with parsley.
Serves 10–12

CAULIFLOWER AND BROCCOLI SALAD

500 g cauliflower
500 g broccoli
1 cup Creamy Vinaigrette Dressing (see recipe)
1–2 teaspoons French mustard
1 teaspoon capers, chopped
Tabasco sauce, to taste
paprika, to taste

Wash cauliflower and broccoli and separate into florets. Cook broccoli and cauliflower separately until tender but still crisp. Drain and cool. Combine dressing with mustard, capers and Tabasco sauce. Adjust seasonings to taste. Arrange cooked vegetables in a serving dish and spoon dressing over. Cover and chill until serving. Serve sprinkled with paprika.
Serves 10–12

RED CABBAGE AND APPLE SALAD WITH HERBED YOGHURT DRESSING

750 g red cabbage
4 green apples, washed and cored
squeeze lemon juice
6 shallots, sliced diagonally
1 cup Herbed Yoghurt Dressing (see recipe)
2 tablespoons chopped dill

Remove hard centre core of cabbage and any wilted outer leaves. Finely shred cabbage, wash well and drain.

Cut apples into thin wedges and sprinkle with a little lemon juice to coat. Combine apple, shallots and cabbage. Arrange in a serving bowl, pour dressing over and toss to coat. Sprinkle with dill and serve chilled.
Serves 10–12

TOMATO AND CAPSICUM SALAD

750 g tomatoes, peeled
1 bunch shallots, thinly sliced
3 green capsicums, sliced
⅓ cup Salad Dressing (see recipe)
⅓ cup Herbed Yoghurt Dressing (see recipe)

Cut tomatoes into wedges, discarding core section. Place in a bowl with shallots and capsicum. Mix dressings together and stir into salad. Serve chilled.
Serves 10–12

Clockwise from top: Tomato and Capsicum Salad, Cauliflower and Broccoli Salad, Salad Greens and Tomato Dressing (p. 155)

SALAD DRESSING

2 tablespoons cornflour
⅔ cup reduced fat milk
1 tablespoon prepared mustard
1 tablespoon polyunsaturated margarine
1 egg, beaten
2 tablespoons vinegar
⅓ cup polyunsaturated oil
salt (optional)
freshly ground pepper, to taste

Mix cornflour with a little milk. Heat remaining milk to simmering. Add cornflour mixture, stir well and simmer until thickened. Remove from heat and stir in mustard and margarine. Beat in egg, then gradually add vinegar and oil. Return mixture to pan and heat gently until thick, stirring constantly. Do not allow to boil. Allow dressing to cool. Add seasonings. Store in an airtight container in refrigerator. Use as directed.
Makes approximately 1¼ cups

HERBED YOGHURT DRESSING

1 cup low-fat yoghurt
2 tablespoons chopped parsley
1 tablespoon chopped chives
1 tablespoon prepared mustard
salt (optional)
freshly ground pepper, to taste

Combine yoghurt, herbs and seasonings in a bowl. Store in an airtight container and refrigerate before using. Use as directed.
Makes approximately 1 cup

Left to right: Creamy
Tomato Dressing, Fren
Yoghurt Dressin

CREAMY VINAIGRETTE DRESSING

This recipe is the basis of many fine salad dressings that add pizzazz to leafy green vegetables. To vary the flavour or add a gourmet touch, use the unique flavours of walnut, almond, or rape oil blended with a little herb or strawberry vinegar. These are all quite strong, so use sparingly and combine with vegetable oil or white vinegar to make the correct proportions.

1/2 cup white wine vinegar
salt and freshly ground pepper
1 cup olive oil (or a combination of 1/2 olive oil and 1/2 vegetable oil)

Combine all ingredients in a screw-topped jar or blender and shake or process until well combined.
Makes 1½ cups.

FRENCH DRESSING

¼ cup white wine vinegar
salt and freshly ground pepper, to taste
½ teaspoon sugar
½ teaspoon mustard powder
1 clove garlic, peeled and lightly pressed
½ cup olive oil

Combine vinegar, salt and pepper, sugar, mustard and garlic in a screw-topped jar or blender. Shake or process until well blended. Gradually add oil and mix until combined.
Makes ¾ cup

Champagne Method
750 mL
12% ALCOHOL BY VOLUME

ORANGE SORBET

10 oranges
1 tablespoon gelatine
2 tablespoons water
½ cup water extra
sugar substitute, to taste
4 egg whites

Squeeze juice from oranges and strain. Sprinkle gelatine over water and leave for a few minutes. Place container of gelatine in hot water and stir until dissolved. Combine with orange juice and add sweetening to taste.

Pour mixture into a cake tin and freeze until half-frozen. Tip mixture into a bowl and beat well to break down ice-crystals. Place in refrigerator.

Whisk egg whites until stiff and fold into orange juice mixture. Return mixture to freezer and freeze until half-frozen. Turn into a bowl again and beat to break down ice crystals. Refreeze. Beat once more if liked.

Note: If you own an ice cream maker, follow the manufacturer's instructions.

Serves 10–12

CHILLED LEMON SOUFFLE

375 mL can evaporated skimmed milk
2 tablespoons gelatine
4 tablespoons water
pinch salt (optional)
grated rind and juice 4 lemons
powdered or liquid sweetener, to taste
4 kiwi fruit, peeled and sliced

Chill evaporated milk in refrigerator for 24 hours. Sprinkle gelatine over water and leave to stand for a few minutes. Place container of gelatine in hot water and stir until dissolved then set aside.

In a large chilled bowl, whisk milk and salt until frothy. Beat in gelatine, lemon rind, juice and sweetener. The dessert should taste lemony — add more juice and rind if necessary. Pour into a serving bowl and refrigerate to set. To serve, arrange kiwi fruit decoratively on top of souffle.

Serves 10–12

Left to right: Chilled Lemon Souffle, Strawberry Snow and Orange Sorbet

STRAWBERRY SNOW

3 punnets ripe strawberries
sugar substitute, to taste
2 tablespoons gelatine
4 tablespoons water
6 egg whites

Wash and hull strawberries, puree and sweeten to taste. Sprinkle gelatine over water and leave to stand for 5 minutes. Place container of gelatine in hot water to dissolve then stir gelatine into strawberry puree.

Whisk egg whites to form stiff peaks; fold into strawberries. Taste and adjust for sweetness. Spoon strawberry snow into a serving bowl, cover and chill until serving time.

Serves 10–12

SUMMER FRUIT PLATTER

Fresh fruits are a good choice for dessert being low in fat and salt and high in fibre. During the summer months we are lucky to have a wide variety of reasonably priced fruits available to choose from. Tropical fruits only can be selected, stone fruits only or a mixture of both. Remember to select fruit that is free from bruises and soft spots. Wash all edible skinned fruit before preparing.

TROPICAL

1 large ripe pineapple
1 ripe pawpaw
3 ripe mangoes
10–12 lychees (optional)

STONE FRUITS

10–12 ripe apricots
10–12 ripe plums
10–12 ripe peaches
250–500 g cherries

MIXED FRUITS

2 punnets ripe strawberries
6 kiwi fruit
1 rock melon
500 g seedless grapes

Tropical selection: Top and tail pineapple. With a sharp knife cut off skin, including all eyes. Halve pineapple lengthways. Cut each half into 6 wedges then cut off core. Halve and seed pawpaw and cut into 12 wedges. Cut mango on each side of stone. Set aside stone section. Cut the flesh on the other sections into diamond shapes. Peel lychees. Arrange fruit on a platter. Cover and chill until serving time.

Stone Fruits: Halve apricots, plums and peaches and remove stones. Arrange all fruits on a platter. Cover and chill until serving time.

Mixed Fruits: Hull strawberries. Peel kiwi fruit and quarter. Halve rock melon, remove seeds and cut into 12 wedges. Cut fruit from rind. Separate grapes into bunches. Arrange fruit on a platter. Cover and chill until serving time.

Each selection serves 10–12

Low Cholesterol

GAZPACHO

1 kg tomatoes, peeled, seeded and chopped
½ cucumber, seeded and diced
3–4 cloves garlic, finely chopped
4 shallots, finely sliced
½ green capsicum, diced
2 tablespoons oil, olive or *polyunsaturated*
1–2 tablespoons white wine vinegar
salt (optional)
freshly ground pepper, to taste
Tabasco sauce, to taste
3 tablespoons chopped parsley
2½ cups iced water

GARNISH

½ cucumber, seeded and diced
½ green capsicum, diced
3 slices wholemeal bread, diced

Combine tomatoes, cucumber, garlic, shallots, capsicum, oil and vinegar with salt, pepper, Tabasco sauce and parsley; chill well. Just before serving stir through iced water.

Serve soup in chilled bowls. Place cucumber, capsicum and bread in small bowls. Guests can help themselves to garnish as liked.

Note: For those people permitted it, 2 eggs, hard-boiled, can be chopped and offered as another garnish.

Serves 10–12

FENNEL AND ORANGE SALAD

3 heads fennel
3 oranges
4–6 tablespoons Tomato Dressing (see recipe)
2 tablespoons chopped parsley

Trim fennel, slice thinly; wash well and discard any discoloured slices. Cut both ends from oranges then cut off all rind and pith. With a small sharp knife, cut between membranes of oranges and free segments. Remove any seeds. Combine oranges, fennel and dressing. Cover, chill and serve sprinkled with parsley.

Serves 10–12

FRUIT AND NUT SALAD

1 cup chopped pineapple
2 grapefruits, segmented
2 oranges, segmented
1 large green apple, diced
1 tablespoon lemon juice
½ cup stuffed olives
½ lettuce, shredded
¼ cup toasted pine nuts
¼ cup toasted almonds
¼ cup chopped walnuts
1 tablespoon olive oil
2 tablespoons vinegar
salt and pepper, to taste
1 tablespoon chopped chives

Combine pineapple, grapefruit and orange segments and chill. Toss apple in lemon juice to prevent browning and add. Top with olives. Place lettuce leaves on serving platter. Spoon fruit mixture over lettuce and sprinkle with nuts. Combine oil, vinegar, salt, pepper, chives and pour over salad just before serving.

Serves 6

SALAD GREENS WITH TOMATO DRESSING

1 cos lettuce, washed
1 butter lettuce, washed
4 shallots, trimmed and sliced
1 green capsicum, sliced
2 tablespoons chopped parsley
4–6 tablespoons Tomato Dressing (see recipe)

Tear both lettuces into pieces. Place in a salad bowl with shallots, capsicum and parsley. Toss lightly. Cover and chill until serving time. Just before serving, add dressing and toss to coat all the ingredients.

Serves 10–12

Fruit and Nut Salad

BROWN RICE SALAD WITH TOMATO DRESSING

2 oranges, segmented
2 cups raw brown rice, cooked
4 shallots, sliced
1 large red capsicum, diced
1 large green capsicum, diced
1 cup Tomato Dressing (see recipe)
salt (optional)
freshly ground pepper, to taste

Cut rind and all pith from oranges. With a small sharp knife, cut between the membrane and flesh of each segment and free the orange flesh. Remove and discard any seeds.

Combine oranges, rice, shallots and capsicums. Pour dressing over and toss lightly. Season to taste. Place in a serving bowl, cover and chill until serving time.
Serves 10–12

TOMATO DRESSING

1 cup tomato juice
juice 1 lime or *½ lemon*
2 shallots, finely chopped
2 cloves garlic, chopped
Worcestershire sauce, to taste
Tabasco sauce, to taste
freshly ground pepper, to taste

Combine all ingredients and mix thoroughly. Store in an airtight container in the refrigerator. Use as directed.
Makes 1 cup

LEMON DRESSING

2 tablespoons lemon juice
finely grated zest 1 lemon
3 tablespoons olive oil
2 teaspoons rum
½ teaspoon brown sugar
freshly ground pepper, to taste

Combine all ingredients in screw-topped jar and shake to mix well. Try this one with avocado slices.
Makes ½ cup

GLOBE ARTICHOKES ROMAN-STYLE

4 large artichokes
lemon juice
70 g breadcrumbs
1 small bunch fresh mint, finely chopped
2 cloves garlic, chopped
6 tablespoons olive oil
salt and pepper, to taste

Discard the outside woody leaves of the artichokes. Trim the stems to 5 cm in length and chop the first 2 cm off the top ends so that the most tender part remains. Put them in a bowl of cold water containing a little lemon juice (to preserve their green colour).

In a bowl, mix breadcrumbs with mint and garlic. With your fingers, ease open the artichokes and push the breadcrumb mixture between the leaves.

Arrange them side by side in a casserole, sprinkle with salt and pepper and pour oil on top. Add enough water to come halfway up the artichokes and cook slowly until nearly all liquid is evaporated and a fairly thick sauce forms. The artichokes are cooked when the leaves can easily be pulled off.
Serves 4

Lemon Dressing

Apple and Onion Bake

APPLE AND ONION BAKE

6 onions, sliced
2 tablespoons polyunsaturated vegetable oil
10 thick slices tomato
½ cup breadcrumbs
4 apples, peeled and sliced
2 green chillies, seeded and finely chopped
2 tablespoons chopped coriander
1 cup hot vegetable stock

Preheat oven to 190°C (375°F).

Lightly fry onions in 1 tablespoon oil. Remove with slotted spoon. Fry tomato slices. Drain off juices through strainer and reserve. Saute breadcrumbs in remaining oil to brown lightly. Grease baking dish and arrange onion, apple and tomato in alternate layers.

Put chillies, coriander and reserved juices in hot stock and pour over vegetables. Sprinkle breadcrumbs over top. Cover and bake for 30 minutes. Uncover and cook another 15 minutes.
Serves 4

BOLIVIAN BEAN STEW

1 cup chick peas, skins removed
1 cup butter beans
1 cup lentils
vegetable stock
1 green capsicum, roughly chopped
1 red capsicum, roughly chopped
4 sticks celery, thickly sliced
2 carrots, chopped
250 g tomatoes, peeled
310 g can corn kernels, drained
2 tablespoons tomato paste
1 bouquet garni

Soak beans and chick peas overnight. Drain and measure liquid, adding vegetable stock to make up 600 mL. Place all ingredients in a saucepan and bring to boil very slowly — this should take about 30 minutes — then simmer for 45–60 minutes, until beans are tender. Remove bouquet garni and season to taste.
Serves 6

Bolivian Bean Stew

Mushrooms with Garlic and Parsley

CAPSICUM CASSEROLE

100 mL olive oil
200 g sliced onions
2 cloves garlic, sliced
2 bay leaves, crushed
880 g large capsicums, a mixture of green, yellow and red, seeded and sliced
salt and pepper, to taste
500 g tomatoes, peeled and chopped

In a heavy frying pan with a lid, heat oil and saute onions, garlic and bay leaves. When the onion is starting to colour, add capsicums, salt and pepper and continue to saute for another 10 minutes on fairly high heat. Now add tomatoes and check seasoning.

Cover pan with a lid and continue cooking until capsicum is soft and tomatoes have formed a thickish sauce. Serve hot or cold.
Serves 4

MUSHROOMS WITH GARLIC AND PARSLEY

800 g field or *cultivated mushrooms*
100 mL olive oil
3 cloves garlic
salt and pepper, to taste
4 tablespoons chopped parsley
juice ½ lemon

Wash mushrooms and drain carefully. If they are large, slice them; if small, leave them whole. Warm the oil (it should not be very hot), add garlic cloves and stir once just to warm through. Then add mushrooms and a little salt and pepper and cook for 4–5 minutes on a medium to high heat until they start to form their own liquid. Do not overcook. Take them off the heat, add parsley and lemon juice, lower heat and cook for another 1–2 minutes. Serve hot or cold.
Serves 4

SPINACH ROLLS

4 dried Chinese mushrooms soaked in water 10 minutes
1 shallot, chopped
1 clove garlic, crushed
2 teaspoons polyunsaturated oil
1 teaspoon ginger
1 cup shredded cabbage
½ cup chopped celery
½ cup grated carrot
1 cup bean sprouts
¼ cup chopped water chestnuts
2 tablespoons soy sauce
1 tablespoon sesame oil
1 tablespoon dry sherry
2 tablespoons cornflour
salt and pepper, to taste
1 bunch spinach

Remove mushroom stalks, drain and slice. Heat oil, stir-fry mushrooms, shallot and garlic 3 minutes. Add ginger, cabbage, celery, carrot, bean sprouts and water chestnuts. Cook 5 minutes. Combine soy sauce, sesame oil and sherry; blend in cornflour and stir into vegetables. Adjust seasoning and cook mixture until it thickens and boils. Allow to cool.

Wash spinach and remove hard stems. If large, cut spinach leaves into shapes about 12 cm square. If small, use whole spinach leaves. Place a tablespoon of mixture on each spinach leaf, roll up and seal ends. Steam rolls over boiling water until spinach is tender. Serve hot.
Serves 4

Capsicum Casserole

Baked Vegetable Ring

BAKED VEGETABLE RING

2 onions, chopped
2 cloves garlic, chopped
1 tablespoon oil
1 bunch spinach
2 cups cottage cheese
2 cups cooked soy beans
½ cup chopped walnuts
½ cup sultanas
¼ cup tomato paste
¼ cup grated carrot
¼ teaspoon dill
pepper, to taste
1 tomato, sliced

FRESH TOMATO FILLING

2 tomatoes, peeled and chopped
¼ cup chopped onion
1 tablespoon chopped mint
1 tablespoon lemon juice
pinch cayenne

Preheat oven to 180°C (350°F). Fry onions and garlic in oil until soft but not brown. Wash spinach and remove stalks. Steam until just tender. Chop finely and drain in a colander. Squeeze spinach to remove all excess liquid. Combine spinach with cooked onion and all remaining ingredients.

Grease and line a ring tin. Place slices of tomato on base of dish. Cover with spinach mixture and press down firmly. Cover tin with foil and bake for 45 minutes, removing foil after 25 minutes. If not firm after 45 minutes, bake 10 minutes more. Allow to stand 10 minutes before turning out onto serving plate.

To make Fresh Tomato Filling, combine all remaining ingredients. Fill centre of vegetable ring and serve.
Serves 6

RATATOUILLE

2 zucchini
2 eggplants (aubergines)
salt
2 green capsicums
1 red capsicum
100 mL olive oil
2 medium-sized onions, chopped
2 cloves garlic, chopped
4 tomatoes, skinned, seeded and chopped
pinch thyme
1 bay leaf
½ teaspoon sugar (optional)
freshly ground pepper, to taste
4 tablespoons flour
1 tablespoon vinegar
juice ½ lemon
½ teaspoon basil, chopped

Cut zucchini and eggplants into slices 1.5 cm thick. Sprinkle with salt and leave for 30 minutes. Wash, drain and dry. Split capsicums lengthways. Remove the seeds and cut in thin slices.

Heat half the oil in a large pan and saute onions for 3 minutes or until tender. Do not allow them to brown. Add the capsicums, zucchini and garlic to pan. Cook for 2 minutes, then add tomatoes, thyme, bay leaf and sugar. Season and cook for a further 6 minutes.

In a separate pan, heat the remaining oil. Coat the eggplant slices in flour. Shake off any excess. If the slices are large, halve or quarter them so that they are equivalent to the zucchini in diameter. Fry for ½ minute on each side or until golden. Remove and drain well.

Combine all the vegetables in a casserole dish. Add vinegar and lemon juice, and mix well. Chill and serve sprinkled with chopped basil.
Serves 4

LIME RICE

juice 4–5 limes
½ coconut, grated
1 teaspoon turmeric
2 cups rice, cooked
¾ cup polyunsaturated vegetable oil
½ cup mustard seeds
1 cup cashews, chopped
2 curry leaves, chopped
6 green chillies, seeded and chopped
1 tablespoon finely chopped coriander leaves
1 lime, sliced, to garnish

Combine lime juice, coconut, turmeric and cooked rice. Set aside. Heat oil and fry mustard seeds until they pop. Add cashews, curry leaves and chillies and cook for 3 minutes, stirring. Combine with rice and coriander leaves and mix well. Cover and cook over low heat for 15 minutes to heat through. Garnish with lime slices.
Serves 6

Lime Rice

Mixed Fruit Curry

MIXED FRUIT CURRY

4–5 pieces crystallised ginger
hot water
2 onions, chopped
60 g polyunsaturated vegetable oil
1 teaspoon crushed coriander seeds
1 tablespoon curry powder
1 tablespoon flour
2 cups vegetable stock
2 teaspoons lemon juice
freshly ground black pepper
3 cups grated coconut
2–3 tablespoons coconut milk
4–5 cups chopped mixed fruits (melons, peaches, plums, grapes, bananas, apples, pears)
rice, to serve

Cover ginger with hot water for a few minutes to remove sugar, drain, pat dry and chop.

Fry onions in oil until soft. Stir in ginger, coriander seeds, curry powder and flour and cook gently for 5 minutes. Gradually add stock, stirring rapidly. Bring to boil, add lemon juice and season to taste. Simmer for 30 minutes. Stir in coconut milk, prepared fruits and serve hot or cold with rice.
Serves 4

MELON SALAD

1 rock melon
1 honeydew melon
½ watermelon
¼ bunch mint, shredded

Halve rock melon and honeydew melon and scoop out seeds. Cut flesh into balls or pieces using a melon baller or knife. Remove as many seeds from watermelon as possible. Cut flesh into balls or pieces.

Place all melon pieces in a serving bowl. Sprinkle mint over and stir. Cover and chill until serving time.

VARIATION
Substitute fresh ginger for mint. Cut 6–8 slices peeled ginger into strips and stir through melon.
Serves 10–12

AVOCADO DIP

1 avocado
1 teaspoon lemon juice
½ teaspoon finely grated lemon rind
1 small onion, grated
1 clove garlic, crushed
½ teaspoon paprika
shredded red cabbage, to garnish
grapes and *melon balls, to serve*

Wash avocado, cut in half and remove seed. Spoon out flesh and mash with remaining ingredients. Spoon back into shells. Garnish with shreds of red cabbage. Serve with grapes and melon balls.
Makes 1 cup

LEMON YOGHURT DRESSING

⅔ cup yoghurt
finely grated rind and juice ½ lemon
1 tablespoon finely chopped parsley
1 tablespoon finely chopped chives
1 tablespoon finely chopped thyme or *mint*
freshly ground pepper

Combine all ingredients and mix well. Season to taste. This is an oil-free dressing, ideal for pawpaw, grapes, melons and strawberries.
Makes ⅔ cup

Lemon Yoghurt Dressing

CHICKEN STOCK

1 kg chicken backs or *stock pieces*
water, to cover
1 onion, studded with 3 cloves
few celery leaves
1 carrot, roughly chopped
bouquet garni
½ teaspoon whole black peppercorns

Wash chicken, discard skin and trim off fat. Place bones in a pan with water to cover and bring to boil, skimming as necessary. Add remaining ingredients, reduce heat and simmer partially covered, for 1½–2 hours. Skim as necessary.

Strain stock and allow to cool. Chill overnight and remove any fat that has risen to the surface. Use stock as directed.

To store: Refrigerate for up to 1 week, simmering every 2–3 days. Alternatively freeze in usable quantities. 250 mL (1 cup) quantities are a useful size. It is always handy to have frozen cubes of chicken stock, so another useful method is to freeze 2 ice-cube trays of stock. Place frozen cubes into a plastic bag, seal and label.

Makes approximately 4 cups

PUMPKIN SOUP

1.5 kg pumpkin, peeled and seeded
1 litre Chicken Stock (see recipe)
2 teaspoons polyunsaturated oil
1 large onion, finely chopped
2 tomatoes, peeled, seeded and chopped
freshly ground pepper, to taste
3 tablespoons chopped basil

Cut pumpkin into pieces and cook in the stock until tender; cool. Puree pumpkin, in batches, and return to the rinsed pan with cooking liquid; stir to combine.

Heat oil, add onion and saute 5 minutes. Add tomatoes and saute a few minutes. Pour tomato mixture into pumpkin mixture and combine. Taste and add pepper.

Reheat soup, stirring occasionally. When soup is completely reheated, stir through basil. Allow to stand for 5 minutes before serving.

Serves 10–12

CREAMY CARROT SOUP

2 teaspoons polyunsaturated oil or *margarine*
1 onion, finely chopped
1 clove garlic, crushed
1 kg carrots, peeled and chopped
1 litre Chicken Stock (see recipe)
freshly ground pepper, to taste
1 cup low-fat yoghurt
1 teaspoon cornflour
3–4 tablespoons chopped parsley
2 tablespoons chopped chives, to garnish

Heat oil in pan, add onion and garlic and saute 5 minutes, stirring occasionally. Add carrots, chicken stock and pepper and bring to boil. Reduce heat and simmer, partially covered, for about 20 minutes until carrot is tender. Cool for a few minutes.

Puree soup, return to rinsed pan and reheat soup gently. Add some hot soup to combined yoghurt mixture and cornflour mixture and stir well. Add yoghurt mixture to soup and heat, stirring.

Just before serving, add parsley. Pour soup into a heated tureen and serve garnished with chives.

Serves 10–12

HERBED YOGHURT AND CUCUMBER SOUP

1 litre low-fat yoghurt
500 mL chicken stock (see recipe)
chopped garlic, to taste
2 cucumbers
100 g pecans, very finely chopped
1-2 tablespoons oil, olive or *polyunsaturated*
1-2 tablespoons chopped mint
1 tablespoon chopped dill
freshly ground pepper, to taste

Place yoghurt in a bowl and beat well. Stir through chicken stock and garlic and chill in refrigerator.

If cucumber has a thick skin, peel it, otherwise leave the skin on. Halve the cucumbers lengthways and scoop out seeds. Dice cucumber flesh. Stir cucumber into yoghurt mixture with remaining ingredients. Serve chilled.

Serves 10-12

CHILLED LEEK AND POTATO SOUP

4 leeks
20 g polyunsaturated margarine or *unsalted butter*
1 kg potatoes, peeled and sliced
2 litres homemade Chicken Stock (see recipe)
freshly ground pepper, to taste
250 g low-fat yoghurt
¼ bunch chives, chopped

Remove darker green leaves from leeks. Halve leeks lengthways almost to the root end. Wash well, separating leaves to clean. Drain, cut off root end and slice.

Heat margarine, add leeks, cover pan and cook for 5 minutes. Add potatoes, and stock and pepper. Bring to boil, reduce heat and simmer for 20–30 minutes until potato is tender. Set aside to cool.

Drain soup, reserving cooking liquid. Puree cooked vegetables in batches, adding reserved liquid as necessary. Combine puree and remaining cooking liquid and adjust seasoning. About 1 hour before serving, add yoghurt. Serve soup chilled, sprinkled with chives.
Serves 10–12

EGG, AVOCADO AND BEET SALAD

500 g cooked beetroot, thinly sliced into matchsticks
4 hard-boiled eggs, chopped into eighths
2 avocados, finely sliced

DRESSING

3 tablespoons wine vinegar
½ cup olive oil
freshly ground pepper to taste
1 tablespoon finely chopped onion

Arrange beetroot strips on a plate, avocado on top and chopped egg on top of that. Spoon over dressing.

To make dressing, combine all ingredients in a bowl and beat with a fork or whisk until well mixed.

Note: Reserve a little cooked egg white which can be very finely chopped and sprinkled over the finished salad.
Serves 4

Egg, Avocado and Beet Salad

BROCCOLI AND CAPSICUM SALAD

750 g broccoli
2 small red capsicums, diced
8–10 fresh lychees, peeled, seeded and halved
1 clove garlic, crushed
½ cup prepared no-oil salt-free French dressing

Trim broccoli and divide into florets. Cook in lightly salted boiling water for 3–5 minutes or until tender but still crisp. Drain and refresh under cold water, drain again. Alternatively, broccoli can be steamed until tender but still crisp. Refresh under cold water and drain.

Combine broccoli, capsicum and lychees in a bowl. Marinate garlic in the dressing for 30 minutes. Pour dressing over and toss to coat. Cover and refrigerate before serving. Drain off any excess dressing before serving.
Serves 10–12

MACARONI AND ZUCCHINI SALAD

250 g zucchini, sliced
1 cup sliced mushrooms
1 cup cooked wholemeal macaroni
¾ cup light cream
¼ cup salt-free peanut butter
½ cup salt-free mayonnaise
1 tablespoon honey
1 tablespoon white vinegar
2 tablespoons lemon juice
½ cup roasted unsalted peanuts, to garnish

Combine zucchini, mushrooms and macaroni in salad bowl. Chill while preparing dressing.

Place all remaining ingredients except peanuts in blender and whip until smooth but not too thick. Coat salad lightly with dressing. Chill well and serve garnished with toasted peanuts. Extra dressing will keep well in refrigerator.
Serves 6

Macaroni and Zucchini Salad

AMBROSIA

1 cup diced orange
1 cup grated coconut
1 cup diced pineapple
1 cup light sour cream
1 cup chopped white marshmallows
4 firm lettuce leaves

Mix together and chill. Serve in lettuce leaf cups.
Serves 4

GLACE GRAPEFRUIT

1 orange
2 large grapefruit, halved
½ cup caster sugar
4 tablespoons sherry

GARNISH

extra orange and *grapefruit segments* and *shredded peel*
mint leaves
4 strawberries

Finely grate orange rind. Segment grapefruit and orange and dice. Reserve grapefruit halves. Blend flesh with sugar, sherry and rind. Fill grapefruit halves with mixture and freeze until set. Garnish with orange and grapefruit segments, shredded peel, mint leaves and halved strawberries.
Serves 4

RHUBARB FOOL

2 bunches rhubarb
sugar substitute, to taste
2½ cups skim milk
5 tablespoons custard powder

Trim rhubarb and cut into 5 cm pieces. Wash and place in a pan with enough water to cover half-way. Bring to boil, reduce heat and simmer, covered, until tender. Drain, reserving liquid. Puree fruit, adding liquid as necessary and sweeten to taste.

Place most of the milk in a pan. Combine remaining milk with custard powder and stir into milk. Bring to boil, stirring, and simmer until thick. Cool slightly. Mix custard and rhubarb, taste and adjust for sweetening. Spoon into a serving bowl. Cover and chill until serving time.
Serves 10–12

APRICOT RICE PUDDING

¾ cup short-grain rice
1¼ cups water
2½ cups milk
½ cup honey
¼ cup gelatine
1 kg apricots
2 tablespoons kirsch
150 mL light cream

Preheat oven to 180°C (350°F).

Put rice and half the water in saucepan and boil until water has been absorbed. Add milk and simmer 25 minutes. Add ¼ cup honey and gelatine to hot rice and stir well until completely dissolved. Place apricots, remaining water and honey in shallow ovenproof dish and bake for 20 minutes. Remove from oven and cool. Take 8 apricots from dish and mash in their syrup. Add kirsch and blend in with rice. Whip cream and fold into rice. Place rice in 2 litre jelly or charlotte mould and set in refrigerator for 2 hours until firm.

Turn pudding onto serving dish and decorate with additional apricots.

Note: To turn out moulded dessert, dip mould briefly in hot water and gently tap sides and base before inverting on to serving plate.
Serves 6–8

BAKED APPLE AND SAGO PUDDING

600 mL milk
¼ cup sago
3 eggs
2 tablespoons honey
pinch nutmeg
pinch cloves
2 apples, peeled, cored and sliced
40 g unsalted butter

Preheat oven to 180°C (350°F). Bring milk and sago to boil and cook 8 minutes. Leave to cool. Beat in eggs, honey and spices. Gently cook apples in butter until soft. Arrange in souffle dish and fill dish with sago mixture. Place dish in baking tray half-filled with hot water and bake for 45 minutes. Serve cold.
Serves 4

Baked Apple and Sago Pudding (above) and Apricot Rice Pudding

Diabetic

CHEESE STRAWS

Total = 143 g carbohydrate
8 straws = 15 g carbohydrate = 823 kJ

1½ cups flour
pinch cayenne pepper
60 g polyunsaturated margarine
1 cup grated tasty cheese
2 egg yolks
2 tablespoons milk
2 tablespoons water
Parmesan cheese (optional)

Preheat oven to 200°C (400°F).

Sift flour and cayenne pepper into mixing bowl. Rub margarine into flour, using fingertips, until mixture resembles breadcrumbs. Mix in grated cheese. Whisk egg yolks, milk and water together.

Make a well in centre of flour mixture, add egg mixture, mixing to a dough consistency. Roll out pastry into an oblong, approximately 18 × 32 cm.

Cut pastry into 18 equal-sized strips, each strip being 1 cm wide and 32 cm long. Cut the length of pastry into 4 equal portions, each 8 cm long, making 72 cheese straws. Use a sharp knife for cutting pastry.

Place cheese straws, slightly apart, on a greased baking tray. Dust with Parmesan cheese and bake for 15–20 minutes or until golden brown and crunchy.

Makes 72

Cheese Straws

FRENCH ONION DIP
Total = 30 g carbohydrate = 4320 kJ

1 300 g carton sour cream
1 packet French Onion Soup

Combine both ingredients and beat until well mixed. For a firm dip, refrigerate before serving.
Makes approximately 1 cup

TACOS
Total = 98 g carbohydrate
1 serve = 8 g carbohydrate = 713 kJ

12 taco shells
20 g polyunsaturated margarine
1 medium-sized onion, chopped
1 clove garlic, crushed
500 g minced beef
2 tablespoons taco seasoning mix
1 tablespoon tomato paste
½ cup water

GARNISH
shredded lettuce
finely chopped tomato
finely chopped onion
grated Cheddar cheese

Place taco shells on a baking tray and bake at 180°C (350°F) for 10 minutes or until crisp.

Melt margarine in a frypan and fry onion and garlic until tender. Add meat and brown well.

In a small bowl blend seasoning mix, tomato paste and water together. Add to mince and mix well. Bring to boil, then reduce heat and simmer for 15–20 minutes until liquid is reduced.

Remove shells from oven, place 2 tablespoons mince in the bottom of each shell. Add prepared garnishes and top with cheese. Serve immediately.
Makes 12

HAMBURGERS
Total = 90 g carbohydrate
1 serve = 30 g carbohydrate = 1907 kJ

250 g mince
1 small onion
¼ cup grated carrot
pinch pepper
3 hamburger buns

GARNISH
shredded lettuce
3 slices tomato
3 slices beetroot
3 slices cheese

In a mixing bowl, combine all ingredients for hamburger rissole. Divide into 3 portions and flatten each portion using the back of an egg slice. Grill patties until browned.

Toast buns and spread with polyunsaturated margarine. Place lettuce, tomato, beetroot and cheese on bun, top with hamburger pattie and serve.
Makes 3

SAUSAGE ROLLS
Total = 188 g carbohydrate
2 sausage rolls = 15 g carbohydrate = 1215 kJ

1 packet frozen ready-rolled puff pastry, thawed

FILLING
500 g sausage mince
1 medium-sized onion, finely chopped
pinch pepper
1 teaspoon mixed herbs
1 tablespoon chopped parsley

Preheat oven to 200°C (400°F).

Place all filling ingredients in a mixing bowl and mix thoroughly. Put mixture into a large piping bag, without a nozzle.

Roll out pastry in a rectangle, 40 × 30 cm. Trim edges. Divide pastry into 3 equal strips lengthways.

Pipe filling along each strip of pastry, slightly towards 1 edge. Glaze 1 edge lightly with milk and fold the other edge over the filling. Seal well. Repeat with remaining strips, then glaze each completed strip lightly with milk.

Cut each strip into 8 equal-sized sausage rolls. Place on an ungreased baking tray. Pierce each sausage roll a couple of times with a fork, to allow the steam to escape.

Bake for 10 minutes, then reduce heat to 180°C (350°F) for a further 15–20 minutes, or until golden brown.
Makes 24

CORNISH PASTIES

Total = 98 g carbohydrate
1 serve = 30 g carbohydrate = 1373 kJ

SHORTCRUST PASTRY

1 cup self-raising flour
20 g polyunsaturated margarine
½ teaspoon lemon juice
2–3 tablespoons water
½ tablespoon flour, for kneading

FILLING

125 g minced steak
½ medium-sized potato, peeled and diced small
1 small onion, chopped finely
½ tablespoon chopped parsley
salt and pepper, to taste
milk, for glazing

GARNISH

parsley sprigs
tomato sauce

Preheat oven to 200°C (400°F). Sift flour into mixing bowl. Rub margarine into flour, using fingertips, until mixture resembles breadcrumbs. Add lemon juice and just enough water to mix to a dry dough.

Place dough on a board that has been dusted with flour for kneading, and knead lightly until smooth. Refrigerate while making filling.

In a bowl combine meat, potato, onion, parsley, salt and pepper and mix well.

Roll out pastry until approx 0.5 cm thick. Place a saucer on the pastry and cut around it. Repeat until there are 3 pieces of pastry. (There will be a small amount of wastage.)

Place a good spoonful of meat mixture on pastry. Wet opposite edge of pastry lightly with water and fold into a half moon shape. Join pastry edges together by pinching a small neat frill.

Place pasties on a lightly greased baking tray. Pierce with a fork to allow steam to escape during baking. Glaze lightly with milk, using a pastry brush.

Bake for 10 minutes, then reduce heat to 160°C (325°F) for a further 25–30 minutes, or until golden brown and meat is tender. Serve hot, garnished with sprigs of parsley and tomato sauce.

Serves 3

Cornish Pasties

EGG AND BACON PIE

Total = 195 g carbohydrate
1 serve = 15 g carbohydrate = 675 kJ

SHORTCRUST PASTRY

2 cups self-raising flour
40 g polyunsaturated margarine
1 teaspoon lemon juice
4–6 tablespoons water
½ tablespoon flour, for kneading

FILLING

2 bacon rashers
2 eggs
160 mL milk
1 teaspoon parsley
salt and pepper, to taste

Sift flour into a mixing bowl. Rub margarine into flour, using fingertips until mixture resembles breadcrumbs. Add lemon juice and just enough water to mix to dry dough.

Place dough onto a lightly floured board, using flour for kneading, and knead lightly until smooth. Line a 20 cm pie dish with two-thirds of the pastry.

To make filling, remove rind from bacon and chop finely. Sprinkle into pastry case. Lightly beat eggs, milk, parsley, salt and pepper together in a mixing bowl. Pour over bacon.

Glaze edge of pastry lightly with milk. Roll out remaining pastry to fit the top of the pie. Press edges together using the back of a fork. Pierce the top of the pie to allow steam to escape during baking. Trim edges using a sharp knife. (There will be a small amount of wastage.) Glaze pie top lightly with milk using a pastry brush.

Bake at 200°C (400°F) for 10 minutes, then reduce heat to 180°C (350°F) for a further 20–25 minutes or until golden brown and set.

Serves 12

ASSEROLE

:0 g carbohydrate
15 g carbohydrate = 1797 kJ

roni, dry
425 g can tuna
1 medium-sized onion, finely chopped
1 carrot, diced
1 celery stick, diced
⅔ cup peas
½ cup corn kernels
40 g polyunsaturated margarine
2 tablespoons flour
pinch pepper
320 mL milk
2 tablespoons dried breadcrumbs
½ cup grated tasty cheese

Preheat oven to 180°C (350°F).

Cook macaroni in boiling water approximately 15–20 minutes until tender. Drain well in a colander.

Drain tuna, place in a mixing bowl and flake using a fork. Add onion, carrot, celery, peas and corn, and mix well.

Melt margarine in a small saucepan, stir in flour and cook for 1 minute. Add seasoning then add milk gradually, stirring continually over a low heat, until sauce boils and thickens. Add macaroni and tuna mixture and heat through.

Transfer to an oven-proof dish. Top with breadcrumbs and grated cheese. Bake for 15–20 minutes, then place under griller and brown the top, just before serving.
Serves 6

WALDORF SALAD

Total = 45 g carbohydrate
1 serve = 8 g carbohydrate = 943 kJ

3 unpeeled red apples, cored and diced
juice 2 lemons
2 sticks celery, sliced
1 cup walnuts, chopped
4 tablespoons mayonnaise
lettuce leaves

Place apples in a mixing bowl and sprinkle with lemon juice. Add celery and walnuts and toss together with just enough mayonnaise to moisten ingredients. Line serving bowl with lettuce leaves. Pile in salad and serve.
Serves 6

POTATO SALAD

Total = 60 g carbohydrate
1 serve = 8 g carbohydrate = 684 kJ

4 small potatoes, peeled
1 hard-boiled egg, peeled and chopped
¼ cup shallots
3–4 tablespoons mayonnaise
¼ teaspoon dried mustard
pinch pepper

Cook potatoes in boiling water until tender (approximately 5 minutes). Drain and allow to cool slightly, then dice. Combine potatoes in a bowl with egg and shallots. Mix mustard and mayonnaise together and blend into potato. Add pepper and serve.
Serves 6

RICE SALAD

Total = 105 g carbohydrate
1 serve = 15 g carbohydrate = 389 kJ

5 tablespoons long-grain rice
⅓ cup peas
1 red capsicum, seeded and chopped
1 small onion, chopped
1 carrot, chopped
¼ cup corn kernels
1½ tablespoons raisins
pinch pepper
squeeze lemon juice

In a saucepan boil 1 litre water, then add rice, peas, capsicum, onion, carrot and corn. Simmer for 10 minutes, without a lid, until rice is just cooked.

Drain in a colander and wash well under cold running water. Drain thoroughly. Place in a serving bowl with chopped raisins and pepper. Toss well and add lemon juice just before serving.
Serves 6

PINEAPPLE VELVET ICE CREAM
Total = 83 g carbohydrate
1 serve = 15 g carbohydrate = 615 kJ

2 eggs
1½ cups unsweetened pineapple juice
½ cup water
½ cup evaporated milk
1 cup chilled evaporated milk extra
2 tablespoons lemon juice

Beat eggs, pineapple juice, water and evaporated milk together in a mixing bowl. Place in the top of a double saucepan, and cook over boiling water until mixture thickens enough to coat the back of a wooden spoon. Pour into a mixing bowl and place in freezer to chill.

In a chilled mixing bowl, whip chilled extra evaporated milk. Add lemon juice and continue beating until very stiff. Fold in chilled pineapple mixture and freeze until half-set, then beat again until smooth to prevent ice crystals forming in the ice cream. Pour into 2 ice cream trays and freeze until firm. Divide each tray into 3 equal serves.
Serves 6

PUMPKIN SCONES
Total = 203 g carbohydrate
1 scone = 15 g carbohydrate = 436 kJ

40 g polyunsaturated margarine
1 cup mashed pumpkin
1 egg
2 cups self-raising flour
pinch cinnamon
pinch nutmeg
1 tablespoon milk (if necessary)
flour, for kneading

Preheat oven to 200°C (400°F).

Beat margarine in mixing bowl until smooth. Beat in pumpkin, add egg and mix well. Sift flour, cinnamon and nutmeg together. Fold through pumpkin mixture and mix to a soft dough. If dough is too dry, add milk.

Turn onto a lightly floured board and knead lightly until mixture holds itself together. Flatten dough with hands until it is about 1.5 cm thick. Cut dough with a 5 cm scone cutter to make 12 scones. Place on a greased floured baking tray, glaze scones lightly with milk and bake for 10–15 minutes until golden brown.
Makes 12

CHRISTMAS PLUM PUDDING
Total = 138.75 g carbohydrate
1 serve = 15 g carbohydrate = 532 kJ

3 teaspoons sago
½ cup fresh brown breadcrumbs
3 tablespoons milk
3 tablespoons self-raising flour
¼ teaspoon allspice
¼ teaspoon cinnamon
¼ teaspoon nutmeg
¼ teaspoon salt
30 g polyunsaturated margarine
2 eggs, beaten
1 tablespoon grated carrot
1 tablespoon grated apple
1 tablespoon grated orange rind
¾ cup mixed dried fruit
1 teaspoon vanilla essence
2 or 3 drops sweetener
1 teaspoon bicarbonate of soda

TO SERVE
custard or ice cream

Place sago, breadcrumbs and milk in a basin. Leave to soak while you prepare the remaining ingredients.

Sift flour with spices and salt, and rub in margarine. Combine sago and breadcrumb mixture with eggs, carrot, apple, orange rind, mixed fruit, vanilla, sweetener and flour mixture. Lastly beat in bicarbonate of soda.

Place mixture in a well-greased bowl or pudding basin. Cover and steam over boiling water for 1½–2 hours. When cooked, remove from basin immediately. Cut into 8 equal slices. Serve with custard or ice cream.
Serves 8

CHRISTMAS CAKE
Total = 488 g carbohydrate
1 slice = 30 g carbohydrate = 1098 kJ

250 g polyunsaturated margarine
½ teaspoon sweetener
2 cups self-raising flour
pinch salt
1 teaspoon allspice
4 eggs
100 mL milk
1 teaspoon parisienne essence
1 teaspoon vanilla essence
rind 1 lemon
2½ cups mixed dried fruit

Preheat oven to 160°C (325°F).

Place margarine and sweetener in a mixing bowl and beat until light and creamy. Sift flour, salt and spices into a mixing bowl. Beat eggs, milk and essences together. Gradually add egg mixture to margarine, beating well. Beat in lemon rind, fold in flour and fruit alternately, starting and finishing with flour. Beat only until the flour disappears.

Grease and flour cake tin. Spread mixture in tin evenly and smooth over top using wet hands. Bake for 1¼–1½ hours or until cake leaves the sides of the tin and is golden brown.
Serves 16

BRUNCHES, LUNCHES AND DINNER PARTIES

The traditional dinner party has always been a great way to entertain a close group of family and friends. Classic entertaining success stories often result from dinners that are a credit to the host and hostess for their imagination, flair and elegance. Yet, as successful as it may be, the dinner party is losing ground as an entertaining favourite. Flexible leisure periods and less structured daily lifestyles allow us to invite guests at almost any hour of the day to dine in style and simplicity — luncheon and brunch are increasingly popular.

Starting the day with a bright and friendly brunch is mostly reserved for the weekend, when the pressures of weekday demands are lifted and the emphasis is on relaxation. There's no need for a very early kickoff; elevenish is popular and offers guests the freedom to stay as long as they wish or simply drop in for a quick hello and a bite to eat. Brunches are usually very casual and food is a variation on breakfast, featuring up-market adaptations of familiar and satisfying dishes. Serve suitably uncomplicated beverages such as fresh juice, coffee and tea and offer a little early-morning bubbly for those who wish to start the day with a giggle!

Lunches, like dinners, can be flexible affairs to suit any day of the week. Take your cue when planning a lunch on your guest's daily schedule; don't expect someone with pressing afternoon engagements to linger long into the sunset. One course meals or buffets are easy with platters of fresh fruit and cheese offered later.

Dinner parties offer the opportunity to let your culinary talents shine with anything from a bowl of homemade soup by the fire to a three or four course spectacular.

Whatever the occasion, relax and enjoy it!

Pies, prawns and sliced meats enhance brunches and lunches

Savoury

TURKISH WEDDING SOUP

500 g boneless mutton or
stewing lamb, diced
1/3 cup seasoned flour
60 mL oil
1.5 litres water
1 marrow bone, cracked or
mutton or *lamb bones*
1 onion, quartered
1 carrot, chopped
6 peppercorns
salt, to taste
2 egg yolks
juice 1 lemon
45 g butter
3 teaspoons paprika

Roll meat in seasoned flour. Heat oil in a large pan, add lamb in batches and cook until browned. Gradually add water, stirring well, then add cracked marrow bone.

Bring to boil, skimming as necessary. Add onion, carrot, peppercorns and salt. Reduce heat and simmer, partially covered, for 1½–2 hours or until meat is tender. Skim occasionally. Remove meat and strain soup, discarding vegetables and bones. Return meat to soup and reheat.

Combine egg yolks with most of the lemon juice in a bowl. Add 1 cup of hot liquid and beat well. Return to soup and cook over a very gentle heat for 1–2 minutes. Remove from heat and cover to keep warm.

Melt butter in a small pan and add paprika. To serve, turn soup into a tureen and pour over butter and paprika. Alternatively, serve soup individually and spoon over a little of the butter mixture. Serve hot.

Note: In Turkey, mutton is always used for this soup, but if you have difficulty purchasing mutton, use lamb instead. Your butcher may be able to order the mutton for you.

Serves 4

CREAM OF SPINACH SOUP

1 kg leaf spinach or
silverbeet
30 g butter
1 small onion, finely
chopped
3 tablespoons flour
1¼ cups chicken stock
1¼ cups milk
¼ teaspoon nutmeg
salt and pepper, to taste

Wash spinach well and place in large pan with about 2 tablespoons water and cook until tender — about 5 minutes. Drain well and puree; set aside.

Melt butter in a saucepan; add onion and cook until soft and transparent. Take pot off heat, stir in flour and blend. Return to low heat, pour in stock and milk, a little at a time, stirring continuously until smooth.

Stir in spinach puree and nutmeg, season to taste, cook gently until hot, then serve immediately.

Serves 4

SORREL AND AVOCADO SOUP

2 avocados
150 mL cream
500 g fresh sorrel leaves or
spinach
50 g butter
600 mL vegetable stock
freshly ground pepper, to
taste
dash lemon juice, if spinach
is used

Mash avocados and mix with a little of the cream. Shred sorrel leaves and gently cook in butter for 5 minutes. Allow to cool. Put stock in blender with cooked sorrel and puree until smooth.

Return to saucepan and heat again over moderate heat, adding cream and pepper at the very end with the mashed avocado. Serve hot.

Serves 4

Turkish Wedding Soup

RED LENTIL SOUP

200 g red lentils
50 g butter
1 large onion, chopped
1 stalk celery, chopped
1.5 litres water or *chicken stock*
salt and pepper, to taste
½–1 teaspoon paprika
1 tablespoon flour
1 cup milk
2 egg yolks
lemon juice, to taste
1 teaspoon ground cumin (optional)

Wash lentils and discard any that float. Heat the butter in a heavy-based pan; add onion and celery and fry until lightly golden.

Add drained lentils, stirring to coat with butter. Pour in 1 litre of liquid, add salt and pepper, paprika and, if desired, cumin. Bring to boil, reduce heat and simmer until lentils are tender, skimming as necessary. Add any extra liquid as required.

Puree lentils by pushing through a sieve or processing in a blender or food processor; use any of the reserved liquid as necessary. Return to pan. In a separate saucepan, heat remaining butter, add flour and cook for 1 minute. Gradually add milk and bring to boil, stirring, and simmer for a few minutes. Season to taste.

Beat egg yolks in a small bowl, add a little hot sauce, combine well and return to sauce. Stir sauce into lentil puree and gently heat. Taste and adjust the seasoning with lemon juice. Serve hot.

Note: Lentil soup is eaten throughout the Middle East; this version is basically Turkish, although the roux and egg yolks are added to thicken it. Red lentils are used in this case but other colours may be substituted.

Serves 4–6

CHILLED CUCUMBER AND TOMATO SOUP

1.5 litres vegetable stock
75 g long-grain rice
4 tomatoes
100 mL cream
pinch cayenne pepper
salt and pepper, to taste
½ cucumber
small bunch chervil, chopped

Bring stock to boil in a saucepan. Wash rice and add to stock; cook 20 minutes. Quarter tomatoes; and squeeze gently to extract the water and pips. Add tomatoes to stock after rice has cooked for 20 minutes. Leave to cook 30 minutes longer.

When cooked, puree soup in a blender or rub through a sieve. Stiffly whip and fold in cream. Add cayenne pepper. Mix well together. Taste and adjust the seasoning; cool.

Remove the end of the cucumber. Cut in 2, lengthways; take out seeds with a small spoon. Cut in thin strips. When the soup is cold, add the cucumber strips and stir. Chill in refrigerator for at least 3 hours.

Ladle chilled soup into individual bowls. Sprinkle with chervil and serve.

RASPBERRY SOUP

3½ cups raspberries
¾ cup water
2 tablespoons finely chopped orange rind
juice 1 orange
2 tablespoons cornflour
½ cup sugar
2 cups rose wine
½ cup sour cream

Set ½ cup raspberries aside for garnish. Puree remainder in blender or food processor. Place in medium-mesh sieve set over bowl. Press puree through sieve with back of large spoon; reserve in bowl.

Spoon leftover seeds into small saucepan, add water and stir. Add orange rind and juice and simmer, covered, 5 minutes. Strain mixture into small bowl; discard seeds. Return liquid to saucepan.

Blend cornflour with 2 tablespoons water to make smooth paste, stir into liquid in saucepan until well blended. Heat mixture over low heat, stirring constantly until thickened, about 3 minutes. Stir in sugar until dissolved; stir in raspberry puree and wine until well blended. Chill thoroughly. To serve, add spoonful sour cream to each bowl and garnish with reserved raspberries.

Serves 6

Raspberry Soup

CHICKEN LIVER PATE

1 kg chicken livers
185 g butter
2 cloves garlic, crushed
4 tablespoons dry sherry
5 tablespoons brandy
1 tablespoon chopped parsley
½ teaspoon fresh thyme leaves
pinch cinnamon
pinch grated nutmeg
salt and freshly ground pepper, to taste
¼ cup thickened cream

Clean chicken livers. Heat 90 g butter, add garlic and cook for 30 seconds. Add chicken livers and cook for 5 minutes or until almost cooked. Puree chicken livers and cooking liquid in a bowl.

Heat remaining butter. Add remaining ingredients except cream and heat through. Pour over chicken livers and beat well. Stir in cream, taste and adjust seasoning. Spoon mixture into a serving container, cover and chill. Serve with crackers.
Serves 10–12

COUNTRY COMBINATION PATE

1 onion, chopped
1 clove garlic, crushed
sprig thyme
sprig parsley
sprig chervil
60 g butter
250 g chicken livers, cleaned
salt and pepper, to taste
125 g fat pork, roughly chopped
125 g lean pork, roughly chopped
6 bacon rashers

Gently cook onion, garlic and herbs in butter for 1–2 minutes, then add livers diced into 2 cm pieces, and cook gently for about 1 minute. Cool, then season and puree with pork.

Line a terrine with rashers of bacon and spoon in meat mixture, covering it with more bacon rashers. Stand terrine in a baking dish half-full of water and bake at 180°C (360°F) for 1 hour. Cool, then refrigerate until firm. When chilled, slice pate and serve on lettuce leaves, accompanied by triangles of toast.
Serves 8

SMOKED FISH PATE

4 smoked mackerel fillets or *2 whole smoked mackerel*
juice 2 limes or *1 lemon*
125 g cream cheese, softened
200 g butter, melted
pepper, to taste
sprigs of fresh herbs e.g. dill, fennel, flat-leaved parsley
lemon slices to garnish
Melba Toast, to serve (see recipe)

Skin and flake mackerel. Place in a blender or food processor with lime juice, cream cheese and butter. Blend to a puree, then season with pepper.

Turn into a suitable size serving dish and chill for several hours. Garnish with fresh herbs and lemon slices. Serve with Melba toast or crackers.
Serves 4–6

JELLIED MEAT LOAF

2 veal knuckles
750 g lean pork
125 g bacon
½ teaspoon mixed herbs
1 clove garlic, crushed
salt and pepper, to taste
300 mL water
3 teaspoons gelatine

Cut meat from veal knuckles. Chop veal, pork and bacon meat into 1.5 cm cubes. Place in a bowl and add herbs, garlic, salt and pepper. Pack meat mixture into 750 mL mould.

Combine water and gelatine in saucepan. Bring to boil and boil 1 minute. Allow to cool slightly then pour over meat.

Place 2 cups water in electric frying pan. Place mould in frying pan. Cover with lid and simmer gently for 2 hours topping up with water as necessary. Stir terrine to separate meat. Refrigerate until set. Unmould and serve sliced with salad.
Serves 6

FILO AVOCADO CHICKEN

2 teaspoons tarragon
2 teaspoons French mustard
salt and freshly ground pepper, to taste
6 chicken fillets or *3 whole chicken breasts with bones removed*
flour, for dusting fillets
2 tablespoons oil
200 g filo pastry sheets
melted butter, for brushing pastry
3 avocados, thinly sliced

Mix tarragon, mustard and seasonings together. Dust chicken fillets with flour and cook in oil until nicely browned on both sides. Allow to cool.

Using 2 sheets of filo pastry for each person, brush 1 sheet with melted butter, cover with second sheet and brush again. Fold in half and brush again.

Place 1 fillet in centre at the end of the pastry, spread over a little tarragon mustard, then top with avocado slices. Fold slices of pastry over the chicken to completely enclose. Repeat with remaining chicken.

Place on greased oven tray, brush pastry tops with butter and bake at 200°C (400°F) for 10 minutes, reducing heat to 180°C (350°F) for a further 10–15 minutes. Filo rolls should be a light golden brown. Serve with seasonal vegetables.

Note: you can prepare this dish up to 2 hours before serving time if it is kept in the refrigerator; heat for 10 minutes before serving.

Serves 6

DEEP-FRIED CHICKEN BALLS

675 g chicken, cooked and minced
¼ cup minced pork fat
4 water chestnuts, minced
1 shallot, minced
1 thin slice ginger root, minced
1 egg
1 tablespoon cornflour
½ teaspoon salt
1 tablespoon sherry
oil, for deep-frying
⅔ cup coating batter

In a bowl, mix chicken, fat, water chestnuts, shallot, ginger, egg, cornflour, salt and sherry until smooth. Form the mixture into balls, 4 cm in diameter.

Heat oil for deep-frying. Dip chicken balls, a few at a time, in batter and fry them in oil until light golden brown; drain and leave to cool. If freezing, place in a container, seal, label and freeze. To serve, re-fry the chicken balls in oil, heated for deep-frying, until dark golden brown. Drain and serve.

Serves 4

CHICKEN BREASTS ROSSINI

4 chicken breasts
4 slices foie gras or *4 slices fresh goose liver*
flour, for dusting chicken
70 g butter
½ cup port or *Madeira*
salt and pepper, to taste

Spread chicken breasts on table. On each put a slice of foie gras. If using fresh goose liver, seal the slices for a minute in butter on high heat before you put them on the chicken breasts.

Fold each breast in two so that you have a kind of chicken roll. Flour the rolls and saute in butter on a lively heat. As soon as they are cooked (this will take no more than 10 minutes), arrange them on a heated serving dish. Add the Madeira to juices in pan to form a rich brown sauce. Pour sauce on chicken rolls and serve immediately.

Serves 4

ROAST BEEF SANDWICHES

1 soft avocado
175 g cream cheese
30 g blue cheese
2 tablespoons chopped walnuts
½ teaspoon Worcestershire sauce
¼ teaspoon Tabasco sauce
12 slices wholemeal bread
12 slices cold roast beef
watercress sprigs, onion slices or *tomato slices, to garnish*

Peel and pit avocado and mash with both cheeses until very smooth. Add walnuts, Worcestershire and Tabasco. Spread evenly on bread and top with roast beef. Decorate with a sprig of watercress, finely sliced onion rings or slice of tomato.

Serves 6–12

Chicken Breasts Rossini

MEAT PLATTER

1 kg piece beef
1 pig's trotter
1 cotechino (from Italian butchers)
1 piece turkey
1 capon
1 small bunch parsley
2 celery stalks
1 clove garlic
2 onions
3 carrots
2 potatoes
2 zucchini
1 piece calf's head

GREEN SAUCE

1 tablespoon breadcrumbs, soaked in
a little vinegar
1 hard-boiled egg, finely chopped
2 anchovy fillets
3 tablespoons finely chopped parsley
2 tablespoons capers, chopped
1 clove garlic, crushed
olive oil
lemon juice, to taste
salt and pepper, to taste

Place beef, pig's trotter, cotechino, turkey and capon in boiling water, together with parsley, celery, garlic, onions and carrots. Add potatoes and zucchini and simmer for 1 hour. Now add calf's head and continue to simmer for a further 2 hours, taking out of the pan the various pieces of meat when you see that they are cooked. Serve all meats on same platter, accompanied by Green Sauce.

To make sauce, in a small bowl or sauceboat, combine breadcrumbs, egg, anchovy fillets, parsley, capers and garlic. Add enough olive oil to achieve consistency of rather thin mayonnaise. Add lemon juice and adjust seasoning. This sauce tastes better if prepared a couple of hours in advance.
Serves 8

HONEYED LAMB KEBABS

1.5 kg lean lamb, trimmed and diced
¼ cup white wine
2 tablespoons Hoi Sin sauce
2 tablespoons sherry
2 tablespoons honey
1 clove garlic, crushed
salt and freshly ground pepper, to taste
1 large onion, cut into wedges

Marinate lamb in combined wine, Hoi Sin sauce, sherry, honey and garlic. Season, cover and refrigerate overnight. Drain and reserve marinade to use as a baste during cooking.

Soak sate sticks in boiling water to cover for 10 minutes. Drain and thread lamb dice onto sate sticks interspersed with wedges of onion. Cook kebabs under a preheated hot grill or over a barbecue, basting occasionally with marinade. Turn to cook and brown each side.
Serves 6–8

LAMB NOISETTES

2 cups chicken stock
2 small onions, chopped
2 cloves garlic, chopped
3 cups chopped turnip
1 cup chopped fennel
2 cups sliced celeriac or *1 leek*
salt and pepper, to taste
nutmeg, to taste
⅓ cup yoghurt
6 lamb noisettes — loin chops boned, rolled and skewered with toothpick
⅓ cup melted butter or oil
12 sheets filo pastry
extra yoghurt and *chives, to garnish*

Bring stock to boil. Add vegetables and simmer 15 minutes until tender. Drain and reserve stock for later use.

Puree vegetables, add seasonings and yoghurt. Allow to cool.

Saute noisettes quickly in pan, browning all over. Cool and remove toothpicks.

Brush melted butter over sheet of filo and fold in half to form a square. Brush again with butter. Place noisette in centre, top with 1 tablespoon of puree. Fold over pastry and twist the top to close. Brush with butter, place on baking dish. Repeat with remaining lamb.

Bake at 190°C (375°F) for 10 minutes, then reduce oven heat to 180°C (350°F) for 15 minutes until golden.

Serve with additional yoghurt and chopped chives.
Serves 3–6

Lamb Noisettes

VINTAGE 1973
Penfolds
KALIMNA DRY RED
BIN 28
PENFOLDS WINES PTY. LTD.
750 ml

VEAL WITH TUNA SAUCE

1.2 kg veal (a boned piece of leg is ideal)
1 carrot, sliced
1 onion, sliced
2 celery stalks, sliced
1 strip lemon or orange peel
⅔ cup white wine
⅔ cup olive oil
salt, to taste
200 g can red tuna in oil
4 anchovy fillets
375 mL mayonnaise
1 tablespoon capers
3 gherkins, sliced

Roll up meat and secure with string or toothpicks to maintain its shape and place it in a deep casserole or pan. Add carrot, onion, celery, strip of lemon peel, wine, olive oil and 300 mL cold water. Salt lightly and cook at 180°C (350°F) for 1 hour or until veal is done. Remove and allow to cool.

Strain cooking liquid and reduce it until concentrated. Blend tuna and its oil with a little cooking broth and anchovy fillets. Add to mayonnaise.

Slice meat and arrange on a serving platter. Pour sauce on top and decorate with capers and gherkins. Refrigerate before serving.

Serves 4

VEAL STEAKS FRANCAIS

6 very lean veal steaks
6 slices cheese
6 slices salami
2 tablespoons chopped onion
2 tablespoons chopped parsley
freshly ground pepper, to taste
¼ cup flour
1 egg, beaten
½ cup toasted breadcrumbs
3 tablespoons oil
60 g butter

SAUCE

60 g butter
60 g can anchovy fillets, drained and chopped
pepper, to taste
¼ cup lemon juice
2 tablespoons chopped parsley

On 1 side of each veal steak, place slice of cheese and salami, a little onion and parsley; season with pepper. Fold veal in half and secure with toothpick. Coat veal steaks in flour then beaten egg and then toasted breadcrumbs.

Melt butter and oil in frying pan. Fry veal steaks until golden brown on each side and drain.

To make sauce, heat butter and anchovy fillets in saucepan. Add pepper, lemon juice and parsley. Pour sauce over veal steaks to serve.

Serves 6

VEAL POT-ROAST WITH S

1.2 kg loin of veal, boned
1 small onion, sliced
100 g bacon, chopped
2 tablespoons oil
30 g butter
100 mL dry white wine
1 cup broth
salt and pepper, to taste

STUFFING

1 bread roll
200 mL milk
1 tablespoon pistachio nuts
200 g minced beef
150 g sausage mince
2 tablespoons chopped parsley
1 egg
salt and pepper, to taste
60 g Parmesan

To prepare stuffing, first soak break in milk. Put pistachios in boiling water for 1 minute, drain and peel. In a bowl, mix together minced beef, sausage mince, soaked and squeezed-out bread, parsley and pistachio nuts, egg, grated Parmesan, salt and pepper.

Open loin of veal on table and flatten with a meat mallet to shape it. Spread stuffing on top, roll up meat firmly to form a big roll and sew untidy ends together with a big needle and thick thread.

Place meat in a heavy casserole with onion, bacon, butter and oil. Let meat brown all over on a lively heat.

Add white wine, let it evaporate, cover casserole and continue to cook on very low heat for about 1¼ hours, basting now and then with cooking juices. To prevent roast from becoming too dry, add a few tablespoons of broth now and then.

Check seasonings and place meat on a wooden board. Let it rest for 5 minutes before carving in neat slices. Serve with its own cooking juices, accompanied with roast potatoes or peas cooked in butter.

Serves 4

Veal with Tuna Sauce

SEAFOOD AVOCADO MILLE-FEUILLE

500 g frozen ready-rolled puff pastry, thawed
2 cups Bechamel Sauce (see recipe)
2 avocados, chopped
juice 1 lemon
2 medium-sized fish fillets (sea perch is very suitable)
4 king prawns
dill sprig, to garnish

Roll out pastry and cut into 4 equal squares. Bake at 200°C (400°F) for 20 minutes or until golden brown. Cut a little slit in top and cool on wire rack.

Fry fish fillets in a little butter until cooked. Break neatly into pieces. Mix cooked fish, cooked prawns and chopped avocado sprinkled with lemon juice into Bechamel Sauce and very gently heat until filling is well-warmed.

This filling is best heated in a frying pan, so that it does not have to be stirred quite as much.

To serve, cut cooked pastry squares in half. Spoon in seafood-avocado filling and replace the lid if desired. Decorate with a little filling around the edge of puff pastry case and then garnish with dill sprig.

Note: Nothing more than a light salad needs to be served with this dish.

Serves 4

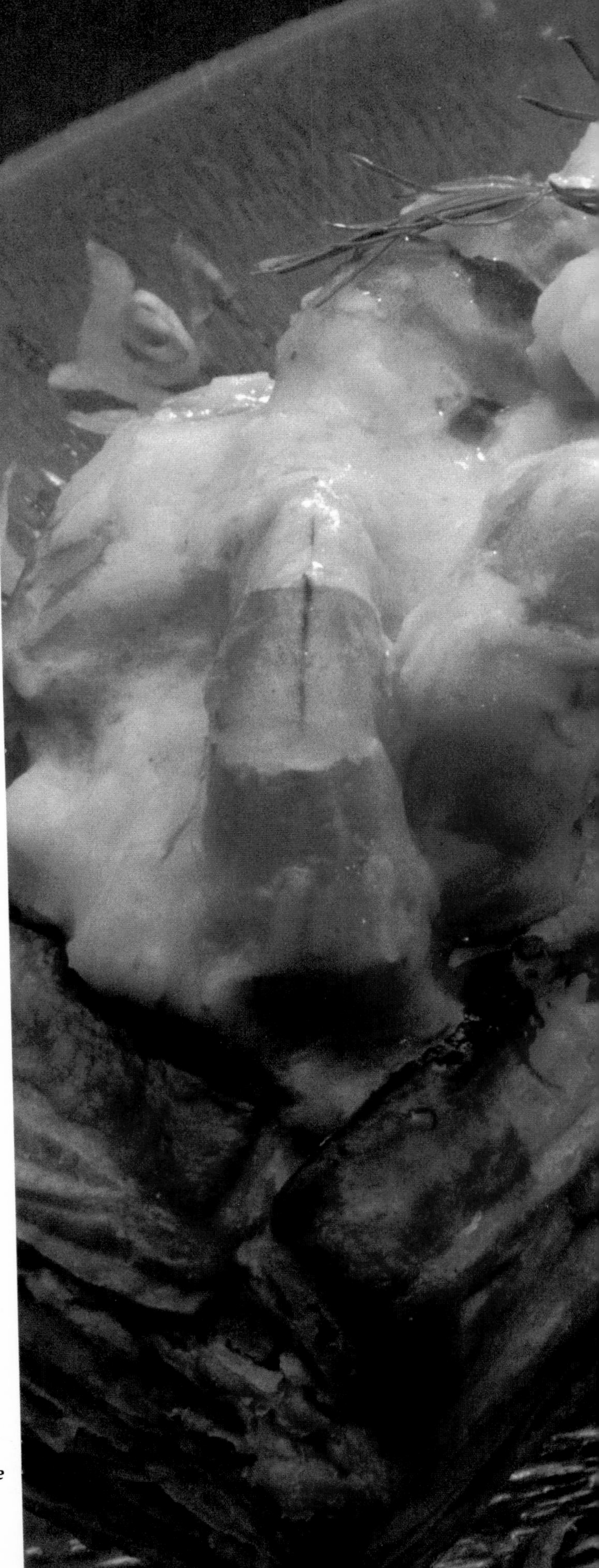

Seafood Avocado Mille- Feuille

PRAWN RISSOLES

2 tablespoons oil
240 g prawns, shelled
1 medium-sized onion, finely chopped
small bunch parsley, finely chopped
3 eggs
2 tablespoons flour
1 teaspoon salt
freshly ground pepper, to taste
4 sheets ready-rolled frozen shortcrust pastry, thawed
oil for deep-frying

Heat oil in a frying pan and fry prawns, onion and parsley 4–5 minutes, stirring constantly.

Put prawn mixture in a large bowl. Separate egg yolks and add to bowl with flour, salt and pepper. In another bowl beat egg whites until they form stiff peaks; gently fold them into prawn mixture, using a spoon.

Roll out shortcrust pastry very thinly and cut into rounds with a 10 cm diameter pastry cutter. Place a little prawn mixture on half of each round. Moisten edges of pastry with cold water and fold it over the filling. Pinch edges together to seal.

Heat oil in a deep saucepan: it is ready when a little flour dropped in sizzles instantly. Put in rissoles a few at a time and fry 4 minutes or until pastry is golden-brown.

Drain rissoles on paper towels and serve hot.

Serves 4

MEXICAN FISH BALLS WITH AVOCADO SAUCE

500 g fish fillets
80 g butter
4 shallots, finely chopped
2 slices day-old bread, with crusts removed
½ cup milk
1 egg, beaten
salt and pepper, to taste
1½ tablespoons tomato puree
1 cup fine dry breadcrumbs
4 tablespoons oil
1 quantity Avocado Sauce (see recipe)

Saute fish fillets in butter for 5 minutes, adding shallots and then cooking for a further 5 minutes. Remove from pan and flake fish finely with fork.

Soak bread in milk for 5 minutes. Squeeze out excess milk and crumble bread into bowl with fish. Add salt, pepper, egg and tomato puree.

Combine thoroughly, shape into walnut-sized balls and coat with breadcrumbs.

Heat oil in frying pan and cook fish balls on all sides till golden brown. Remove with slotted spoon and drain on paper towels or brown paper. Serve hot with Avocado Sauce.

Serves 4

FISH LASAGNE

1 kg cooked fish, scaled, boned and flaked
½ teaspoon basil
2 cloves garlic, crushed
salt and pepper, to taste
1 teaspoon dried oregano
1 tablespoon chopped parsley
240 g can tomato paste
1 teaspoon Worcestershire sauce
825 g can whole tomatoes
500 g green ribbon noodles, par-cooked
500 g cottage cheese
2 eggs
¼ teaspoon dry mustard
125 g blue vein cheese, crumbled
200 g cheddar cheese, grated

Preheat oven to 180°C (350°F). Combine fish, basil, garlic, salt and pepper. Add oregano, parsley, tomato paste, Worcestershire sauce and tomatoes. Place into base of large baking dish. Add layer of noodles.

Combine cottage cheese, eggs and mustard and spread over noodles. Top with combined cheeses. Bake for 30 minutes. Stand 10 minutes before slicing. Serve hot with salad.

Serves 6

FILLETS OF SOLE WITH ZUCCHINI

350 g zucchini, sliced
oil, for frying
1 sprig rosemary
1 teaspoon chopped fresh basil
salt and pepper, to taste
150 g tomatoes, peeled and chopped
a little flour
8 fillets of sole (whiting, dory or barramundi)
80 g butter
1 cup breadcrumbs
12 basil leaves
1 lemon, sliced

Saute zucchini in a little oil with rosemary, basil, salt and pepper. When nearly done, add tomatoes and saute a further 2 minutes.

Flour fillets of sole and brown in butter. Butter an ovenproof dish and arrange fillets in 1 row if possible. Cover with zucchini mixture, sprinkle with breadcrumbs, dot with butter and bake at 225°C (425°F) for a few minutes until brown. Serve decorated with basil leaves and lemon.

Serves 4

Mexican Fish Balls

SEAFOOD STUFFED SNAPPER WITH CURRY SAUCE

1.5 kg whole snapper, cleaned
lemon juice
salt and pepper, to taste
1 rasher bacon, chopped
2 tablespoons chopped onion
1 tablespoon chopped green capsicum
1 tablespoon chopped celery
1 cup cooked rice
250 g cooked prawns, shelled
½ cup oysters, reserve liquid
3 tablespoons sherry

CURRY SAUCE

60 g clarified butter
1 small onion, finely chopped
1 clove garlic, crushed
4 green chillies, finely chopped
1 teaspoon mustard seeds
1 teaspoon turmeric
4 curry leaves
1 teaspoon coriander
1 teaspoon cumin
1 tablespoon lemon or lime juice
1½ cups unsweetened coconut milk

Preheat oven to 200°C (400°F). Wash and dry snapper thoroughly. Season with lemon juice, salt and pepper.

Gently fry bacon in frying pan for 3 minutes. Add onion, capsicum and celery and cook a further 3 minutes. Combine with rice, prawns and oysters. Place filling mixture into cavity of fish. Secure with toothpicks. Place fish in greased casserole dish. Pour over sherry and reserved oyster liquid, cover dish and bake for 25 minutes.

To make Curry Sauce, melt butter in a frying pan and saute onion until golden. Add garlic, chillies and spices and cook 4 minutes. Add lemon juice and cook 1 minute. Add coconut milk and heat through. Serve immediately in a sauce boat.

Serves 4

STUFFED BAKED SQUID

800 g calamari (a 15 cm hood is ideal)
1 clove garlic
1 small bunch parsley
2–3 tablespoons fresh breadcrumbs
1 tablespoon olive oil
salt and pepper, to taste
1 egg yolk
melted butter, for brushing
½ cup dry white wine

Clean calamari, leaving head intact. Chop tentacles finely, together with garlic and parsley. Add breadcrumbs, oil, salt and pepper and egg yolk.

Stuff heads with this mixture and close them with a toothpick. Arrange stuffed calamari in an oven dish, moisten with melted butter and sprinkle a little white wine and some salt and pepper on top. Bake at 180°C (350°F) for 40–50 minutes. Serve hot.

Serves 4

Stuffed Baked Squid

Hot Tuna Bread

HOT TUNA BREAD

1 short loaf French bread
300 g can tuna fish, drained
100 mL mayonnaise
2 tablespoons chopped chives
juice 1 lemon
salt and pepper, to taste

TO SERVE

lettuce leaves
tomato quarters

Remove breadcrumbs in the centre of the bread with a knife, leaving approximately 1.5 cm of bread around the crust.

In a bowl, combine tuna, mayonnaise, chives, lemon juice and seasoning.

Fill the hollow in the bread with this mixture and chill in refrigerator. Serve cut into rounds on a bed of lettuce with fresh tomato.

Serves 4

FRESH ANCHOVY CUTLETS

800 g fresh anchovies or *sardines*
150 g butter
2 eggs
1 cup breadcrumbs
salt, to taste

ANCHOVY SAUCE

3 hard-boiled eggs
4 anchovy fillets
oil and
white wine vinegar, to taste

Clean anchovies and open them to remove the backbone. Wash and dry them carefully.

Beat eggs with salt and coat anchovies first with egg mixture and then breadcrumbs. Fry them slowly in butter until golden. Serve with anchovy sauce.

To make sauce, pass hard-boiled yolks through a sieve together with anchovy fillets. Add oil and vinegar to taste. Use finely chopped whites for decoration.

Serves 4

Fresh Anchovy Cutlets

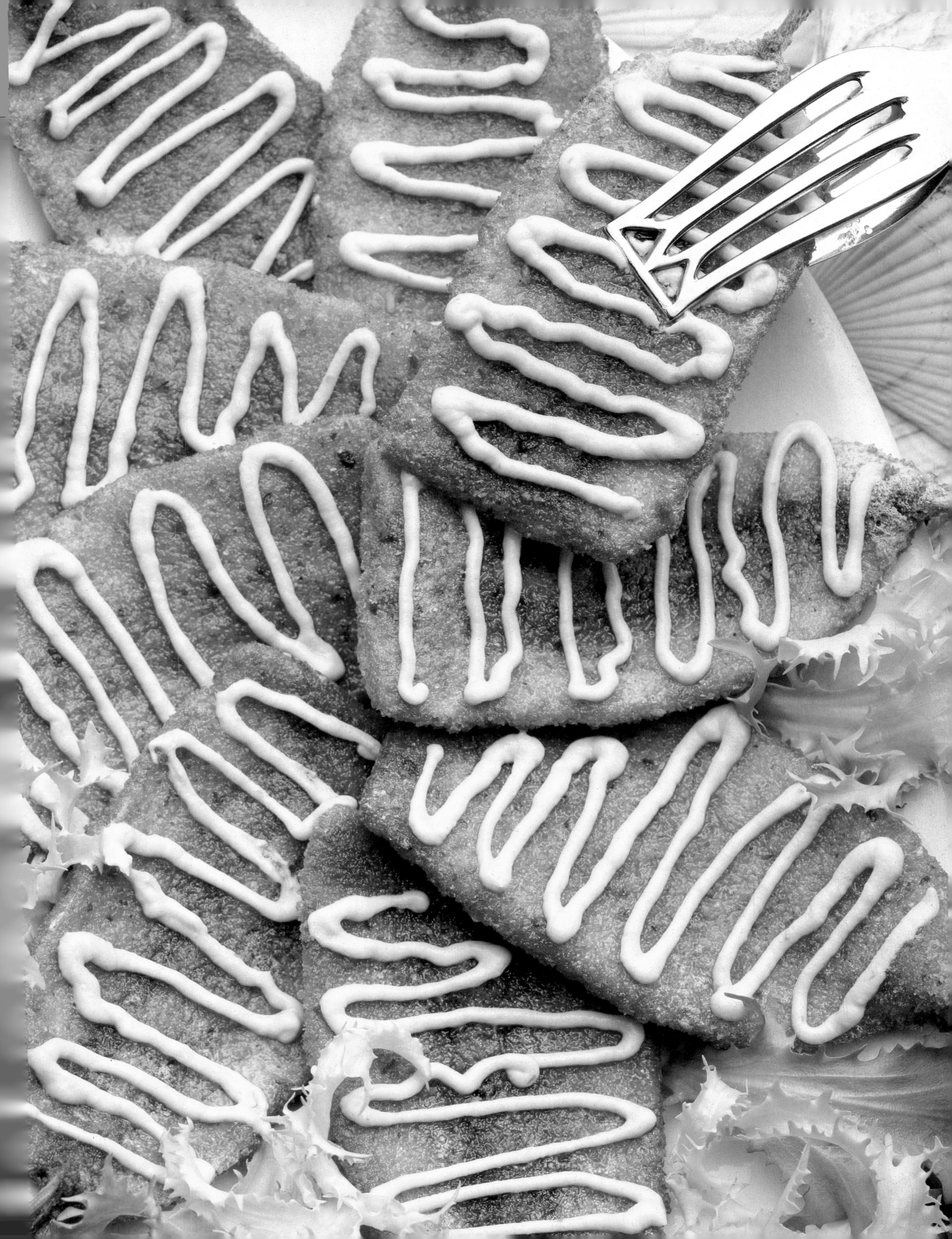

CHINESE SPRING ROLLS

8 spring roll wrappers
1 onion, finely chopped
1 tablespoon oil
125 g lean ham, diced
125 g bean sprouts
1 teaspoon soy sauce
oil, for deep-frying

ALTERNATIVE FILLING

125 g minced pork
2 teaspoons soy sauce
1 tablespoon oil
4 Chinese dried mushrooms, soaked in water 20 minutes and sliced
60 g Chinese cabbage, shredded
125 g water chestnuts

Heat oil in wok and stir-fry onions until clear. Add ham and bean sprouts, stir-fry gently for 1½ minutes. Stir soy sauce through mixture. Allow to cool.

Spoon 2 tablespoons ham and onion filling onto each spring roll wrapper, fold over at ends and roll up, pressing edges in firmly. Stand for 15 minutes.

Heat oil in wok. Deep-fry spring rolls until golden.

Note: To cook alternative filling, season pork with soy sauce. Heat oil in wok and stir-fry. Stir in mushrooms and cabbage and cook for 4 minutes. Stir in water chestnuts.

Serves 4

BASIC PIZZA DOUGH

4 cups flour
salt
30 g dry yeast
1 teaspoon sugar
300 mL warm milk
4 tablespoons olive oil

Sift flour and salt into a bowl. Combine yeast, sugar, warm milk and olive oil in a separate bowl. Make a well in centre of flour, pour in milk mixture. Sprinkle with flour, cover with plastic wrap and leave in a warm place for 15 minutes or until yeast mixture bubbles.

Work mixture to form dough. Knead dough on floured board for 10 minutes. Halve dough and roll out each half to 20 cm round. Place dough on greased baking tray.

Add topping of your choice *(see recipes following).* Allow pizzas to stand for 15 minutes. Bake at 200°C (400°F) for 40 minutes and serve hot.

VARIATION:

To make brown pizza dough, use half wholemeal flour and half white flour.

Makes 4

PIZZA NAPOLETANA

1 quantity Basic Pizza Dough (see recipe)

TOPPING

500 g tomatoes, fresh or *canned, peeled and coarsely chopped*
2 small mozzarellas or *1 large one*
1 can anchovies
oregano and
olive oil, to taste

Prepare dough and place on greased oven tray.

Cover pizzas with tomatoes and then arrange thick slices of mozzarella on top. Decorate with anchovies in a criss-cross pattern, sprinkle generously with oregano and olive oil and cook in the oven at 200°C (400°F) for 30–40 minutes. Eat hot.

Serves 4

PIZZA MARGHERITA

1 quantity Basic Pizza Dough (see recipe)

TOPPING

500 g tomatoes (or canned peeled tomatoes)
2 large mozzarellas
300 g green olives
oregano and
olive oil, to taste

Prepare dough and place on greased oven tray.

Cover pizzas with tomatoes, then thick slices of mozzarella and finally stoned green olives. Sprinkle with oregano and olive oil and bake.

Note: Margherita was the first Queen of Italy and this pizza reflects the colours of the Italian flag: white, red and green.

Serves 4

Pizza Napoletana

PIZZA WITH HAM AND OLIVES

1 quantity Basic Pizza Dough (see recipe)

TOPPING

200 g ham, cut in strips
200 g Gruyere, grated
120 g black olives
olive oil and
salt and pepper, to taste

Prepare dough and place on greased oven tray.

Cover pizzas with ham and cheese. Dot with olives and season with a little salt and plenty of freshly ground pepper. Sprinkle generously with olive oil and bake.
Serves 4

FOUR SEASONS PIZZA

1 quantity Basic Pizza Dough (see recipe)

TOPPING

2 tablespoons tomato paste
1 teaspoon dried oregano
300 g button mushrooms
150 g ham
pinch oregano
1 onion
500 g chopped tomatoes
1 large mozzarella
10 peeled uncooked king prawns
1 tablespoon chopped parsley
2 tablespoons olive oil

Prepare dough and place on greased oven tray.

Spread tomato paste over dough and sprinkle with oregano.

With a sharp knife, make a slight incision on the pizza and divide into 8 sections.

On the first section arrange some sliced mushrooms. On the second, diced ham, oregano and chopped onion. On the third, chopped tomatoes and grated mozzarella and on the fourth, chopped tomatoes, sliced prawns and parsley. Repeat for remaining 4 sections of pizza.

Sprinkle with olive oil and bake.
Serves 4

LASAGNE

Each family and region have their own preferred recipe for lasagne. The principle remains the same, but the flavour can be varied as you wish. Here are a few suggestions:
* Layer the lasagna with Bolognese sauce and slices of mozzarella cheese. Finish with Parmesan and butter.
* Layer green lasagne with a sauce made with minced beef or veal and 100 g chicken livers. Use the same ingredients and method as for Bolognese sauce, omitting the tomatoes.
* Layer green or yellow lasagne with a mixture of seafood lightly cooked in butter added to a thick bechamel sauce. Sprinkle each layer with parsley and Parmesan or Gruyere.

LASAGNE WITH HAM AND MUSHROOMS

PASTRY

400 g flour
4 eggs
salt
1 tablespoon oil

SAUCE

100 g butter
1 small onion, chopped
1 carrot, chopped
1 celery stalk, chopped
250 g lean minced veal or *beef*
300 g fresh mushrooms, finely sliced
1 small bunch parsley, chopped
200 g tomatoes, peeled and chopped
salt and pepper, to taste
100 g ham
100 g grated Parmesan cheese

Sift flour and form into a mound on a bench, make a well in the middle and break in the eggs. Add salt and oil and mix and knead until you have an elastic ball. Wrap it in a slightly wet towel and let it rest for 30 minutes.

With a rolling pin, roll out pastry until it is as thin as a piece of cloth, keeping it lightly floured all the time. Now cut it into 8 cm squares and arrange them flat on a floured surface to dry. Saute onion, carrot and celery in 15 g butter. Add minced meat, mushrooms, parsley and tomatoes. Add salt and pepper and a little water and let it cook for 25 minutes.

Cook lasagne, a few at a time, in plenty of boiling salted water, being most careful not to overcook (it will take only about 2 minutes). Lift out and arrange on paper towel to dry.

Butter an ovenproof dish and arrange in layers lasagne, some sauce, strips of ham and some Parmesan and dot each layer with butter. Finish with Parmesan and butter. Bake at 225°C (425°F) until it is brown on top.
Serves 4

Lasagne

Boda Nova
STAINLESS
JAPAN

BACON AND ASPARAGUS QUICHE

PASTRY

1¾ cups flour
salt, to taste
60 g butter
1 egg yolk, beaten
cold water

FILLING

2 rashers bacon, chopped and rind removed
2 shallots, chopped
20 g butter
5 eggs
100 mL cream
60 g grated Cheddar cheese
15 g blue vein cheese, crumbled
1 medium-sized tomato, sliced
8–10 canned asparagus spears

Preheat oven to 220°C (425°F).

Sift flour and salt into a bowl and rub in butter to resemble breadcrumbs.

Stir in egg yolk and sufficient water to form soft dough. Knead dough on lightly floured board. Roll out to fit 23 cm flan tin, trimming to fit. Prick base of pastry and bake blind for 10 minutes.

Saute bacon, shallots and butter for 2 minutes. Beat eggs and cream together, then strain. Fold in grated cheeses and bacon mixture.

Place tomato slices on pastry base, top with asparagus spears and pour over egg mixture. Reduce oven temperature to 190°C (375°F) and bake for 45 minutes or until set and browned on top. Serve hot or cold.

Serves 6–8

MUSHROOM QUICHE

375 g ready-rolled frozen shortcrust pastry, thawed
40 g butter
1 large onion, finely chopped
1 clove garlic, crushed
375 g button mushrooms, sliced
juice ½ lemon
4 eggs
1½ cups cream
salt and freshly ground pepper, to taste

Halve pastry, roll out and line 2 × 23 cm flan tins. Preheat oven to 200°C (400°F). Place greaseproof paper over pastry and weigh down with rice grains. Bake blind for 10 minutes. Remove paper and rice and bake pastry a further 5 minutes then set aside.

Heat butter and saute onion and garlic for 5 minutes. Add mushrooms and saute 3–5 minutes. Off the heat add lemon juice.

Beat eggs, add cream and beat again. Season with salt and pepper. Spoon mushrooms onto pastry bases then pour over cream mixture. Bake quiches for 15 minutes. Reduce temperature to 180°C (350°F) and bake a further 20–25 minutes until cooked when tested. Allow to cool then serve sliced.

Serves 12

Clockwise from top: Chicken and Mushroom Pie, Bacon and Asparagus Quiche and Mushroom Quiche

CHICKEN AND MUSHROOM PIE

1.5 kg chicken
2 tablespoons dry sherry
6 black peppercorns
½ tablespoon chopped fresh herbs
¼ teaspoon dried sage
½ teaspoon salt
¼ cup sliced leek
½ cup chopped onion
1 clove garlic, crushed
60 g butter
250 g fresh mushrooms, sliced
freshly ground pepper
12 sheets filo pastry
90 g butter, melted
1 tablespoon sesame seeds

Clean and rinse chicken. Place in large saucepan with sherry, peppercorns, herbs and salt. Cover with cold water and bring to boil. Simmer for 45 minutes. Allow to cool in liquid then drain, discarding stock.

Remove skin and bones from chicken and discard. Cut up chicken meat and set aside.

Saute leek, onion and garlic in butter until transparent. Add mushrooms and pepper and cook 2 minutes. Add mushroom mixture to chicken meat, stirring to blend. Place chicken mixture in 20 cm pie plate.

Cut pastry sheets in half to cover top of pie plate. Place between 2 dry tea towels and cover with a just damp tea towel to keep pastry moist. Layer pastry over filling, brushing every second sheet with butter. Roughly tuck pastry around edge of dish. Brush with butter and sprinkle with sesame seeds.

Bake on top shelf at 200°C (400°F) for 45 minutes or until golden brown. Serve hot.
Serves 6–8

VEGETARIAN PIE

PASTRY

1½ cups flour
¼ teaspoon baking powder
pinch salt
2 teaspoons curry powder
125 g butter
2 tablespoons chopped onion

FILLING

250 g spinach, washed and chopped
1 onion, chopped
20 g butter
225 g can mixed beans, drained
200 g can creamed corn
1 tablespoon chopped parsley
1 teaspoon salt
1 tablespoon tomato sauce
dash Tabasco sauce
600 g cottage cheese
1 egg
paprika, to taste

Preheat oven to 200°C (400°F). Sift flour, baking powder, salt and curry powder into a bowl. Rub in butter to resemble breadcrumbs. Add onion and sufficient water to form dough. Knead dough lightly on floured board. Roll out to fit 23 cm flan dish. Trim edges and prick with fork. Bake blind for 10 minutes.

Saute spinach and onion in butter over low heat for 2 minutes. Drain excess liquid. Layer spinach, onion, mixed beans, creamed corn and parsley on base. Combine salt, tomato sauce, Tabasco, cottage cheese and egg. Pour over vegetable filling and sprinkle with paprika. Return to oven and bake for 30 minutes. Serve hot or cold.
Serves 6

AVOCADO AND LETTUCE SALAD WITH MUSTARD SEED DRESSING

1 lettuce
2 avocados, peeled, sliced and sprinkled with
juice ½ lemon
1 small cucumber, peeled and sliced
6 shallots, trimmed
alfalfa sprouts

MUSTARD SEED DRESSING

2 tablespoons natural yoghurt
1 tablespoon vegetable oil
2 teaspoons mustard seeds
1 teaspoons grated ginger root

Wash and dry lettuce. Refrigerate 30 minutes until crisp then tear into bite-sized pieces. Place in salad bowl. Top with avocado slices. Add cucumber and garnish with shallots and alfalfa sprouts.

To make dressing, combine all ingredients mixing until smooth. Just before serving pour over salad and toss.
Serves 8–10

TUNA OLIVE SALAD WITH GARLIC TOAST

1 eggplant, peeled and diced
salt
2 tablespoons oil
3 tablespoons olive oil
1 tablespoon vinegar
1 clove garlic, crushed
½ teaspoon mustard
salt and pepper, to taste
225 g canned tuna
2 sticks celery, chopped
8 black olives
stick French bread

GARLIC BUTTER

4 garlic cloves
50 g butter, softened
salt and pepper, to taste

Sprinkle eggplant with salt and leave for ½ hour. Wash and drain, then fry quickly in the oil. Allow to cool. Mix olive oil, vinegar, garlic, mustard, salt and pepper, and pour over tuna, celery and eggplant in a bowl. Garnish with black olives. Chill until ready to use. Before serving, preheat oven to 190°C (375°F). Slice bread and toast each piece. Spread with Garlic Butter and heat in oven for about 10 minutes, until all the butter is soaked up.

To make Garlic Butter, pound garlic to a paste. Cream butter and combine with garlic, salt and pepper.

Serve hot garlic toast with chilled tuna mixture.
Serves 4

Tuna Olive Salad with Garlic Toast

1 Pat eggplant dry

2 Make dressing from olive oil, vinegar and mustard

3 Place tuna in bowl with celery and eggplant

Peasant Salad

PEASANT SALAD

1 round Lebanese bread, toasted
2 cucumbers, peeled and sliced
½ lettuce, washed and shredded
2 shallots, chopped
½ cup finely chopped parsley
¼ cup finely chopped mint
juice 1 lemon
½ cup olive oil
2 cloves garlic, crushed
salt and pepper, to taste
red capsicum or cucumber, to garnish

Cut bread into cubes and sprinkle with a little water. Place in a bowl with cucumber, lettuce, shallots, parsley and mint and toss all ingredients together.

Place lemon juice, oil, garlic, salt and pepper in a jar and shake well. Pour dressing over salad, garnish with shredded red capsicum or thinly sliced unpeeled cucumber and serve.

Serves 4

MULTI-GRAIN HEALTH BREAD

3 teaspoons dry yeast
2 teaspoons sugar
2 tablespoons warm water
200 g wholemeal flour
1½ tablespoons gluten
1⅕ cups soy flour
⅘ cup flour
2 teaspoons salt
3 tablespoons millet meal
3 tablespoons sunflower seeds
3 tablespoons bran
30 g butter, melted
300–450 mL lukewarm milk
1 egg
2 tablespoons cracked wheat

Combine yeast, sugar and warm water. Set aside in a warm place until bubbling. In a bowl, sift wholemeal flour, gluten, soy flour, flour and salt. Stir in millet meal, sunflower seeds, bran, butter and 200 mL lukewarm milk. Pour yeast mixture into flour. Sprinkle a little flour over mixture, cover with plastic wrap and stand in a warm place for 10 minutes. Add remaining milk and combine to form dough.

Knead dough on floured board for 10 minutes. Return dough to clean greased bowl and cover with plastic wrap. Stand in warm place 30 minutes or until dough doubles in size.

Punch down dough and divide into 4. Knead and roll each portion into log shape. Place on greased baking tray leaving a 1.5 cm gap between each loaf. Glaze with egg and sprinkle with cracked wheat. Preheat oven to 220°C (425°F).

Cover with plastic wrap. Allow to rise for 10 minutes. Bake for 15 minutes, reduce heat to 200°C (400°F) and bake a further 30 minutes. Allow to cool on cake rack.
Makes 4 loaves

WHOLEMEAL NUT BREAD

3 teaspoons dry yeast
2 teaspoons sugar
2 tablespoons warm water
2¼ cups wholemeal flour
1 cup flour
3 tablespoons wheatgerm
2 teaspoons salt
3 tablespoons crushed pecan nuts
30 g butter, melted
300–450 mL lukewarm milk
1 egg, beaten

Combine yeast, sugar and warm water. Leave in a warm place for a few minutes to bubble. Sift flours and salt in bowl, stir in wheatgerm and yeast mixture, pecan nuts, butter and 200 mL milk. Sprinkle surface with flour. Cover with plastic wrap and stand in warm place for 15 minutes.

Combine enough of remaining milk with flour mixture to form dough. Place on floured board and knead for 10 minutes. Place in greased bowl. Cover with plastic wrap. Stand 30–40 minutes in warm place until mixture doubles in quantity. Punch dough down. Divide in half and knead each into log shape.

Place in 2 greased loaf tins. Cover with plastic wrap. Allow dough to rise to top of tin. Preheat oven to 220°C (425°F). Glaze with beaten egg and bake for 15 minutes; reduce heat to 200°C (400°F) and continue cooking 30–40 minutes. Cool on cake rack.
Makes 2 loaves

MELBA TOAST

sliced white bread

Remove crusts from 5 mm thick slices of white bread. Toast until a pale brown, then cut through the middle of each to give extra-thin slices. Toast again, white sides up, until golden. Or bake thinly-cut slices in the bottom of a very slow oven 120°C (250°F) until very crisp and curled; then brown under grill.

Sweets

PARIS BREST WITH COFFEE CREAM FILLING

60 g butter
1 cup water
1 cup self-raising flour
3 eggs
150 mL cream, whipped
1 punnet strawberries, hulled and sliced
icing sugar, for sprinkling

COFFEE CREAM FILLING

300 mL thickened cream, well chilled
2 tablespoons caramel sauce
few drops vanilla essence
1½ tablespoons Tia Maria or other coffee liqueur

Preheat oven to 220°C (425°F). Place butter and water in saucepan. Heat until butter melts then bring to boil. Remove from heat and stir in flour. Return to heat and cool for 2 minutes, stirring constantly. Cool slightly then beat in eggs one at a time. Place mixture in piping bag with large fluted tube. Pipe large rosettes in circle next to each other on greased baking tray.

Bake for 40 minutes then remove from oven. Carefully cut pastry in half and return to oven for 5 minutes. Remove any moist dough from centre of pastry with a teaspoon.

To make Coffee Cream Filling, combine cream and caramel sauce in a large, well-chilled bowl and whip until soft peaks form. Add remaining ingredients and continue to whip until just stiff. Do not beat past this stage or the mixture will curdle.

Spoon filling into centre of pastry and sandwich together. Decorate with whipped cream and strawberries and sprinkle with icing sugar to serve.
Serves 6

ZABAGLIONE

4 egg yolks
⅔ cup sugar
grated peel ½ lemon
8 tablespoons dry Marsala

Put egg yolks and sugar in a bowl and beat until mixture forms a ribbon. Add lemon peel and Marsala and place bowl over heat in a double boiler. Keep beating with a whisk or egg beater until you have obtained a rich, frothy consistency and the volume of the eggs has doubled.

Pour into wine glasses and serve hot.

Accompany with home-made biscuits, such as Pine Nut Macaroons *(see recipe)*.
Serves 4

ZABAGLIONE ICE CREAM

4 egg yolks
⅘ cup sugar
2 cups milk
½ cup Marsala

In a bowl, beat yolks with sugar until creamy. Place bowl in a double boiler, add milk and Marsala. Continue beating until very hot. Let mixture cool.

If you have an ice cream maker, pour mixture into it and churn until frozen. Otherwise, pour mixture into ice cube trays and place in the freezer. Stir it through after the first hour, to break up any icy particles that might have formed, and finish the freezing process.
Serves 4

STRAWBERRIES IN RED WINE

400 g fresh strawberries
½ cup red wine
juice 1 lemon
⅗ cup sugar

Hull and wash strawberries, drain carefully and arrange in a glass bowl. Refrigerate for 2 hours. Mix wine and lemon juice and add sugar. Stir to dissolve sugar. A little before serving, pour wine mixture on strawberries.
Serves 4

Strawberries in Red Wine

PEARS IN WHITE WINE

12 small cooking pears, peeled (leave stems on)
½ cup honey
300 mL white wine
300 mL water
1 lemon
1 stick cinnamon
4 whole cloves

Arrange pears in shallow ovenproof dish. Boil honey, wine and water together for 3 minutes and pour it over pears. Slice lemon and add to dish with spices. Cover and bake at 180°C (350°F) for 1 hour, turning pears occasionally. Leave to cool.

Arrange pears in serving dish, strain juice and pour around pears.

Serves 6

PINE NUT MACAROONS

2 cups sugar
3 cups ground almonds
1 teaspoon vanilla essence
4 egg whites
1 cup pine nuts

In a food processor place sugar, ground almonds, vanilla and egg whites. Whirl for a minute or so, to form a smooth paste. Mix whole pine nuts into this mixture and with the help of a spoon form walnut-sized balls and place on greased biscuit tray. Bake at 160°C (325°F) for 10–12 minutes.

Serves 4–6

FUDGE CAKE

180 g butter
¾ cup sugar
1 tablespoon honey
3 eggs
2 cups self-raising flour
1 tablespoon baking powder
⅔ cup milk
½ teaspoon almond essence

CREAM FILLING

125 g butter
1½ cups icing sugar
juice ½ lemon

FUDGE ICING

125 g butter
1 tablespoon honey
2 tablespoons milk
2 cups icing sugar
flaked almonds and *chocolate curls, to garnish*

Preheat oven to 200°C (400°F). Cream butter and sugar until light and fluffy. Add honey and eggs, beating well. Sift flour and baking powder and add to butter mixture alternately with milk and almond essence.

Divide mixture between 3 × 20 cm greased and lined cake tins. Bake for 18–20 minutes or until cooked when tested. Remove from tins to cake rack and allow to cool.

To make filling, beat butter and icing sugar together with lemon juice. Sandwich cake layers together with cream mixture.

To make Fudge Icing, combine butter, honey and milk in saucepan. Gently heat until butter melts, then heat until nearly boiling. Remove from heat and sift in icing sugar, beating until icing thickens. Spread icing over top of cake and allow to drizzle down the sides. Cool and decorate with flaked almonds and chocolate curls.

Pine Nut Macaroons

ELEGANT AFTERNOON TEAS AND LATE-NIGHT SUPPERS

'Anyone for tea?'
Ahhh! Even the mere mention of the word brings a smile to the lips! The soothing civilised ritual of afternoon tea can provide a welcome relief from the pressures of everyday life. It can also be an elegant and rewarding way to entertain.

Afternoon tea and its sophisticated older sister, supper, provide the perfect times for relaxing and enjoying pleasant company and conversation with the minimum of fuss. Although they're both essentially informal gatherings, there's a certain ceremonial charm that prevails, offering the opportunity to lay the table with your finest linens, freshly polished tea service and prettiest serving plates.

Food for both occasions is usually light and sweet, so as not to spoil dinner or disturb sleep, with delicate pastries, tiny iced cakes and savoury-filled finger sandwiches always popular.

Theme teas can be fun and memorable, so why not treat your guests to a real event? A traditional Devonshire tea with baskets of fresh hot scones, rich plump jams, whipped and clotted cream and cups of steaming brew is always inviting; or perhaps an elegant tea party on the lawn with cucumber sandwiches, lemon tea and croquet is more your style? Suppers usually set their own mellow mood, as guests wind down after dinner or a night on the town.

Traditionally, the host or hostess serves fresh coffee and a selection of fine Indian and Chinese teas such as Darjeeling, Oolong, Jasmine and Assam.

British Prime Minister William Gladstone once stated that if you are cold, tea will warm you; if you are heated, it will cool you; if you are depressed, it will cheer you and if you are excited, it will calm you.

Whether you choose to entertain with afternoon tea or supper, you'll reap the benefits of this low-key style of party where everyone — including the host and hostess — can sit back, unwind and relax!

Delicious cakes and buns are a tempting treat at teatime

Savoury

APPLE, CHEESE AND OLIVE SAVOURIES

4 wholemeal bread rolls
3 red-skinned apples, cored and chopped
1½ cups grated cheese
salt and pepper, to taste
4 stuffed olives, sliced
parsley, to garnish

Cut thin slice off top of each roll and scoop out centre. Spoon apple into each and cover with cheese and season. Bake at 190°C (375°F) for 20 minutes, until golden and bubbly. Garnish with olives and parsley.
Makes 4

CHEESE AND MUSHROOM SAVOURIES

8 slices wholemeal or *rye bread*
150 g butter
4 eggs, beaten
1 cup grated Gruyere cheese
300 g button mushrooms, sliced
1 clove garlic, crushed
parsley, to garnish

Toast bread and lightly butter. Blend eggs and three-quarters cup cheese together. Melt remaining butter and gently fry mushrooms and garlic for 3 minutes, until soft. Stir in cheese mixture, season to taste and cook, stirring until eggs are scrambled.

Divide mixture between toast. Sprinkle over remaining cheese and cook under grill until golden. Garnish with parsley and serve immediately.
Serves 4

SPINACH TURNOVERS

500 g frozen ready-rolled puff pastry, thawed
750 g frozen spinach, thawed
¾ cup grated Cheddar cheese
pinch nutmeg
salt and pepper, to taste
2 egg yolks, beaten
juice 1 lemon
1 egg, beaten
1 tablespoon sesame seeds

Preheat oven to 200°C (400°F). Roll out pastry 3 mm thick. Using a round pastry cutter, cut out circles of 10 cm diameter.

Drain spinach and squeeze to extract as much water as possible, then chop finely. Place in a bowl and add grated cheese, nutmeg and seasoning. Add egg yolks and lemon juice and mix well.

Divide spinach mixture between pastry circles. Brush edges of pastry with water. Fold pastry over spinach and press edges together firmly. Brush turnovers with beaten egg and sprinkle with sesame seeds. Place turnovers on a greased baking tray and bake for 20 minutes.
Serves 4

1 *Place spinach mixture on pastry circles*

2 *Fold over pastry edges and press together firmly*

Spinach Turnovers

HAM AND MUSHROOM PASTIES

4 sheets frozen ready-rolled puff pastry, thawed
1 egg, beaten

FILLING

125 g ham, diced
1 onion, chopped
125 g mushrooms, sliced
40 g butter
1 stick celery, chopped
1 tablespoon chopped parsley
2 teaspoons tomato puree
pepper, to taste

Fry ham, onion and mushrooms in butter until onion is transparent. Add celery, parsley, tomato puree and pepper. Heat until mixture is dry and liquid evaporates. Remove from heat and allow to cool.

Cut pastry sheets into 9 rounds with 10 cm cutter. Place a tablespoonful of mixture on one half of each round. Fold over pastry to form semi-circle. Press edges together to seal, using prongs of fork for decoration. Brush with beaten egg. Place pastries on baking tray. Bake at 220°C (425°F) for 15–20 minutes. Serve hot or cold.
Makes 36

CORNISH PASTIES

375 g frozen ready-rolled shortcrust pastry, thawed
1 swede, coarsely grated
2 potatoes, coarsely grated
250 g lean chuck steak, finely diced
1 large onion, finely chopped
salt and freshly ground pepper, to taste
80 g butter
1 egg, beaten

Preheat oven to 200°C (400°F).

Roll out pastry to a thickness of 5 mm. Using a small plate about 15 cm in diameter as a pattern, cut 4 circles with a knife.

Sprinkle swede over centre of each round of dough. Then add potato. Spread diced beef on top then onion. Season generously. Top each with 20 g butter.

Dampen edges of pastry with water and fold them together. Press to seal and crimp edges to make a fluted pattern. Glaze with beaten egg. Place on baking tray and bake for 15 minutes. Then reduce heat to 180°C (350°F) and bake for further 30 minutes till crisp and golden. Serve hot or cold.
Serves 4

HAM AND CHEESE SLICE

1 tablespoon oil
1 small onion, finely chopped
2 cups chopped mushrooms
½ cup diced ham
salt and pepper, to taste
⅔ cup Bechamel Sauce (see recipe)
1 tablespoon chopped chives
pinch nutmeg
500 g frozen ready-rolled flaky pastry, thawed
1 egg beaten

Heat oil in frying pan. Gently fry onion for 3 minutes, until soft but not coloured. Add mushrooms and cook for 1 minute more, then add ham. Season and cook for a further 2 minutes. Stir in Bechamel Sauce and bring to the boil. Crumble in ½ cup grated cheese, stirring until dissolved. Remove from heat, check seasoning, and leave until cold and firm. Stir in chives and nutmeg.

Preheat oven to 220°C (425°F).

Roll out pastry to 5 mm thick. Prick over with a fork. Cut into 3 equal-sized rectangles and place on a greased baking tray. Bake for 15 minutes.

Place ½ the sauce on 1 slice of pastry, sprinkle with grated cheese. Place the second slice on top, and spoon over rest of sauce. Add more grated cheese. Place third slice on top and brush with beaten egg. Top with remaining grated cheese. Return to oven for 8 minutes, or place under grill. Serve.
Serves 6

Ham and Cheese Slice

Farmer's Pie

FARMER'S PIE

500 g frozen ready-rolled shortcrust pastry, thawed
1 egg, beaten
250 g beef sausage mince
1½ cups diced mushrooms
1 onion, chopped
1 egg, beaten
1 tablespoon chopped fresh parsley
1 clove garlic, crushed
salt and pepper, to taste
pinch ground mace
½ cup chopped gherkin or *pickled cucumbers*
2 tablespoons port wine

TO SERVE

tomatoes
potato salad

Preheat oven to 180°C (350°F). Roll out ⅔ of the pastry to 5 mm thick on a floured board. Cut a 23 cm circle to line a greased 20 cm flan tin. Brush inside of pastry with beaten egg.

In a bowl, combine other ingredients to form a smooth mixture. Spread mixture evenly over flan shell.

Roll remaining one-third of pastry and cut a circle 20 cm in diameter. Cover filled flan shell. Pinch edges together to seal, brushing with beaten egg if necessary. Use pastry trimmings to make leaves or twisted strips to decorate top of pie. Brush top with remaining beaten egg.

Bake 1 hour. Serve hot, with fresh tomatoes and a new potato salad.

Serves 6

TOMATO PIE

1 packet frozen ready-rolled shortcrust pastry, thawed
2 tablespoons chopped chives
2 tablespoons cornflour
1½ tablespoons sugar
salt and pepper, to taste
6–8 medium-sized tomatoes, sliced
1 egg, beaten

Preheat oven to 200°C (400°F). Roll out two-thirds of the pastry and use to line a 20 cm flan dish.

Mix chives, cornflour and sugar with seasoning to taste. Arrange a layer of sliced tomatoes in pastry case and sprinkle with chive mixture. Continue to layer the tomatoes, sprinkling the chive mixture between layers. Brush edges of pie lightly with water. Roll out remaining pastry. Trim pastry edge and flute. Decorate with 'leaves' made from pastry trimmings.

Brush pie with a little beaten egg and bake for 40–45 minutes, until golden brown. Serve hot or cold, with cold meat or salad.

Serves 6–8

Tomato Pie

WHOLEMEAL SALAD TARTLETS

PASTRY

1 cup flour
1 cup wholemeal flour
1 tablespoon chopped herbs
125 g butter
1 egg yolk
2 tablespoons lemon juice
salt and pepper, to taste
iced water, to mix

FILLING

½ cup asparagus cuts
¼ cup steamed peas
1 cup chopped tomatoes
¼ cup chopped celery
2 tablespoons chopped chives
¼ cup grated carrot
¼ cup corn kernels
natural yoghurt

Preheat oven to 200°C (400°F).

Place flours and herbs in a bowl and rub in butter. Add egg yolk, then lemon juice, salt and pepper and enough water to form dough. Wrap in plastic and place in refrigerator for 20 minutes. Take out and knead on a lightly floured board until smooth. Roll pastry to 0.5 cm thickness and cut out with 8 cm cutter. Place in patty tins and bake 10 minutes. Allow to cool.

To make filling, combine all vegetables and stir in enough yoghurt to hold filling together. Spoon into baked pastry shells and chill thoroughly before serving.

Makes 12

COTTAGE CHEESE PANCAKES

3 eggs, separated
125 g low-fat cottage cheese, sieved
1 tablespoon flour
pinch cinnamon
butter, for frying
honey, sour cream or *yoghurt, to serve*

Blend egg yolks with cheese, flour and cinnamon. Whisk egg whites until stiff peaks form and fold gently into cheese mixture. Melt a little butter in frying pan. Drop batter by the large spoonful into pan and fry until golden brown on both sides, turning once. Serve immediately with honey, sour cream or yoghurt.

Serves 4

Cottage Cheese Pancakes

POTATO PANCAKE

500 g jacket potatoes, baked
salt and pepper, to taste
80 g butter
½ cup oil
1 cup grated cheese

When potatoes are cool, halve, scoop out pulp and mash coarsely. Season with salt and pepper.

Heat butter and oil in a frying pan about 22 cm in diameter. Stir two-thirds of the grated cheese into mashed potato. Spread evenly across pan. When pancake is golden brown underneath, turn and cook other side.

Sprinkle with remaining grated cheese and place under a hot grill until cheese melts and bubbles. Cut pancake into 4 and serve with grilled meat or salad.

Serves 4

AUSTRALIAN WELSH RAREBIT

250 g grated Cheddar cheese
30 g butter
2 tablespoons flour
⅓ cup beer or *milk*
1 teaspoon Worcestershire sauce
½ teaspoon dry mustard
salt and freshly ground pepper, to taste
1 egg yolk, beaten
8 slices toast, crusts removed

Combine all ingredients, except egg yolk and toast, in saucepan. Stir over low heat until cheese is melted. Add egg yolk and continue to heat and stir. Do not boil.

Remove from heat. Spread cheese mixture evenly over toast. Place under grill until golden brown and serve at once.

Serves 4

ASPARAGUS ROLLS

8 slices wholemeal bread
75 g cream cheese
1½ teaspoons chopped chives
8 slices prosciutto ham
8 slices processed Swiss cheese
8 asparagus spears, cooked or *canned*
toothpicks

Remove crust from bread. Combine cream cheese and chives. Spread each slice of bread with cheese mixture. Cover with a slice of prosciutto then Swiss cheese. Top with asparagus spear. Roll up bread from corner to corner and secure with toothpick.
Serves 6

PISSALADIERE

QUICK SCONE DOUGH

50 g butter
2 cups self-raising wholemeal flour
⅓ cup milk

TOPPING

3 onions, sliced
¼ cup oil
250 g tomatoes, peeled and sliced
freshly ground pepper
250 g mozzarella cheese, sliced

GARNISH

50 g anchovy fillets, drained
20 stuffed green olives

Preheat oven to 220°C (425°F).

Rub butter into flour and mix in milk to make a firm dough. Turn dough onto lightly floured board and knead until there are no cracks. Pat out to round shape 23 cm in diameter. Place on greased baking sheet. Using forefinger and thumb, raise edge slightly by pinching the dough.

To make topping, fry onions until soft but not browned. Spread onions over top of dough, cover with tomato slices, sprinkle with pepper and top with cheese slices. Bake for 20 minutes, until base is browned and cheese bubbling. For extra taste add garnish of anchovy fillets and olives, and cook further 10 minutes.
Serves 2–3

Pissaladiere

Cakes, biscuits and slices

PLAIN SCONES

2 cups flour
1 teaspoon cream of tartar
½ teaspoon bicarbonate of soda
½ teaspoon salt
60 g butter, cut in pieces
⅔ cup milk
milk or *beaten egg, to glaze*

Preheat oven to 200°C (400°F). Grease a baking sheet.

Sift flour, cream of tartar, bicarbonate of soda and salt into a bowl. Add fat and rub in with fingertips until mixture resembles fine breadcrumbs.

Add enough milk to form a soft dough. Bring mixture together lightly with fingertips. Roll or pat out dough to 1.5 cm thickness and cut 10 scones, using a floured 5 cm cutter.

Place scones on baking sheet, brush tops with milk and bake for 12–15 minutes. Cool on rack.

Note: To achieve perfect scones, handle the mixture very lightly. To split scones, pull them gently apart with the fingers — cutting with a knife gives them a doughy texture.
Makes 10 scones

MANDELBRODT

3 eggs
2 tablespoons sugar
1½ cups flour
½ tablespoon baking powder
2 tablespoons chopped almonds

Preheat oven to 180°C (350°F). Combine eggs and sugar. Beat until thick. Sift flour and baking powder. Add to eggs with the almonds.

Pour batter into greased and lined loaf tin. Bake for 45 minutes. Turn out to cool on cake rack. When cold, cut into slices about 1.5 cm thick and serve with coffee.
Makes 24

CHEESE SCONES
Add 1 cup grated cheese and a good pinch dry mustard to the rubbed-in mixture.

FRUIT SCONES
Add 2 tablespoons sugar and ⅓ cup sultanas or raisins to the rubbed-in mixture.

OATY SCONES
Use half plain white flour and half rolled oats.

PEANUT AND ORANGE SCONES
Add ½ cup chopped unsalted peanuts and ½ teaspoon finely grated orange rind to the rubbed-in mixture, with 2 tablespoons sugar.

TANGY APPLE SCONES
Peel, core and finely chop half cooking apple and add to the rubbed-in mixture with finely grated rind ½ lemon and 2 tablespoons sugar.

WHEATMEAL SCONES
Use half wheatmeal flour and half plain flour. Fill scones with whipped cream and chopped pineapple.

DATE WHOLEMEAL SCONES

½ cup wholemeal flour
2¼ cups flour
2 teaspoons baking powder
½ cup oatmeal
100 g butter
½ cup brown sugar
2 eggs, beaten
1 teaspoon allspice
2 cups chopped dates
⅔ cup milk
little milk

Preheat oven to 190°C (375°F).

Sift flours and baking powder. Add oatmeal and rub in butter. Add sugar, eggs, spice and dates and combine. Gradually add milk to make a smooth dough.

Knead lightly and divide into 20 scones about 6.5 cm in diameter and 1 cm thick. Grease baking tray, arrange scones on it close together and brush lightly with milk. Rest for 10 minutes. Bake for 15 minutes.
Makes 20

Date Wholemeal Scones

BERRY MUFFINS

3 cups flour
½ cup sugar
1 tablespoon baking powder
½ cup brown sugar
125 g butter, melted
3 eggs
1 cup milk
1–1½ cups berries in season
icing sugar

Preheat oven to 200°C (400°F). Sift flour, sugar and baking powder into bowl. Stir in brown sugar. Combine butter, eggs and milk and stir into dry ingredients until just blended. If large berries such as strawberries are used, cut into dice. Fold in berries very lightly and carefully. Spoon into greased muffin tins until two-thirds full. Bake for 20 minutes until browned. Sprinkle with icing sugar while hot. Serve hot with butter.
Makes 20–24

PARKIN

100 g butter
½ cup brown sugar
½ cup golden syrup
2 tablespoons treacle
2¼ cups oatmeal
½ cup flour
1 teaspoon baking powder
1 tablespoon ginger
1 egg, beaten
1 tablespoon milk

Preheat oven to 140°C (275°F). Melt butter, sugar, syrup and treacle over low heat without boiling. Sift dry ingredients and stir in melted ingredients with egg and milk.

Pour into greased and lined 20 cm square cake tin and bake for 1¾ hours until cooked. Cool in tin.
Makes 8

CARAWAY SEED CAKE

2 cups flour
2 teaspoons nutmeg
1 teaspoon bicarbonate of soda
1 teaspoon baking powder
125 g butter
1 teaspoon vanilla
1 cup caster sugar
½ cup brown sugar
3 eggs
1 teaspoon caraway seeds
½ cup sour milk

TOPPING

4 tablespoons sugar
1½ teaspoons cinnamon
2 teaspoons grated orange rind
¾ cup soft breadcrumbs
40 g butter, melted

Preheat oven to 200°C (400°F). Sift flour, nutmeg, bicarbonate and baking powder twice. Cream butter, vanilla and sugars until light and fluffy. Beat in eggs. Fold in flour mixture and caraway seeds, alternately with sour milk. Place mixture into a 20 cm greased and lined cake tin.

To make topping, combine all ingredients and sprinkle over top of cake. Bake for 20–25 minutes or until cooked. Cool on cake rack and serve.

COFFEE CREAM CAKE

1 quantity Victoria Sandwich mixture (see recipe)
2 tablespoons cornflour
2 tablespoons caster sugar
2 tablespoons instant coffee powder
300 mL milk
250 g butter
2 tablespoons icing sugar
2 tablespoons flaked almonds
glace cherries

Preheat oven to 220°C (425°F). Prepare Victoria Sandwich mixture. Spread mixture evenly into greased and lined Swiss roll tin. Bake for 10–12 minutes.

Turn the cake out onto greaseproof paper and remove the lining paper. Leave to cool, then cut into 3 even strips lengthways.

Blend cornflour, sugar and coffee with 2 tablespoons milk. Heat the remaining milk, stir in cornflour mixture and return to heat. Bring to boil, stirring until thickened. Place a piece of wet greaseproof paper or plastic wrap on the surface of 'sauce' and leave to cool.

Cream butter and icing sugar. Beat gradually into coffee sauce. Spread mixture over 2 of the cake layers, then sandwich together. Cover top and sides with coffee cream and sprinkle with flaked almonds. Decorate with piped rosettes of coffee cream and glace cherries.

Coffe Cream Cake (left) and Caraway Seed Cake

APPLE SPICE CAKE

500 g Granny Smith apples, peeled, cored, sliced
4 tablespoons water
juice ½ lemon
175 g butter
½ cup brown sugar
3½ cups wholemeal flour
1 teaspoon bicarbonate of soda
1 teaspoon cinnamon
½ teaspoon nutmeg
½ teaspoon mace
¼ teaspoon ground cloves
1 cup chopped walnuts
1 cup chopped dates
⅓ cup raisins
3 tablespoons milk

TOPPING

1 tablespoon brown sugar
¼ cup chopped walnuts
½ teaspoon cinnamon

Preheat oven to 170°C (340°F). Cook apples over low heat in water and lemon juice until soft. Mash with wooden spoon and leave to cool. Cream butter and sugar. Sift flour with bicarbonate of soda and spices into creamed mixture. Stir in with walnuts, dates, raisins and milk. Spoon into greased 1 kg loaf tin.

Combine topping ingredients, sprinkle over cake and bake for 1¼–1½ hours. Leave to rest for 15 minutes then cool on wire rack.

APRICOT BANANA BREAD

1 cup chopped dried apricots
¼ cup sherry
1¼ cups flour
2 teaspoons baking powder
½ teaspoon bicarbonate of soda
¼ teaspoon salt
90 g butter
grated rind 1 lemon
⅔ cup caster sugar
2 eggs
½ cup mashed banana

Preheat oven to 180°C (350°F). Soak apricots in sherry for 1 hour. Drain and discard sherry. Sift flour, baking powder, bicarbonate of soda and salt twice. Cream butter, lemon rind and sugar. Beat in eggs one at a time. Fold in fruits alternately with flour mixture. Place mixture into a greased and lined loaf tin. Bake for 1 hour or until cooked. Cool on cake rack. Ice if desired, with icing of your choice.

MANGO BREAD

2 cups flour
1½ cups sugar
2 teaspoons bicarbonate of soda
2 teaspoons cinnamon
3 eggs
1½ cups diced mangoes
1 cup salad oil
½ cup grated fresh coconut
½ cup raisins
½ cup chopped macadamia nuts
1 teaspoon vanilla essence

Preheat oven to 180°C (350°F). Sift flour, sugar, bicarbonate of soda and cinnamon. Add to remaining ingredients and mix well. Pour into two 19 × 9 cm or one 23 × 12 cm greased loaf tins. Bake for 55 minutes until bread shrinks away slightly from sides of tin.

DATE AND ORANGE RAISIN TEABREAD

1 teaspoon sugar
¾ cup warm water
1 tablespoon fresh yeast
1 tablespoon lard
3½ cups wholemeal flour
1 teaspoon salt
2 tablespoons caster sugar
grated rind 1 orange
⅓ cup raisins
1 cup chopped dates
1 egg, beaten with
1 tablespoon water

Dissolve sugar in warm water, crumble in yeast and leave for 10 minutes in warm place until frothy. Rub lard into flour, add salt, caster sugar, orange rind, raisins and dates and mix well.

Make well in centre, pour in yeast mixture and mix to combine. Knead for 10 minutes until smooth. Place dough in warmed, lightly greased bowl and cover with damp cloth or greased plastic wrap, and leave in warm place until doubled in size.

Preheat oven to 190°C (375°F). Knock back dough and knead until smooth. Shape to fit 450 g loaf tin or 20 cm cake tin, and leave to rise to top of tin.

Brush loaf with egg and water glaze and bake for 40–45 minutes.

Apple Spice Cake

SUGAR BUNS

2 cups self-raising flour
½ teaspoon salt
125 g butter
1 cup milk
extra melted butter
½ cup sugar combined with
3 teaspoons cinnamon

Preheat oven to 220°C (425°F). Sift flour and salt. Rub in butter to resemble breadcrumbs. Add milk to form dough. Knead lightly on floured board.

Roll dough to 6 mm thickness and cut into 5 cm rounds. Brush top with melted butter and fold each round in half. Dip in melted butter then toss in combined sugar and cinnamon. Place on greased baking trays and bake 15–20 minutes until cooked. Serve hot or cold.
Makes 24

PETITS FOURS

2 quantities Victoria Sandwich mixture (see recipe)

FILLING
1¾ cups apricot jam
250 g almond paste

ICING
1½ cups icing sugar
1–2 tablespoons water
1 tablespoon rum
food colouring

DECORATIONS
glace cherries
chocolate vermicelli
candied coffee beans
crystallised violets
chopped pistachios
silver confectionery balls

Prepare 2 quantities Victoria Sandwich *(see recipe)* and divide between 3 greased and lined Swiss roll tins. Bake at 220°C (425°F) for 10–12 minutes.

Remove cakes from tins while still warm. Turn out onto clean greaseproof paper, removing paper lining. Carefully halve each cake lengthways, giving 6 layers. Spread each layer of cake with apricot jam. Layer cake together.

Roll out almond paste to the size of the cake. Place on top of cake. Cover with foil or greaseproof paper, weight down with a heavy wooden board and leave for 24 hours. Cut the cake into 3.5 cm squares or shapes.

Beat icing sugar with water and rum till smooth. Colour icing as desired. Coat cake squares in icing. Place on cake rack to dry. Pipe decorations with remaining icing and decorate with cherries, vermicelli etc. When dry, place each square in paper cases to serve.
Makes 28

FRUIT AND NUT TWIST

20 g fresh yeast
¼ cup sugar
¾ cup warm milk
40 g butter
2 cups wholemeal flour
pinch salt
½ teaspoon allspice
½ cup mixed dried fruit
½ cup chopped mixed nuts
1 egg

GLAZE
1 tablespoon water
2 tablespoons sugar

Dissolve yeast with a little sugar in ¼ cup warm milk and allow to stand in a warm place until frothy.

Combine remaining milk with butter. Place flour, salt, allspice, fruit and nuts and remaining sugar in a bowl. Beat egg into milk and butter mixture. Pour all liquid into bowl and combine to form a smooth dough.

Cover with a damp cloth or plastic wrap and set in a warm place until dough doubles in size.

Turn out onto floured board and knead thoroughly. Roll dough into a long sausage shape and then loop it into half. Take ends of dough and twist.

Place on well-greased oven tray. Cover with a damp cloth and set in a warm place for 20 minutes. Preheat oven to 220°C (425°F).

Bake for 15–20 minutes. As soon as twist is removed from oven, glaze with a lightly warmed mixture of water and sugar.

CARAMEL CHELSEA BUN

150 g butter
½ cup brown sugar
¼ cup chopped walnuts
½ cup chopped glace cherries
3½ cups self-raising flour
½ teaspoon salt
2 eggs, beaten
1¼ cups milk
30 g extra butter, melted
½ cup sugar
2 teaspoons cinnamon
1 cup raisins, finely chopped

Preheat oven to 220°C (425°F). Cream 60 g butter and all the brown sugar. Spread over base of a 23 cm square cake tin. Sprinkle with walnuts and cherries and set aside.

Sift flour and salt. Rub in remaining butter to resemble breadcrumbs. Combine eggs and milk. Add to flour mixture to form soft dough. Knead dough lightly on floured board. Roll out to rectangle shape, 6 mm thick.

Brush surface with melted butter. Sprinkle with sugar, cinnamon and raisins. Roll up dough from longest side to form log shape. Cut into 2.5 cm pieces. Place cut side down into tin. Bake 25-30 minutes until cooked. Invert onto plate to cool. Serve sliced.

Left to right: Citrus Ring Biscuits , Caramel Chelsea Bun and Apricot Banana Bread

Lamingtons

LAMINGTONS

175 g butter
¾ cup caster sugar
3 eggs, beaten
2 cups self-raising flour
⅔ cup milk
½ teaspoon vanilla essence

ICING

25 g butter
¼ cup boiling water
2 tablespoons cocoa
2 cups icing sugar
2 cups desiccated coconut

Preheat oven to 180°C (350°F). Grease a 30 × 25 cm lamington tin, line it with greaseproof paper and regrease.

Cream butter and sugar until light and fluffy. Gradually add eggs, beating well after each addition. Alternately fold in flour and milk, stir in vanilla essence.

Place mixture in greased, lined lamington tin and bake for 30–35 minutes. Cool cake on wire rack. Cut cake into cubes.

To prepare icing, place butter in a bowl and pour in boiling water. Add cocoa and, beating continuously, gradually add icing sugar. Place bowl of icing over pan of hot water. Using a long, pronged fork to hold cubes of cake, dip each piece into icing and roll immediately in coconut. Leave lamingtons to set.

Note: It is best to make the cake 2 days before making lamingtons.

Makes 12

ORANGE ROCK CAKES

2 cups self-raising flour
pinch salt
125 g butter
½ cup sugar
125 g mixed dried fruit
1 egg, beaten
2 tablespoons milk
2 tablespoons orange juice
½ teaspoon vanilla
whipped cream, to serve

Preheat oven to 200°C (400°F). Sift flour and salt into a bowl. Rub in butter until mixture resembles breadcrumbs. Add sugar and fruit. Combine egg, milk, orange juice and vanilla. Stir into flour mixture.

Place tablespoons of mixture onto 2 greased baking trays. Bake 15–20 minutes or until cooked. Cool on cake rack. When cold, split and fill with whipped cream to serve.
Makes 15

COCONUT PLUM FINGERS

BASE

¾ cup wholemeal flour
¾ cup self-raising flour
125 g butter
¼ cup caster sugar
vanilla, to taste
1 egg
¼ cup milk

TOPPING

½ cup plum conserve
1 cup chopped raisins
1 egg
2 tablespoons sugar
1¼ cups coconut

Preheat oven to 220°C (425°F). Sift flours together twice. Cream butter and sugar together. Blend in vanilla and egg. Fold in flour mixture and milk alternately. Press mixture evenly into greased 30 × 25 cm lamington tin. Spread with plum conserve and sprinkle with raisins. Combine egg, sugar and coconut. Spread carefully over top of raisins.

Bake for 10 minutes then reduce heat to 180°C (350°F) for further 10–15 minutes. Allow to cool in tin 10 minutes before cutting into 24 thin fingers. Allow to cool a further 5 minutes before removing from tin to cake rack to cool completely. Store in airtight container.
Makes 24

STRAWBERRY JELLY ROLLS

1 packet red jelly crystals
1½ cups boiling water
1 cup desiccated coconut

SPONGE

4 eggs, separated
2 egg yolks extra
grated rind 1 lemon
½ cup caster sugar
4 tablespoons flour
1 tablespoon cornflour

FILLING

60 g butter
3 tablespoons sugar
1 tablespoon boiling water
1 tablespoon milk
vanilla, to taste
1 cup chopped strawberries

Dissolve jelly crystals in boiling water by stirring well. Refrigerate to cool but not set. Preheat oven to 220°C (425°F).

Whisk egg yolks, lemon rind and half the sugar till creamy. Whisk egg whites till stiff, add remaining sugar and fold into egg yolk mixture. Sift flour and cornflour and fold into egg mixture.

Spread evenly in a greased and lined Swiss roll tin. Bake for 10–12 minutes or until cooked. Remove from oven and cover with a damp tea towel until cold.

To make filling, cream butter and sugar for 5 minutes. Gradually add boiling water, milk and vanilla, beating thoroughly. Stir through strawberries.

Turn cake out and remove lining paper. Spread with strawberry cream, cut into 12 squares and roll each one up. Dip into cold jelly, roll in coconut and place on greaseproof paper to set.
Makes 12

MELTING MOMENTS

100 g butter, softened
⅓ cup caster sugar
1 egg yolk
few drops vanilla essence
grated rind ½ lemon
1¼ cups self-raising flour, sifted

BUTTERCREAM FILLING

125 g butter, softened
¼ cup icing sugar, sifted
grated rind ½ orange
few drops orange food colouring

Cream butter until light and fluffy. Add caster sugar and beat until dissolved. Beat in egg yolk, vanilla essence and lemon rind. Fold in sifted flour gradually to form a stiff dough. Divide dough into 20 walnut-sized balls.

Place biscuit balls on greased baking tray, flattening slightly to allow for spreading. Bake at 190°C (375°F) for 15 minutes. Cool on a wire rack before sandwiching biscuits together with buttercream.

To make filling, cream butter, add icing sugar and beat until smooth. Add grated rind and food colouring. Spread cream on flat side of 10 biscuits and sandwich together with remaining biscuits.

Makes 20

Melting Moments

CREAMED AVOCADO PUFFS

PUFF MIXTURE
1 cup water
70 g butter, cut in small pieces
1 tablespoon raw sugar
1 cup sifted flour
4 eggs

CUSTARD
⅔ cup raw sugar
5 egg yolks
⅔ cup flour
1½ cups milk
1 teaspoon vanilla essence

AVOCADO CREAM
2 cups chopped avocado
Creme de Menthe, to taste (optional)
1 cup whipped cream sweetened with
honey, to taste

GARNISH
avocado slices
strawberry slices
icing sugar

Preheat oven to 200°C (400°F).

Place water, butter and sugar in pan and stir to completely melt butter. Bring to boil and remove from heat. Add flour all at once and stir vigorously. Reheat mixture for 2 minutes until the dough forms a ball.

Remove from heat and beat each egg well into mixture, one at a time. Butter and flour oven trays and, using 2 spoons, form balls about the size of an egg. Place 8 cm apart on tray.

Bake for 20 minutes or until puffed and golden brown.

To make custard, beat sugar and yolks until thick and lemon-coloured. Beat in flour. Heat milk and add to egg, sugar and flour mixture. Cook over moderate heat, stirring, to form a thick custard. Allow to cool.

To make avocado cream, blend avocado, Creme de Menthe and sweetened whipped cream until smooth.

Slice top off each puff. Fill with cooled custard and top with avocado cream. Garnish with avocado slices and finely sliced strawberries. Replace cream puff lid. Dust with sifted icing sugar before serving.

Serves 8

Creamed Avocado Puffs

CUSTARD VANILLA SQUARES

1 × 375 g ready-rolled packet frozen puff pastry, thawed

CUSTARD

4 cups milk
2/3 cup sugar
60 g butter
1 cup cornflour
1 teaspoon gelatine
1 tablespoon hot water
2 egg yolks, beaten
2 teaspoons vanilla

ICING

200 g icing sugar, sifted
1 tablespoon water
2 tablespoons passionfruit pulp

Preheat oven to 220°C (425°F). Roll out pastry to a 60 × 30 cm rectangle. Cut in half widthways. Place on 2 baking trays, sprinkle with cold water and prick with fork. Stand pastry for 10 minutes. Bake 12–18 minutes and cool on cake rack.

Combine 3 cups milk with sugar and butter in a pan. Dissolve sugar over low heat, stirring, then bring to boil. Blend remaining milk with cornflour. Dissolve gelatine in hot water and add to cornflour mixture. Add cornflour mixture to hot milk and heat, stirring until thick and smooth. Remove from heat and beat in egg yolks and vanilla. Allow to cool.

Blend icing sugar, water and passionfruit pulp. Trim pastry layers to fit Swiss roll tin. Spread icing over 1 layer of pastry and allow to set. Place second layer of pastry on bottom of Swiss roll tin. Spread with very cool custard mixture. Top with iced pastry layer. Allow to set for 20 minutes before cutting into 5 cm squares to serve.
Makes 32

LEMON CHEESE TARTLETS

PASTRY

1 cup flour
pinch salt
90 g butter
squeeze lemon juice
1 egg yolk

FILLING

1/2 cup sugar
2 tablespoons cornflour
2 tablespoons flour
2/3 cup water
2 egg yolks
grated rind 1 lemon
40 g butter
1/3 cup lemon juice

Preheat oven to 230°C (450°F). Sift flour and salt in a bowl. Rub in butter. Add lemon juice and egg yolk to form dough. Knead on lightly floured board. Roll out dough to 3 mm thickness. Cut with fluted scone cutter into 5 cm rounds.

Line patty tins with pastry rounds. Prick base and sides of pastry shells. Bake for 8–10 minutes. Cool on cake rack. Cut pastry strips from remaining dough, twist and bake on tray for 6–8 minutes.

To make filling, combine sugar, cornflour, flour and water. Stir over low heat until mixture simmers and thickens. Remove from heat. Add yolks, lemon rind, butter and lemon juice. Set aside to cool. Spoon lemon cheese mixture into tartlet cases. Decorate with pastry twist. Allow to cool completely to serve.
Substitute lemon cheese filling with raspberry jam or caramel-butterscotch filling.

CARAMEL-BUTTERSCOTCH

1 cup brown sugar
1/3 cup flour
3 tablespoons cornflour
pinch salt
4 egg yolks
2 1/4 cups milk
60 g butter
2 teaspoons vanilla
3 tablespoons golden syrup

Combine brown sugar, flour, cornflour, salt in a pan. Beat egg yolks and milk together and add to pan. Beat mixture till smooth. Gently heat, stirring until mixture thickens. Remove from heat. Beat in butter, vanilla and golden syrup. Allow to cool. Use as desired.
Makes 18

CHOCOLATE NUT SLICE

125 g butter
1/2 cup brown sugar
1 tablespoon golden syrup
2 tablespoons cocoa
1 egg, beaten
1/2 teaspoon vanilla
250 g plain sweet biscuits, crushed
1/2 cup chopped nuts (walnuts, almonds or *pecans)*
2 tablespoons desiccated coconut

ICING

90 g chocolate
3 tablespoons water
1 teaspoon oil
2 cups icing sugar, sifted
1/4 cup finely chopped nuts (walnuts, almonds or *pecans)*

Combine butter, sugar, golden syrup and cocoa in saucepan. Stir over low heat to dissolve sugar, then heat until bubbling. Remove from heat and add beaten egg and vanilla, stirring until thick. Add crushed biscuits, nuts and coconut and mix well. Press mixture into greased 28 × 18 cm lamington tin. Chill until firm.

To make icing, combine chocolate, water and oil in a bowl. Place over hot water to melt. Add icing sugar and stir well to combine. Spread chocolate icing over slice. Sprinkle with nuts. Allow icing to set before cutting into squares or fingers to serve.
Makes approximately 20

HAZELNUT SHORTBREAD

250 g butter
⅓ cup caster sugar
90 g ground hazelnuts
1⅔ cups flour
100 g chocolate
30 g extra ground hazelnuts

Preheat oven to 180°C (350°F). Beat butter and sugar until creamy. Mix in hazelnuts and sifted flour. Put mixture into piping bag with fluted tube and pipe rounds into base of greased patty tins. Bake for 15 minutes. Remove from patty tins to cake rack to cool. Melt chocolate in bowl placed over hot water and stir. Dip shortbread half-way into chocolate. Place on aluminium foil to set. Sprinkle chocolate with extra ground hazelnut. Store in airtight container.
Makes 25

COCONUT MACAROONS

2 egg whites
½ cup caster sugar
1¼ teaspoons cornflour
vanilla essence, to taste
2 cups desiccated coconut
90 g chocolate
40 g butter

Preheat oven to 150°C (300°F). Beat egg whites till stiff. Gradually add sugar, beating well. Fold in cornflour. Place bowl over saucepan of hot water. Bring water to boil and beat egg white mixture until thick. Remove from heat. Fold in vanilla and coconut. Spoon walnut-sized drops of mixture onto trays lined with dampened greaseproof paper. Bake for 25 minutes. Carefully remove and cool on cake rack.

Melt chocolate and butter over hot water. Dip each macaroon half-way in melted chocolate. Place on aluminium foil and allow chocolate to set.
Makes 40

Hazelnut Shortbread and Lemon Cheese Tartlets

FRUITY COCONUT BARS

½ cup wholemeal flour
1½ teaspoons baking powder
½ teaspoon cinnamon
¼ teaspoon ginger
pinch nutmeg
½ cup brown sugar
½ cup sultanas
½ cup chopped dried apricots
1 cup desiccated coconut
2 eggs, beaten
75 g butter, melted
1 tablespoon milk

Preheat oven to 180°C (350°F). Sift flour with baking powder and spices. Combine with sugar, fruit and coconut. Beat in eggs, butter and milk. Spread mixture in greased and lined 18 × 27 cm shallow tin and bake for 30 minutes. Leave to cool in tin then cut into 16 bars.
Makes 16

CAROB COOKIES

150 g butter
¾ cup brown sugar
1 egg
¼ cup carob powder
2 cups self-raising wholemeal flour
½ cup raisins
½ cup chopped walnuts

Preheat oven to 180°C (350°F). Cream butter and sugar, beat in egg and stir in remaining ingredients until well-mixed. Roll into walnut-sized balls and place on lightly greased baking sheet. Flatten lightly with fingertips or fork.

Bake for 12–15 minutes. Cool on baking sheet 2–3 minutes then lift onto cake rack to cool completely.
Makes 45

OATY DATE SQUARES

finely grated rind and juice 1 orange
1½ cups chopped dates
100 g butter
¾ cup brown sugar
¾ cup rolled oats
½ cup wholemeal flour

Preheat oven to 180°C (350°F).

Make up orange juice to 100 mL with water. Cook dates and rind in orange water over low heat until soft and pulpy.

Blend butter and dry ingredients and press half into lightly greased 18 cm square tin. Spread date mixture over, top with remaining oat mixture and press down. Bake for 35–40 minutes. Cool in tin then cut into 16 squares.
Makes 16

Oaty Date Squares (top), Carob Cookies (left) and Fruity Coconut Bars (right)

MONKEY FACE BISCUITS

1 cup flour
½ teaspoon baking powder
pinch each cinnamon and *ground cloves*
¼ cup sugar
grated rind ½ small lemon
90 g unsalted butter
1 egg yolk
milk, to glaze
¼ cup desiccated coconut, toasted
¼ cup raspberry jam

Preheat oven to 180°C (350°F). Sift flour, baking powder and spices into a bowl. Add sugar and lemon rind. Rub butter into flour mixture. Mix in egg yolk to form a soft dough. Knead dough lightly on floured board. Divide dough in 2 and wrap in plastic; chill 15 minutes.

Roll out dough to 3 mm thickness. Cut into 3 cm rounds with a fluted cutter. Using 6 mm round cutter, cut 3 rounds in centre of half the biscuits.

Place whole biscuit rounds on lightly greased baking tray. Brush cut-out rounds with milk and sprinkle with toasted coconut. Bake biscuits for 8–10 minutes until golden. Spread whole rounds with jam and top with cut-out biscuits. Store in airtight container.
Makes 36

CITRUS RING BISCUITS

1 cup flour
¼ teaspoon allspice
150 g butter
½ cup caster sugar
1 egg
grated rind 1 lemon
1 cup ground almonds
2 cups soft breadcrumbs
1 egg yolk, beaten

ICING

200 g icing sugar, sifted
2 tablespoons lemon juice
60 g candied orange and lemon rind

Preheat oven to 200°C (400°F). Sift flour and spice together twice. Cream butter and sugar. Beat in egg and lemon rind. Fold in ground almonds and breadcrumbs to form dough. Wrap dough in plastic wrap and chill for 1 hour.

Divide dough into 30 pieces and roll each piece until 10 cm long. Brush ends with egg yolk and join together to form ring. Place on greased baking trays. Bake 10–15 minutes. Remove to cake rack to cool.

Combine icing sugar and lemon juice. Ice biscuits and decorate with strips of candied rind.
Makes 30

TURKISH BONNETS

5 egg yolks
pinch salt
3 tablespoons caster sugar
1 tablespoon brandy
2½ tablespoons yoghurt
4 cups self-raising flour
oil for deep-frying
icing sugar, for sprinkling

Beat egg yolks and salt until thick and lemon-coloured. Add sugar and brandy. Continue to beat and add yoghurt. Stir in sifted flour, working by hand into a dough.

Knead on a floured board until dough blisters, then roll out as thinly as possible. Cut into ribbons about 2.5 cm wide, then divide into 7.5 cm strips. Make a 2.5 cm slit down the centre of each strip and pull 1 end through.

Fry in heated oil until pastries are puffed and golden, turning once. Drain on paper towel and sprinkle with sifted icing sugar.

Makes about 30

QUINCE PASTE

Quinces, when being cooked in sugar, turn a beautiful purple colour, making this paste both attractive in appearance and delicious to eat. It is also excellent if served with a cheese platter.

1 kg fresh quinces, washed
granulated sugar
caster sugar, for tossing

Place whole quinces in a saucepan with just enough water to cover. Bring to boil, reduce heat and cook gently for 45 minutes or until soft when tested. Remove cores, mash and puree. Measure puree in a cup measure and combine with an equal amount of sugar in a saucepan. Cook over a moderate heat, stirring constantly for 20 minutes or until mixture is thick and comes away from sides of pan. Care should be taken to regulate to prevent scorching.

Spread mixture into a wet, shallow pan and leave to set overnight. When set, cut into squares, toss into caster sugar and leave to dry on a cake cooler. When dry, wrap in greaseproof paper and store in a cool place. Serve with coffee.

Note: Use a long-handled wooden spoon for stirring the boiling mixture because it has a tendency to form large bubbles and spatter.

Makes about 1 kg

Clockwise from top right: Turkish Bonnets, Quince Paste, Almond Sweetmeats, Date Halva and Coffee Rolls

ALMOND SWEETMEATS

250 g ground almonds
125 g icing sugar
4–6 tablespoons orange-blossom water
125 g pistachio nuts, peeled and finely chopped
1½ tablespoons caster sugar
extra 125 g icing sugar
extra 125 g pistachio nuts, peeled

Combine ground almonds and icing sugar with enough orange-blossom water to form a stiff paste. Knead until smooth and allow to rest. Shape paste into small walnut-sized balls.

Using a teaspoon handle, make a small hole in each ball and fill it with combined pistachio nuts and caster sugar. Close hole over filling and reshape. Roll balls in icing sugar and place in small paper cups. Decorate the top of each ball with a peeled pistachio nut. Serve with coffee.

Note: To peel pistachio nuts, simmer for 3 minutes, drain and slip off skins. Dry on a paper towel before use.

Makes about 40

DATE HALVA

4 cups dates
5 cups walnuts
finely grated rind 1 lemon
pine nuts, to garnish (optional)

Chop dates and walnuts and knead together with lemon rind. Press into a slab tin. Cut into squares, decorate each square with a pine nut if desired and serve.

Note: For a lovely flavour combination, try using half dried and half fresh dates.

Makes about 20 pieces

PUFTALOONS

2½ cups self-raising flour
½ teaspoon salt
⅔ cup water
3 tablespoons oil
golden syrup, to serve

Sift flour and salt into a bowl. Add water to form dough. Knead lightly on floured board. Pat out to 1.25 cm thickness. Cut in rounds or squares.

Heat oil in frying pan. Fry puftaloons 1 minute each side or until golden. Drain on paper towels and serve hot with golden syrup.

Makes 24

THE COCKTAIL HOUR

Popular during the 1920s and '30s, the cocktail party is enjoying a comeback as an easy way to entertain large and small groups of people. New generations are discovering the delights of experimenting with exotic mixed drinks that tantalise the tastebuds and whet the appetite for a delicious selection of bite-sized snacks and finger food — an important point to note as guests will invariably be balancing a glass in one hand and food in the other!

The main ingredient for a great cocktail party should be fun, but one mistake made by many hosts is to try to serve almost every drink imaginable. There's really no need, as your guests won't expect it and you'll end up spending a fortune. Simply stock the bar with a reasonable selection of spirits, liqueurs and mixers for basic cocktail recipes and add a few specialty ingredients upon demand. A well-stocked bar will include a good quality scotch or whiskey, vodka, gin, light rum, brandy, white wine and sherry. You should also consider a bottle of vermouth and some inexpensive champagne. Remember that some compromise between quality and price must be made otherwise you're bound to break even the most flexible budget! If you don't want to serve bulk liquor from its original container, use your best jugs and carafes instead.

For a crowd of over 12, limit the range of cocktails to 3 or 4, mix them in the kitchen and serve them from jugs on a tray. Popular standards include champagne and orange, Bloody Marys (vodka and tomato juice), Brandy Alexanders and martinis.

A word of warning about the use of potent liqueurs and spirits. Some cocktails contain very high levels of alcohol (a factor that's often masked by the addition of fruit juices, cream and soft mixers) and party-goers may lose track of just how much they're consuming. Offer an alcohol-free cocktail at regular intervals to help water down a possibly potent party. Your guests will thank you for it in the morning!

Drinks and nibblies — perfect companions for the cocktail hour

Nibbles

COCKTAIL PLATTER

Make up an inexpensive and colourful cocktail platter with a selection of cheeses, cold meats such as ham, roast beef, turkey or smoked salmon, salamis, little cocktail sausages and onions, olives, nuts and *crudites* — crispy sticks of raw sliced vegetables like cauliflower, carrot, celery or mushroom which make a perfect foil for dips. Accompany these with a wide variety of interesting breads — French, Italian, Lebanese and herb for example, or crackers, water biscuits and Melba Toast.

TARAMASALATA

2 slices stale wholemeal bread
75 g smoked cod's roe
1 clove garlic, crushed
pinch cayenne pepper
1–2 lemons, juiced
paprika, to taste
⅔ cup oil

Remove crusts from bread and soak slices in a little water. Remove skins from cod's roe and pound to a smooth paste. Squeeze bread dry and add to roe with garlic and cayenne pepper. Continue to pound mixture until it is really smooth. Gradually stir in lemon juice and oil and beat vigorously. Transfer to serving dish, sprinkle with paprika and serve with toast.
Note: All ingredients can be put in a blender or food processor and blended until smooth.
Serves 4

TARAMA CAVIAR

2 slices white bread, crusts removed
150 g tarama
juice 1½ lemons
1 small onion
1 clove garlic
½ cup olive oil

Soak bread in water, squeeze out excess. Puree bread, tarama, lemon juice, onion and garlic until smooth and add olive oil. Leave to chill and thicken. Serve as a dip or spread on savoury biscuits.
Note: Tarama is smoked fish roe which can be bought from most continental delicatessens. For the best flavour, use Greek olive oil which is green in colour and has a distinctive flavour without being oily on the palate.
Makes 1½ cups

Taramasalata

HUMMUS

440 g can chick peas, drained
2 cloves garlic, crushed
½ teaspoon ground cumin
½ teaspoon salt
3 tablespoons sesame or *olive oil*
¼ cup lemon juice
1 tablespoon chopped coriander or *parsley*

Pound chick peas until smooth and stir in garlic, cumin and salt. Add alternate tablespoons of oil and lemon juice, stirring well after each addition, until mixture forms a smooth, thick paste. Transfer to serving dish, chill and garnish with a sprig of coriander. Serve with pita bread and raw vegetable sticks.
Note: All ingredients can be put in a blender or food processor and blended until smooth.
Serves 4

GUACAMOLE

4 ripe avocados
juice 2 lemons or *limes*
1 teaspoon salt (optional)
2 large onions, grated
2 cloves garlic, crushed
2 teaspoons curry powder
pinch cayenne
few drops Tabasco sauce (optional)
chopped red chillies, to garnish
taco or corn chips, to serve

Mash avocados with fork or blend in food processor. Add lemon juice and salt. Add remaining ingredients to avocado. Cover with plastic wrap and chill to serve. Spoon into 2 bowls before serving. Garnish with chopped red chillies. Serve with taco chips and vegetable sticks.
Note: For this versatile Mexican dish it is good to look for over-ripe avocados. If preparing in advance mash avocados with a wooden spoon and store the finished guacamole in a jar with the avocado seeds. This will prevent discolouring.
Makes 4 cups

TOMATO MOUSSE

1 cup clear aspic, flavoured with sherry
250 g tomatoes, cored, peeled, seeded and diced
3 tablespoons tomato sauce
2 tablespoons tomato juice
3 tablespoons tomato paste
cayenne pepper, to taste
pinch sugar
1 teaspoon gelatine
3 tablespoons hot beef stock
1 cup cream, whipped
fresh dill, to garnish

Pour a little of the clear aspic into 6 × 250 mL moulds and tilt from side to side to coat evenly. Place in refrigerator while preparing mousse.

Rub 125 g tomatoes through a sieve, add sauce, juice, paste and season. Dissolve gelatine in stock and whisk into mixture. Set to a soft gel and whisk in one quarter of the whipped cream and then fold in remainder. Fold in remaining diced tomato. Pour into moulds. Set in refrigerator until firm.

Unmould and serve with prawns and cherry tomatoes. Garnish with fresh dill.
Serves 6

HOT DIP FOR RAW VEGETABLES

5 cloves garlic
2 tablespoons milk
1¼ cups olive oil
60 g butter
120 g anchovies, finely chopped

Chop garlic very finely and leave it in the milk for a few hours to take away some of its pungency. Put oil and butter in a heatproof earthenware pot, add anchovies and drained garlic and cook on very low heat for about 15 minutes, stirring from time to time. Serve immediately, with prepared vegetables.
Serves 4

Tomato Mousse

FRENCH TERRINES

BASIC FORCEMEAT FILLING

750 g pork
375 g veal
2 tablespoons fresh spices
3 eggs
½ cup brandy, port or *Madeira*

ASPIC

1 tablespoon gelatine
2 cups chicken stock
1 tablespoon brandy

Preheat oven to 180°C (350°F). Place forecemeat in food processor or blender and grind finely a little at a time.

Line terrine with strips of pork fat (optional). Pack a layer of forcement on base and then strips of veal or chicken, then another layer of forcemeat. Sprinkle with fresh herbs. Cover with wet greaseproof paper. Top with lid or aluminium foil.

Cook terrine in a bain-marie in the oven for 1–1½ hours. When firm to touch and liquid runs clear, remove and cool.

Cover with a flat board and weigh down with something heavy. A day later remove any excess fat and herbs.

Dissolve gelatine in chicken stock and brandy. Pour over terrine and fill in sides. Garnish top of terrine with sliced vegetables if desired.

VARIATIONS:

Suggestions for layers of meat to be used with forcemeat:
• Chicken breasts, cut into long strips. Marinate for at least 1 hour in 2 tablespoons brandy, 1 tablespoon green peppercorns, and 1 tablespoon chopped parsley. Place crushed juniper berries, thyme and bayleaf on top of terrine before cooking.
• Two chicken supremes cut into long strips with 125 g cooked ham cut into long strips and 60 g pistachio nuts, peeled and blanched.
• Four rashers of bacon, rind removed, with 3 chicken livers, cleaned but uncut, and sauteed with 2 cloves finely chopped garlic. Place 2 rashers on base of terrine, then some forcemeat, then chicken livers down the centre, then remaining forcemeat. Cover with left-over bacon.

Note: Once cold, terrines will turn out easily for slicing. Store 2–3 days before serving.
Serves 10

TERRINE OF DUCK

1 carrot, peeled and diced
1 turnip, peeled and diced
1 small onion, peeled and diced
1 stalk celery, diced
60 g butter
1.5 kg duck

FORCEMEAT

2 tablespoons sultanas
2¼ tablespoons brandy or *port*
100 g lean veal
320 g duck livers, fatty threads removed
2 teaspoons salt
¾ teaspoon pepper
pinch fresh spices
1 cup cream
3 egg yolks

Preheat oven to 225°C (425°F). Saute vegetables in butter until brown and tender.

Remove legs from duck. Remove backbone from carcase to lie flat in a baking dish, spoon over cooked vegetables and bake for 15 minutes. Allow to cool. Turn oven down to 150°C (350°F).

Soak sultanas in brandy. Process meat from duck legs and the veal until creamy smooth. Add livers and seasoning, followed by cream, egg yolks and soaked sultanas.

Remove skin from breast of duck and slice into strips. Place half forcemeat into terrine. Top with strips of breast, placed lengthways down centre. Cover with remaining forcemeat. Cover with oiled greaseproof paper and lid with foil.

Bake in bain-marie at 180°C (350°F) for 1–1½ hours. Allow to cool and then place in refrigerator. Store 24 hours before serving.
Serves 8

PRAWN AND AVOCADO PATE

60 g butter
3 tablespoons flour
1 cup milk
½ cup sour cream
2 avocados
250 g small prawns, shelled
½ teaspoon Dijon mustard
freshly ground pepper
2 teaspoons gelatine
¼ cup water
¼ cup mayonnaise
1 tablespoon lemon juice
chopped parsley and *½ avocado, to garnish*

Prawn and Avocado Pate

Melt butter and add flour. Remove from heat and gradually stir in milk and sour cream. Stir until well combined and sauce thickens. Simmer for 5 minutes over low heat. Cool slightly.

Puree sauce and avocado until smooth. Chop prawns finely, reserving 12 for garnish. Mix through avocado sauce. Add mustard and pepper.

Sprinkle gelatine over water and dissolve over hot water. Add gelatine to avocado mixture. Cool to lukewarm. Mix through mayonnaise and lemon juice.

Spoon into 6 individual dishes or pate bowls and refrigerate for a few hours. Garnish with chopped parsley, 2 prawns per person and a little finely sliced avocado.

Serve with Melba Toast *(see recipe)* or crudites.

Note: a slight discolouration can occur if avocados are not freshly ripened.

Serves 6

CREAMY CHICKEN AND BACON PATE

2 small rashers bacon, rind removed and chopped
1 small onion, chopped
1 clove garlic
500 g chicken livers, fatty threads removed and halved
2 tablespoons cream cheese
2 tablespoons yoghurt
125 g butter, cut in pieces
1 tablespoon brandy
freshly ground pepper

Cook bacon a few minutes over moderate heat to release fat. Add onion and garlic and continue cooking until soft. Discard garlic and place bacon and onion in processor or blender.

Using same pan, saute livers a few at a time, until just cooked but still pink inside. Add to processor and blend.

With motor running, add cream cheese, yoghurt and butter. Season with brandy and pepper. Pour into containers and seal well.

Serves 10

CHICKEN LIVER MOUSSE

125 g chicken livers, trimmed and soaked in milk to cover
1 cup milk
1 egg
½ clove garlic, ground to a paste with salt
pepper, to taste
2 teaspoons parsley
30 g cooked spinach, chopped and moisture removed (optional)

OPTIONAL GARNISH

8 fresh prawns sauteed in butter
fresh tomato sauce

Allow livers to soak 1–2 hours then discard milk. Preheat oven to 200°C (400°F). Place livers in processor or blender with egg, garlic, pepper, parsley and spinach and blend. Mixture may be left 2–3 hours, covered, in refrigerator.

Lightly oil 4 × 7 cm ramekins and fill with mixture. Bake in bain-marie for 30 minutes covered with buttered greaseproof paper or foil.

Saute prawns in warm sauce. When mousses are cooked, leave in pots for a few minutes, then turn out by running knife around edge. Top with prawns and sauce.

Serves 4

CAVIAR MOUSSE

1 tablespoon gelatine
4 tablespoons water
1 cup cream
2 tablespoons horseradish cream
2 × 50 g jars lump fish roe
2 hard-boiled eggs, quartered
4 very thin slices lemon

Stir gelatine in water and dissolve over hot water in a pan. Allow to cool. Whip cream, fold in horseradish cream and cooled gelatine. Reserve a little lump fish roe for decoration and carefully fold remainder into cream mixture. Spoon into individual souffle dishes or 1 large one.

To serve, quickly dip dishes into hot water and turn out onto serving dishes. Garnish with reserved lump fish roe, egg and lemon slices and serve with toast.

Serves 4

ROQUEFORT MOUSSE

2 tablespoons gelatine
1 cup cream
3 eggs, separated
300 g Roquefort or *Danish blue cheese*
2 tablespoons chopped chives
2 tablespoons extra cream

Tie a double band of greaseproof paper around each of 6 individual souffle dishes to come 2.5 cm above the rim. Lightly oil inside of paper. Soften gelatine in cream for 5 minutes. Stand mixture in a pan of hot water and stir until gelatine has completely dissolved.

Whisk egg yolks until pale, then gradually whisk in cream and gelatine mixture. Pour into saucepan and stir over very low heat until thickened. Mash cheese and add thickened mixture and chives. Leave to cool, then chill until beginning to set. Beat egg whites until peaks form. Beat cream until it is just thick. Fold cream and egg whites through the cheese mixture and divide between prepared souffle dishes. Chill until set. Before serving, remove paper.

Serves 6

Roquefort Mousse (top) and Caviar Mousse

ANCHOVY AND EGG MOUSSE

8 canned anchovy fillets soaked in milk
1/3 cup mayonnaise
2 tablespoons cream
2 tablespoons parsley
1 teaspoon anchovy essence (optional)
chilli sauce, to taste
pepper, to taste
4 hard-boiled eggs
1 egg white
watercress leaves, to garnish

TO SERVE

crudites — raw vegetables of your choice

Cover anchovies in milk and allow to soak for 10 minutes. Drain well.

In a blender or food processor, combine anchovies with mayonnaise, cream, parsley, anchovy essence, chilli sauce and pepper. Add boiled eggs and beat well to combine. Taste and adjust the seasonings.

Whisk egg white until stiff. Fold into anchovy mixture using a spatula. Spoon into a serving dish and level the top. Cover with plastic wrap and refrigerate for several hours.

Garnish with watercress and serve with crudites, such as sticks of celery, carrot, shallots, wedges of cucumber and button mushrooms.

Serves 4

ANCHOVY AND GARLIC STUFFED EGGS

4 eggs
4 large cloves garlic, peeled
45 g butter
salt and pepper, to taste
8 olives
8 anchovy fillets
parsley, chopped
4 small tomatoes

Put eggs in pan of cold water and bring to boil. Add garlic, then remove after 7 minutes and pound in mortar.

After water has boiled 10 minutes, take out eggs, cool in cold water and remove shells. Cut shelled hard-boiled eggs in half lengthways, without damaging their surfaces and leave them to cool.

Put butter in a bowl and beat with a spoon. Remove yolks from eggs, without damaging whites. Mash yolks and add to butter with garlic puree, salt and pepper.

Spoon paste into egg whites. Decorate with an olive with an anchovy fillet wrapped around it. Place on a serving platter with tomatoes and garnish with parsley. Serve cold.

Serves 4

Anchovy and Egg Mousse

CUCUMBER AND GRAPE MOULD

1 large cucumber, peeled and thinly sliced
500 g seedless grapes, halved
450 mL water
1 packet lemon jelly
5 tablespoons lemon juice
3 tablespoons orange juice
1 tablespoon grated onion
pinch cayenne pepper

MARINADE

3 tablespoons olive oil
1 tablespoon wine vinegar
1/4 teaspoon mustard
1/4 teaspoon freshly ground pepper
1/4 teaspoon powdered kelp or *ground sea salt*

Thoroughly mix marinade ingredients and marinate cucumber and grapes for 30 minutes. Heat 150 mL water to near boiling and stir in jelly until dissolved. Add remaining water, lemon and orange juices, onion and cayenne pepper and chill until almost setting.

Drain cucumber and grapes well and reserve a few for garnish. Stir remainder into jelly. Pour into 1.5 litre mould and chill until set. Dip mould in hot water and turn out onto serving plate. Fill centre with reserved cucumber and grapes.

Serves 6–8

PROSCIUTTO AND MELON

300 g prosciutto, in very thin slices
1 honeydew or *rock melon*

Arrange slices of melon on a serving platter and top them with slices of ham. Serve very cold.
Note: Prosciutto crudo, or raw ham can now be found easily in Australia. It should not be too salty, and must always be sliced very thin. A good substitute is *coppa,* which is the shoulder of pork, cured in the same way.
Serves 6

SAVOURY BEIGNETS

oil, for frying
cayenne pepper
½ cup Parmesan cheese

CHOUX PASTRY

1¼ cups water
2 teaspoons caster sugar
100 g butter
2 cups flour, sieved
1 tablespoon Parmesan
pinch salt
5–6 eggs, beaten

Preheat oven to 200°C (400°F). In a large saucepan, bring water, sugar and butter to boil. Remove from heat immediately. Add sieved flour, Parmesan and salt. Mix in well. Return pan to heat and stir continuously until mixture leaves sides of pan. Remove from heat and leave to cool. Gradually add beaten eggs, mixing well, until paste is of a dropping consistency.

Taking teaspoonfuls of choux mixture, deep-fry for 4–5 minutes until golden. Drain on paper towel. Sprinkle with cayenne pepper and Parmesan cheese. Serve piping hot.
Makes 40

CHEESE TWISTS

250 g ready-rolled frozen puff pastry, thawed
⅓ cup grated Parmesan cheese
½ cup grated hard cheese
pinch cayenne
pinch paprika
1 egg, beaten

Preheat oven to 200°C (400°F). Grease baking sheet. Roll out pastry to a 3 mm thick rectangle. Mix cheeses with cayenne and paprika and sprinkle over pastry. Fold pastry over and roll out again to same thickness and width of baking sheet. Brush surface of pastry with egg. Cut into strips 1 cm wide. Twist strips, then arrange on baking sheet.

Bake for 8 minutes or until golden brown. Cut strips in 10 cm lengths. It is usual to bake some of the pastry in 5 cm diameter rings into which bundles of cheese twists can be inserted.
Makes 30 twists

CHEESE-FILLED PASTRIES

125 g feta cheese, well crumbled
2 tablespoons chopped parsley
1 egg yolk
pepper, to taste
5 sheets filo pastry
100 g unsalted butter, melted

Preheat oven to 180°C (350°F). Combine feta, parsley and egg yolk with pepper.

Cut pastry sheets widthways into 3 strips. Place on a dry towel and cover with first a dry and then a damp towel while working. One at a time brush each sheet of pastry with butter and place teaspoonful of filling at 1 end. Fold in sides and roll up. Curve slightly to form a half-moon shape and place on a greased baking sheet. Brush with any remaining butter. Bake for 15–20 minutes or until golden. Serve warm.
Makes 15

Prosciutto and Melon

SAVOURY CHEESE PUFFS

CHOUX PASTRY

50 g butter
½ cup water
60 g flour
2 eggs
60 g grated Gruyere cheese
cayenne

Preheat oven to 220° (425°F). Grease and flour baking trays.

Place butter and water in small saucepan and boil until butter dissolves. Add sifted flour all at once. Stir with wooden spoon until mixture leaves sides of pan and rolls into a ball. Stir over heat 1 minute. Allow to cool.

Combine dough with eggs, grated cheese and cayenne pepper. Using 2 teaspoons or piping bag, place small amounts on prepared trays. Bake 15 minutes, reduce heat to 200°C (400°F) for further 10 minutes until firm.

Serve with cooked chicken or prawns and sauteed mushrooms or the filling of your choice.
Makes 40 small puffs or 8 large ones.

DOLMADES I

250 g vine leaves, fresh or preserved
1 tablespoon oil
1 onion, finely chopped
½ cup long-grain rice
1 cup water
60 g pine nuts
pinch cinnamon
salt and pepper, to taste
1 tablespoon chopped parsley
1 tomato, peeled, seeded and chopped (optional)
1 lemon
extra ½ cup oil

To prepare vine leaves: vine leaves are available in packets, loose, or fresh if you grow your own grapes.

Packaged vine leaves are usually preserved in brine. Rinse them carefully in hot water, snip the stem and place, shiny side down, on a work surface. Loose leaves should be rinsed carefully, blanched in boiling water for 1 minute, then drained. Remove fresh leaves from vine, snip stalk off. Wash very well, then blanch in boiling salted water 3–4 minutes. If the vines have been sprayed, refer to instructions on the can for length of time before grapes, and therefore leaves, are safe to use.

Heat oil, add onion and cook until transparent. Add rice and cook until it absorbs the oil. Add water, pine nuts, cinnamon, and salt and pepper to taste. Bring to boil, cover and simmer over a gentle heat until rice is cooked. Gently stir through parsley and, if desired, tomato.

Place a teaspoon of filling in centre of each leaf. Fold over top and sides and roll up. Place, seam side down, in a heavy-based pan. Any torn leaves should be used to line base of pan and to cover dolmades.

Slice lemon and place on top of dolmades. Pour in oil and add sufficient water to cover. Invert a plate over the vine leaves. Cover pan and gently bring to boil, reduce heat and simmer for 45 minutes.

Allow to cool in pan. Remove plate and drain dolmades. Place on a serving plate, sprinkle with a little extra oil and chill. Serve cold.
Note: When stuffed with rice, dolmades are served cold. Dolmades that have a meat filling are always served hot.
Serves 4–6

DOLMADES II

90 g lentils, washed and picked over
⅓ cup burghul, preferably coarse
1 onion, finely chopped
2 tablespoons oil
60 g dried apricots, finely chopped
2 tablespoons currants
1 tablespoon finely chopped fresh mint
1 tablespoon finely chopped fresh savory or pinch dried savory
salt and pepper, to taste
500 g packet vine leaves
juice 1 lemon
2 tablespoons pine nuts (optional)

Cover lentils with water, bring to boil and simmer, covered, until tender. Drain and place in a bowl. While lentils are cooking, soak burghul in warm water for 30 minutes. Drain in a sieve and press out excess water. Place in bowl with lentils. Fry onion in oil until transparent. Drain and add to lentils and burghul. Add dried fruits, herbs, salt and pepper and combine well.

Place prepared vine leaves, shiny side down, on a work surface. Place a spoonful of filling onto each leaf, fold over top and sides and roll up. Line a saucepan with any damaged leaves. Place stuffed leaves, seam side down, in layers in the pan. Sprinkle with lemon juice. Invert a saucer over leaves and carefully add sufficient water to cover. Bring to boil, reduce heat and simmer, covered, for 45 minutes. Allow to cool to room temperature.

Carefully remove to a serving platter, cover and chill until serving time. For variation, pine nuts can be fried in oil and added to filling.
Note: This version of stuffed vine leaves comes from the Caucasian region of Armenia. If neither fresh nor dried savory is available, it is preferable to omit it rather than substitute another herb.
Makes about 35

Savoury Cheese Puffs with Prawns

BAKED OYSTERS

36 oysters in shell
3 tablespoons finely chopped parsley
freshly ground pepper, to taste
6 tablespoons olive oil
3 tablespoons breadcrumbs
1½ lemons

Arrange oysters in a single layer in an oven dish. Sprinkle parsley on top. Grind a generous quantity of black pepper over them and pour on a little olive oil. Add breadcrumbs, more black pepper and remaining olive oil. Put oysters in a preheated oven at 160°C (325°F) for 15 minutes. Serve very hot with lemon wedges.
Serves 6

ANGELS ON HORSEBACK

12 fresh oysters
6 bacon rashers, rinds removed

Cut bacon into 8 cm long strips and roll 1 around each oyster. Secure with a small skewer and barbecue about 5–10 minutes taking care not to let the bacon burn. Serve hot with seafood sauce.
Makes 12

OYSTERS ROCKEFELLER

24 oysters in the shell or *bottled*
½ bunch spinach
30–60 g butter
6 shallots, finely chopped
5 tablespoons finely chopped parsley
½ cup fine dry breadcrumbs
salt and freshly ground pepper, to taste
cayenne pepper, to taste

Separate oysters from the shell, wash and dry shells well and then place oysters back in shell. Place oysters in baking dish lined with rock salt. If using bottle oysters, drain well and divide between 4 ovenproof serving dishes.

Separate spinach leaves and stalk, roll up leaves and shred finely. Wash and drain leaves then pack into a pan and steam, covered, until tender. Drain well and finely chop.

Melt 30 g butter, add shallots and cook until softened. Add spinach and remaining ingredients and stir to combine. If necessary, add remaining butter to bind mixture. Taste and adjust seasoning. Divide between oysters and bake in a preheated oven at 230°C (450°F) for 7–10 minutes. Arrange on serving plates and serve immediately.
Serves 4

Oysters Rockefeller

HONEYED PRAWNS

1 cup dark honey
1 cup tomato sauce
½ cup salad oil
freshly ground black pepper
1 tablespoon dry mustard
Tabasco sauce, to taste
1 kg cooked large prawns, shelled and deveined

Combine honey, tomato sauce, salad oil, pepper, mustard and Tabasco and blend well. Marinate prawns 15–30 minutes then thread 2–3 prawns on each skewer and grill or barbecue 5–6 minutes. Brush with remaining marinade and turn.
Serves 6–8

Prawn Piggybacks and Honeyed Prawns

PRAWN PIGGYBACKS

500 g uncooked prawns, shelled and deveined, tails on
125 g streaky bacon

MARINADE

juice 2 lemons
equal quantity olive oil
1 tablespoon dried tarragon
freshly ground pepper, to taste
2 cloves garlic, crushed (optional)

Combine lemon juice, oil, tarragon, pepper and garlic and marinate prawns for at least 1 hour, turning occasionally. Thread 4 prawns on each skewer in pairs, turning the second one upside down and reversing direction. Cover with streaky bacon. Grill or barbecue over hot fire, 5–6 minutes taking care not to overcook. Prawns are ready when they turn pink. Just before serving, brush quickly with marinade.
Serves 6–8

PACIFIC PUFFS

25 g butter
50 g white button mushrooms, thinly sliced
2 tablespoons flour
150 mL milk
75 g cooked, peeled prawns
75 g corn kernels
pinch chilli powder
salt and pepper
450 g frozen ready-rolled puff pastry, thawed
beaten egg
oil, for deep-frying

Melt butter in pan and fry mushrooms lightly. Stir in flour and cook 1 minute. Add milk, bring to boil and simmer 1 minute, stirring. Add prawns, corn, chilli and seasoning. Cool until ready to make puffs.

Roll out pastry thinly and cut about 16 × 10 cm rounds. Put a spoonful of mixture in the centre of each round. Brush edges with beaten egg, fold in half and press edges together, crimping them decoratively. Chill for 15 minutes or until you are ready.

Heat oil to 190°C (375°F). Fry puffs in hot oil for 5 minutes, until golden-brown. Drain on paper towel. Makes about 16 puffs.

BARRAMUNDI ROSSINI

625 g barramundi fillets
court bouillon or *vegetable stock*
1 small can crabmeat, drained and flaked or *fresh cooked crab* or *chopped cooked prawns*
3 teaspoons tomato paste
1⅓ cups mayonnaise
3 teaspoons chopped chives
6 anchovy fillets, drained
2 canned pimientos, sliced thinly
salt and pepper, to taste

Poach fish fillets 5 minutes in court bouillon. Drain, cut into bite-size pieces and refrigerate until cold. Combine fish and crab. Mix tomato paste with two-thirds cup mayonnaise, add chives and season to taste. Stir in. Divide into 6 small serving dishes. Pipe or spoon remaining mayonnaise over top. Decorate with anchovies and pimiento slices.
Serves 6

CROSTINI WITH HOT SEAFOOD

50 g butter
250 g (net weight) seafood: prawns, scallops, oysters, etc
1 clove garlic, crushed
1 teaspoon tomato paste
1 tablespoon chopped parsley or *chopped basil*
3 tablespoons white wine
salt and pepper, to taste
8 slices French bread

Melt butter in a small pan and add finely chopped seafood, garlic, tomato paste and chopped parsley. Moisten with white wine and simmer 2 minutes. Add freshly ground pepper and a little salt if necessary.

Fry bread in a little oil and top it with mixture. Serve immediately.

Note: Crostini are a typical feature of Italian snack bars, and the variety of their toppings is endless. At home they are often served between meals or as a light first course.
Serves 4–8

Crostini with Hot Seafood

Barramundi Rossini

DRINKS FOR ALL

A party is not a party without a selection of appetising drinks to embellish your delicious food. With originality and flair, you can concoct your own thirst-quenchers, whether innocuous non-alcoholic drinks or something packing a little more punch.

Raise party spirits with the compelling flavour of Strawberry Daiquiri — it lingers on long after thirst has been satisfied. Your guests will be unable to resist Paradise Pineapple — an exotic blend of brandy, rum and liqueur with pineapple nectar. Zesty Bloody Mary is sure to please — the ultimate tomato and vodka pick-me-up.

Alcoholic amounts are entirely up to you and can be omitted entirely if you would rather serve tangy, refreshing, non-alcoholic fruit cups.

For those extra special effects, serve drinks in long-stemmed glasses pre-chilled in the freezer to add a light frosting of ice. A sprinkling of fresh herbs or ground spices and a wedge of fruit add the perfect finishing touches.

Mango and Coconut Delight (rear) and Zesty Bloody Mary

Drinks

Paradise Pineapple

ZESTY BLOODY MARY

2¼ cups tomato juice
1¼ cups vodka
1½ teaspoons Worcestershire sauce
½ teaspoon chilli sauce
¾ teaspoon celery salt
¼ teaspoon garlic powder
juice 3 limes or lemons
ice cubes

Mix all ingredients together, then pour over ice cubes into tall glasses.
Makes 3½ cups

MANGO AND COCONUT DELIGHT

2 mangoes, peeled, seeded and roughly chopped
1 cup coconut milk
1 large lemon, juiced
½ lemon, finely grated
1 tablespoon honey or to taste
1 teaspoon vanilla essence
1 cup crushed ice

GARNISH

6 slices lemon, sliced thinly
mint sprigs

Combine all ingredients and process for 20–30 seconds until smooth and creamy. Pour into tall chilled glasses. To serve, garnish with lemon and mint.
Serves 6

SUNDOWNER

ice cubes
1 jigger Galliano
1 jigger Cointreau
1 jigger brandy
2 jiggers lemon juice
lemon slices, to serve

Pre-chill goblets. Crush enough ice to half-fill glasses. Blend remaining ingredients and pour over ice in goblets. Decorate with lemon.
Serves 4–6

PINEAPPLE NECTAR

1 large ripe pineapple

Peel, core and chop pineapple. In a processor, puree until smooth. Strain through fine sieve, pressing down well on pulp with back of spoon. Sealed in a jar this will keep up to 7 days in refrigerator.
Makes 3 cups

MULBERRY FRUIT CUP

500 g ripe mulberries
1 cup sugar
2 litres water
juice 1 lemon
strip lemon rind
sherry (optional)

Boil all ingredients except sherry together for 20 minutes. Strain and chill thoroughly. Serve with 1 teaspoon sherry per glass, if liked, and ice cubes.
Makes 2.5 lites

PASSIONA PUNCH

1½ cups water
1½ cups sugar
1½ teaspoons tartaric acid
pulp 48 passionfruit

Boil water, sugar and tartaric acid until sugar dissolves. While still boiling add passionfruit, beating with a fork for 3 minutes to extract all the juice. Pour into bowl, mix well and bottle.

To serve, add a small quantity to a glass of water or soda water. If well corked it will keep for some time.
Makes 2½ cups

PLANTATION PUNCH

dash Angostura bitters
1 banana
1 teaspoon caster sugar
dash vanilla
¼ cup milk
1 jigger light rum
3 ice cubes
nutmeg, to serve

Pre-chill tall glasses; when lightly frosted combine all ingredients and blend. Decorate with a sprinkling of nutmeg to serve.
Serves 1

JAMAICAN FLOAT

1½ tablespoons fresh orange juice
1½ tablespoons fresh lemon juice
2 teaspoons Orgeate or Maraschino
3 teaspoons brandy
1½ tablespoons light rum
3 ice cubes

TO SERVE:

2 ice cubes
3 teaspoons rum Negrita
dash grenadine
2 ice cubes

Blend first 6 ingredients, increasing quantity as required. Half-fill a tall chilled glass.

To serve, blend remaining 4 ingredients, float on top of prepared drink and serve garnished with a thin slice of orange.
Serves 1

STRAWBERRY DAIQUIRI

8 ice cubes
1 punnet strawberries, hulled
2 tablespoons caster sugar
6 jiggers white rum
juice 2 limes or *1 lemon*

Crush ice and place in well-chilled glasses. Blend all remaining ingredients and pour over crushed ice. Serve immediately.
Serves 4–6

PARADISE PINEAPPLE

2 jiggers pineapple nectar
2 slices fresh pineapple
dash Orgeate or *Maraschino*
½ jigger brandy
1 jigger light rum
3 ice cubes
mint sprigs, to serve

Pre-chill goblets; when lightly frosted, blend all ingredients. Decorate with mint sprig to serve.
Serves 1

ALOHA PUNCH

⅓ cup sugar
⅓ cup water
8 whole cloves
1 stick cinnamon
3 cups pineapple juice
3 cups orange juice
⅓ cup lemon juice
2 tablespoons rum
1 litre bottle ginger ale
ice cubes

Combine sugar, water, cloves and cinnamon stick and simmer for 5 minutes. Allow to cool then strain into fruit juices. Chill thoroughly. To serve, mix with rum, ginger ale and ice cubes.
Makes 2.5 litres

SPECIAL OCCASIONS MENUS

Special occasion parties are times of particular good cheer and good company — particularly when it's been a while since you were last together. Nothing is more heart-warming than being welcomed into someone's home to share a festivity or special date. Gathering for a celebration gives entertaining spirits added boost.

Because of its intimacy, Dinner for Two is the occasion to go all out with foods which in larger quantities would wreck the budget — a rack of hothouse lamb and hearts of palm. It goes without saying that a dinner for two should be easy on the cook, who is also a guest, so this menu can be prepared ahead in part and quickly put together. The aperitif is, of course, champagne. The lighting style — low.

A Mother's Day Breakfast offers an extravagant way to say thank you for everything, with a flexible menu that can be stretched or shortened with ease. The food can range from something as simple as fruit and champagne to eggs and baked goods or both. Seldom does breakfast involve complex dishes that take a long time to cook, but few other 'special' meals are more appreciated. Flowers on the tray are obligatory.

A Family Celebration for Four is one of the easiest of all special occasion meals, not because you've hardly troubled yourself, but because everyone knows and loves one another. In this menu, the accent is French. The chicken was created in the French province of Normandy to make the best use of native products such as apples, cider, cream and apple brandy. The combination of sweet and ordinary potatoes to make a smooth puree is an inspired combination, as is the tropical entree combining avocados and quail eggs. The Black Forest Gateau is a silk purse concocted with a little patience from ingredients everyone has on hand. A light white wine such as fume blanc would be good with the chicken or cider if you prefer.

Forks and Fingers Party for Four uses a variety of Indonesian dishes perfect for relaxed informal entertaining. A fine selection of sambals is followed by one of the world's favourite dishes, Nasi Goreng, and finished off with an exotic dessert.

South of the Border Teenage Party offers spicy Mexican food ideal for a teenage buffet with dips, corn chips, substantial snacks and a delectable Fruit Flan that can be prepared in minutes.

Buffet for Ten to Twelve gives the adults a most sophisticated menu from which to sample such delights as Ham Mousse, Seafood Fettuccine, Turkey Breasts with Sour Cherry Sauce and two wonderful desserts.

Lunch in the Garden for Eight provides sparkling dishes for no-fuss al fresco entertaining. Delicious to look at and to eat, they take little time to prepare yet give your guests much to appreciate and remember.

A Family Celebration for Four — one of the easiest of all special occasion menus

BUFFET
FOR TEN TO TWELVE

Buffets are the ideal solution when entertaining larger groups. The following recipes help make the table a feast for the eyes, and the appetite. Most of the recipes can be made the day before.

MENU

Ham Mousse with Cumberland Sauce
Seafood Fettuccine
Turkey Breast with Sour Cherry Sauce
Broccoli with Horseradish
Cassata Torte

Served with Chardonnay and
Cabernet Sauvignon

PREPARATION TIMETABLE

1 day ahead: prepare Ham Mousse and refrigerate until ready to unmould and serve. Prepare Cumberland Sauce, cover and refrigerate. Prepare turkey breasts. If serving cold, bake, cool, cover and refrigerate. Prepare Sour Cherry Sauce. Cover and refrigerate. Prepare Cassata Torte cakes and buttercreams. Store cakes in an airtight container. Cover and refrigerate buttercreams.
6 hours ahead: Prepare and bake Seafood Fettuccine. Cover and refrigerate. Blanch broccoli and prepare horseradish sauce. Cover and refrigerate. Chill beverages.
3 hours ahead: Assemble and decorate Cassata Torte. Chill in refrigerator. Prepare garnishes.
1 hour ahead: Remove Seafood Fettuccine from refrigerator to return to room temperature. If serving turkey breasts hot, bake in oven and keep warm until ready to carve. If serving cold, carve, arrange on serving platter, cover and refrigerate until serving time.
30 minutes ahead: reheat Seafood Fettuccine. Unmould Ham Mousse onto a serving plate. Decorate and chill until serving time. Open red wine.
15 minutes ahead: carve hot turkey breasts and keep warm in a low oven. Reheat broccoli. Arrange in a serving dish mask with sauce.
Time for dinner: arrange hot turkey breasts on a serving platter. Dress hot or cold turkey breasts with sauce. Garnish and serve.
Dessert: Transfer the Cassata Torte to a serving platter. Slice this impressive dessert at the table.

Clockwise from far left: Cassata Torte, Cumberland Sauce, Ham Mousse, Turkey Breast with Sour Cherry Sauce, Broccoli with Horseradish, Seafood Fettuccine

HAM MOUSSE

¾ cup finely minced ham
1 cup beef consomme
1 cup tomato juice
½ teaspoon paprika
1½ tablespoons gelatine softened in *4 tablespoons cold beef stock*
2 cups cream, beaten to hold shape
1 tablespoon sherry
salt, to taste

TO SERVE

sprigs fresh watercress
cherry tomatoes

Precoat a 6-cup mould with clear aspic. Allow to set. Process the ham and mix with consomme, tomato juice and paprika. Bring to the boil in saucepan. Add gelatine mixture and stir until dissolved. Strain mixture through fine sieve. Cool, stirring, over ice. When thickened slightly, add beaten cream flavoured with sherry and salt to taste.

Fill the mould with mousse and chill thoroughly until set. Unmould onto a serving plate. Decorate with watercress and cherry tomatoes. The cherry tomatoes may be hollowed out and filled with piped cream cheese with tiny shreds of preserved ginger mixed through.

Serve with Cumberland Sauce *(see recipe)*.

CUMBERLAND SAUCE

1 cup redcurrant jelly
1 shallot
1 tablespoon chopped lemon and orange rind, mixed
¼ cup port
1 tablespoon lemon juice
1 tablespoon orange juice
¼ teaspoon dry mustard
salt and cayenne pepper, to taste

Melt the redcurrant jelly, add the remaining ingredients and simmer gently for 3–4 minutes. Allow to cool and thicken.

BECHAMEL SAUCE

20 g butter
1 tablespoon flour
1 cup milk

Melt butter in a medium-sized pan. When foaming, add flour and stir over low heat 3 minutes. Remove from heat and gradually add milk, stirring constantly. Return to heat and cook, stirring until boiling. Cook a further 3 minutes.

SEAFOOD FETTUCCINE

500 g thin egg noodles
245 g butter
700 g filleted white fish, cut into 2 cm pieces
white part of 1 small leek, sliced
⅔ cup dry white wine
1 cup fish stock
1 cup Bechamel Sauce (see recipe)
1 cup cream
½ teaspoon salt
pinch cayenne pepper
1 teaspoon lemon juice
250 g prawns and scallops
180 g parmesan cheese, grated

Cook noodles in boiling water 8 minutes. Drain, rinse and cool slightly. Toss 40 g butter through and cover.

Heat 80 g butter in pan, add fish and saute with sliced leek. Add wine and fish stock, bring to boil and simmer 1 minute. Remove fish and reduce liquid by half. Add Bechamel Sauce, cream, salt, and cayenne and cook gently until sauce is smooth and glossy but not thick. Remove from heat, add lemon juice and strain.

Saute prawns and scallops gently in 125 g butter. Do not overcook. Combine fish, prawns and scallops.

Place one-third of noodles in an oblong casserole, cover with half the fish mixture and one-third of the grated cheese, sauce and melted butter. Repeat for second layer. Top with the remaining noodles, sauce and melted butter.

Bake in a hot oven 200°C (400°F) for 10–15 minutes until golden.

Note: This dish may be prepared earlier in the day, covered with aluminium foil and kept in refrigerator. Allow to return to room temperature before reheating.

SOUR CHERRY SAUCE

450 g can pitted sour cherries
2 tablespoons brandy
2 tablespoons brown sugar
2 tablespoons malt vinegar
1 cup strong chicken stock
½ cup orange juice
2 tablespoons grated orange rind
grated rind and juice ½ lemon
2 tablespoons cornflour

Drain cherries and set aside, reserving 1 tablespoon juice for turkey forcemeat. Mix remaining cherry juice with brandy.

Boil brown sugar and malt vinegar until caramelised. When cool add chicken stock, orange juice and rind, lemon juice, brandy and cherry juice.

Dissolve 2 tablespoons cornflour with water, add to sauce and cook to thicken. Stir in pan juices from turkey, first removing fat and straining. Add cherries and serve.

TURKEY BREAST

4 whole turkey fillets
½ cup brandy
2 tablespoons dry mustard
20 g butter, melted
watercress, for garnish (optional)

FORCEMEAT

4 cups breadcrumbs or *cooked rice*
60 g chopped prunes
60 g chopped dried apricots
2 small onions, chopped and sauteed
salt and freshly ground pepper, to taste
finely grated orange rind and *lemon rind, to taste*
mixed herbs
1 egg, beaten
1 tablespoon sour cherry juice, reserved from sauce recipe

Mix all the forcemeat ingredients together, binding with the egg and 1 tablespoon sour cherry juice.

Open out the turkey fillets and flatten slightly. Brush the inside of the breast with half the brandy and sprinkle over the mustard. Stuff with the forcemeat and skewer in place. Brush with remaining brandy and mustard. Place in baking pan, cover with greased aluminium foil and bake at 160°C (325°F) for 20–30 minutes basting during cooking time.

Remove the breasts from oven. Allow to stand 10 minutes before carving. Slice and arrange on serving platter. Dress with a little Sour Cherry Sauce and serve rest separately. Garnish with watercress if desired.

Note: The dish may be prepared beforehand if it is served cold.

Large turkey breasts may be used for this recipe to give your buffet a more lavish approach. These need to be ordered at least 1 day in advance from a fresh chicken shop or frozen foot outlet. Chicken breasts make a suitable substitute. Use 8 breasts, make a pocket in 1 side of each breast and stuff. Secure with toothpicks and bake according to the recipe. Carve each breast on the diagonal for serving.

BROCCOLI WITH HORSERADISH

100 g butter
¾ cup mayonnaise
2 tablespoons horseradish cream
2 tablespoons grated onion
¼ teaspoon salt
¼ teaspoon dry mustard
paprika, to taste
1 large bunch fresh broccoli or *2 packets frozen*
1 tablespoon lemon juice

Combine 80 g melted butter, mayonnaise, horseradish, grated onion, salt, mustard and paprika and chill.

Boil broccoli 8 minutes, or until crispy tender. Drain and refresh in cold water. Reheat with a little lemon and 20 g butter and serve with sauce.

CASSATA TORTE

8 eggs
1 cup caster sugar
160 g unsalted butter
1½ cups flour, sifted
1 teaspoon baking powder

BUTTERCREAM

2 tablespoons instant coffee powder
½ cup warm milk
300 g butter
5 cups icing sugar, sieved
200 g glace cherries
325 g can pineapple pieces, drained
60 g angelica, chopped
3 tablespoons Kirsch
⅔ cup chopped nuts
½ cup cream, whipped

Preheat oven to 190°C (375°F). Place eggs and sugar in a heatproof bowl over hot water. Whisk until thick and whisk leaves trail when removed from mixture. Remove from heat and continue to whisk until cool.

Melt unsalted butter and cool but do not allow to set. Gently fold small quantities of flour into egg mixture alternately with melted butter. Finish with flour and baking powder. Pour mixture into 2 × 20 cm greased and paper-lined cake tins, bake for 35–40 minutes. Cool cake on wire rack.

To make buttercream, dissolve coffee powder in a little of the warm milk. Cream butter and beat in sugar a little at a time. Beat in coffee flavouring. Add sufficient warm milk to soften mixture. Reserve 9 cherries and 9 pineapple pieces. Stir chopped angelica, and remaining cherries and pineapple into half of the buttercream.

Split each cake into 2 layers. Sprinkle with Kirsch and sandwich together with fruity buttercream. Coat top and sides with plain buttercream, reserving some for piping. Decorate cake with reserved buttercream and fruit. If the weather is hot keep refrigerated until serving.

SOUTH-OF-THE BORDER TEENAGE PARTY

Here is an ideal menu for a buffet with flavours that will find favour with all age groups. There's ample food to satisfy hungry teenagers and the Fruit Flan and Sangria Punch are absolute winners for this age group. In fact, just looking at such a delectable and colourful array of food is enough to stimulate young appetites.

MENU

Guacamole
Hot Bean Dip

Mexican Chicken
Chilli con Carne
Spicy Mexican Rice and Sausages
Mexican Corn on the Cob

Fruit Flan

Served with non-alcoholic Sangria Punch

PREPARATION TIMETABLE

Make ahead and freeze: Mexican Chicken, Chilli con Carne.
1 day ahead: prepare Guacamole and store in a screwtop jar (including avocado seed) in refrigerator. Prepare and cook Mexican Chicken and Chilli con Carne. Cover and refrigerate until ready to reheat and serve. Prepare and bake pastry bases. When cool, cover flan tins and refrigerate until ready to fill. Prepare and briefly cook vegetable sticks to serve with Guacamole and refrigerate in a plastic bag. Fill ice cube trays and freeze for Sangria Punch.
6 hours ahead: prepare Spicy Mexican Rice and Sausages up to stage of adding tomatoes. Cover and refrigerate until ready to reheat and serve. Prepare topping mixture and corn cobs for Mexican Corn on the Cob. Chill beverages.
3 hours ahead: prepare filling and fruit topping for Fruit Flan. Puree peaches, slice apples and squeeze juices for Sangria Punch.
1 hour ahead: fill and decorate Fruit Flan. Prepare garnishes. Slice avocado (pour over lemon juice to prevent browning) and grate cheese for Hot Bean Dip.
30 minutes ahead: Spoon Guacamole into serving bowl and arrange vegetable sticks on a platter. Assemble and bake Hot Bean Dip. Cook Corn Cobs and keep warm in oven. Reheat Mexican Chicken, Chilli con Carne, Spicy Mexican Rice and Sausages.
15 minutes ahead: make glaze for Fruit Flan and brush over fruit. Refrigerate until serving time. Combine Sangria Punch ingredients in a punch bowl.
Time for dinner: spoon topping over corn cobs, garnish and serve immediately. Garnish other dishes and serve.
Dessert: transfer flan to serving plates, slice and serve.

Clockwise from left: Chilli con Carne, Sangria Punch, Mexican Corn on the Cob, Hot Bean Dip (centre), Fruit Flan, Mexican Chicken, Guacamole

GUACAMOLE

4 ripe avocados
juice 2 lemons or *limes*
1 teaspoon salt (optional)
2 large onions, grated
2 cloves garlic, crushed
2 teaspoons curry powder
pinch cayenne
few drops Tabasco sauce (optional)
chopped red chillies, for garnish
taco or *corn chips, for serving*

Mash avocados with fork or blend in food processor. Add lemon juice and salt. Add remaining ingredients to avocado. Cover with plastic wrap and chill to serve. Spoon into 2 bowls before serving.

Note: If guacamole is to be used for salad dressing, omit curry and blend in a little olive oil to dilute the mixture, or mayonnaise instead of oil may also be used. Garnish with chopped red chillies. Serve with taco chips and vegetable sticks.

For this versatile Mexican dish, it is good to look for over-ripe avocados. These can often be purchased cheaply, and the mixture can be made and frozen for later use. Guacamole can be served as a starter on a lettuce leaf, or as a party dip to be eaten with taco chips. If preparing in advance, mash avocados with a wooden spoon and store the finished guacamole in a jar with the avocado seeds. This will prevent discolouring.

HOT BEAN DIP

2 packets corn chips
250 g Cheddar cheese, grated
300 mL sour cream
425 g can refried beans
1 avocado, peeled, seeded and sliced

Place a layer of corn chips on a heatproof serving platter. Sprinkle with some Cheddar cheese and top with alternating layers of sour cream, refried beans and more corn chips. Sprinkle remaining cheese on the top.

Bake at 150°C (300°F) for 30 minutes or until heated through and cheese has melted.

Serve garnished with avocado.

CHILLI CON CARNE

¼ cup oil
3 onions, chopped
2 cloves garlic, crushed
1 kg minced beef
780 g canned red kidney beans, drained
800 g can peeled tomatoes
2 teaspoons paprika
2 teaspoons chilli powder, or to taste

Heat oil in large pan, add onions and garlic and gently saute until soft. Add minced beef and fry until evenly browned. Stir in beans, tomatoes, paprika and chilli powder. Cover and simmer gently for 45–50 minutes. Adjust seasoning and serve hot.

SPICY MEXICAN RICE AND SAUSAGES

500 g pork sausages
150 g butter
500 g frankfurts
2 large onions, chopped
1 red capsicum, seeded and finely chopped
1 green capsicum, seeded and finely chopped
1½ cups long-grain rice
chilli powder, to taste
1 litre chicken stock
2 tablespoons tomato paste
1 cup canned corn kernels, drained
freshly ground black pepper, to taste
4 tomatoes, cut into wedges
2 teaspoons snipped chives, for garnish

Boil pork sausages in water for 10 minutes (to remove excess fat) and drain.

Melt butter and fry frankfurts and sausages over medium heat 4–5 minutes, shaking pan to prevent sticking. Remove sausages from pan and cut into chunks.

Fry onions and capsicums until onions are lightly golden. Add rice and chilli powder and cook over gentle head 2–3 minutes, stirring all the time.

Add stock, tomato paste, corn, sausage pieces and seasoning. Bring to boil, stir well, reduce heat and simmer gently for 15 minutes until rice is tender and liquid is thoroughly absorbed.

Add tomatoes to pan for the last 5 minutes of cooking. Sprinkle with snipped chives and serve.

MEXICAN CHICKEN

14 chicken pieces
seasoned flour
¼ cup oil
3 large onions, sliced
2 cloves garlic, crushed
½–1 teaspoon chilli powder, to taste
1 tablespoon sesame seeds
½ teaspoon oregano
¾ cup dry red wine
1 cup chicken stock
1 cup slivered almonds
1 cup stuffed olives, sliced
450 g can corn kernels, drained
1 red capsicum, diced
1 teaspoon cornflour

Dust chicken pieces lightly in flour. Heat oil and brown chicken in pan on both sides. Place in casserole.

Add onions and garlic to pan. Cook till soft, stirring to prevent sticking. Stir in chilli powder, sesame seeds, oregano, wine and stock. Pour this over chicken pieces.

Cover casserole and cook in preheated oven at 180°C (350°F) for 1 hour. Add remaining ingredients except cornflour.

Fifteen minutes before serving, blend cornflour with a little liquid from the casserole dish, pour over chicken. Return chicken to oven for 10–15 minutes or until sauce has thickened. Serve hot.

MEXICAN CORN ON THE COB

4 hard-boiled eggs
40 g butter, softened
4 tablespoons thickened cream
½ teaspoon Tabasco sauce
2 tablespoons chopped parsley
salt and freshly ground pepper, to taste
5 corn cobs
4 teaspoons sugar

Mash eggs with fork till smooth. Blend in butter then stir in cream, Tabasco, parsley and seasoning to taste.

Cut each corn cob into 3 pieces. Cook in boiling water with sugar 20–30 minutes or until tender. Drain.

Serve cobs hot, topped with egg and butter mixture.

FRUIT FLAN

PASTRY BASES

4 sheets ready-rolled shortcrust pastry
1 egg, beaten

FILLING

500 g cream cheese, softened
1 teaspoon cinnamon
1 cup caster sugar
juice and grated rind 1 lemon

TOPPING

1 honeydew melon, seeded and scooped into balls
300 g muscat grapes, stems removed
½ rock melon, seeded and scooped into balls
½ honeydew melon, seeded and scooped into balls
2 punnets strawberries, hulled
2 kiwi fruit, peeled and sliced

GLAZE

1 cup apricot jam, warmed and sieved
½ cup orange juice or *water*

Preheat oven to 200°C (400°F). Join 2 pastry sheets together, pressing join firmly. Repeat with remaining 2 sheets. Grease 2 × 22 cm flan tins, press pastry gently into base and bake blind 10 minutes. Remove baking beans and prick pastry base with fork. Return to oven for a further 5–10 minutes. Cool completely before filling. Do not fill more than 3 hours before serving.

Combine filling ingredients and beat until smooth and creamy. Spoon equal amounts into the flan cases and smooth top of each with a spatula. Refrigerate until firm — about 1 hour.

Top with decoratively arranged fruit.

Combine glaze ingredients and lightly brush over fruit. Chill before serving.

SANGRIA PUNCH

1.6 kg canned peaches, pureed and chilled
2 apples, cored and thinly sliced
2 bottles non-alcoholic red wine, chilled
1 teaspoon allspice
sugar (optional)
juice 4 oranges
½ cup lemon juice
ice cubes

Place the peach puree and apples in a punchbowl and pour in the wine. Add the allspice and a few teaspoons of sugar if a sweeter drink is preferred. Add the orange and lemon juices and plenty of ice cubes and stir gently with a wooden spoon until the wine is thoroughly chilled.

LUNCH IN THE GARDEN FOR EIGHT

Eating out-of-doors always makes you appreciate good food even more. Finding a shady part of the garden, decorating an elegant table and serving colourful food will be more inviting to your guests than a no-fuss lunch inside. The no fuss menu will care for itself so relax in the fresh air without worrying about stove top failures.

MENU

Gazpacho

Cannelloni with Olives
Tomato and Feta Cheese Salad

Paella
Baked Bream and Orange

Creme Caramel

Served with Rose

PREPARATION TIMETABLE

1 day ahead: prepare Gazpacho. Store in a covered container in refrigerator. Prepare garlic flavoured croutons and keep in an airtight container. Fill ice cube trays and freeze. Prepare Cannelloni with Olives. Cover and refrigerate until ready to heat and serve. Prepare Creme Caramel and cook. When cooled, chill in refrigerator.
6 hours before: prepare vegetables for garnishing and serving with Gazpacho. Chill in refrigerator. Prepare stuffing mixture for Baked Bream and Orange. Refrigerate until ready to use. Prepare fish. Cover and refrigerate. Chill beverages.
3 hours ahead: prepare Tomato and Feta Cheese Salad. Prepare salad dressing. Prepare seafood, chicken and other ingredients for Paella.
1 hour ahead: prepare garnishes. Whip cream for Creme Caramel.
30 minutes ahead: cook Paella and Cannelloni with Olives. Complete preparation of Baked Bream and Orange.
15 minutes ahead: Bake fish. Place prepared vegetables to accompany Gazpacho into serving bowls.
Time for dinner: pour soup over ice cubes and top with croutons. Garnish and serve Paella, Cannelloni with Olives and Baked Bream and Orange. Pour dressing over salad and serve.
Dessert: turn out Creme Caramel moulds onto serving plates, garnish and serve.

Clockwise from left: Cannelloni with Olives, Gazpacho, Baked Bream and Orange, Tomato and Feta Cheese Salad, Paella

GAZPACHO

2–3 cloves garlic, crushed
1 teaspoon salt
1 tablespoon sugar
2 teaspoons cumin
1 tablespoon paprika
120 mL olive oil
2 tablespoons wine vinegar
pinch cayenne pepper
1.6 kg canned peeled tomatoes
1 litre chicken stock (can be made with stock cubes)
1 cucumber, peeled and diced
1 bunch shallots, chopped
1 green capsicum, diced
2 cups croutons

Combine and blend first 8 ingredients. When thick, add tomatoes and blend. Pour into large bowl and add stock. Add cucumber dice, cover and place in refrigerator for several hours to chill.

To serve place ice cubes in a bowl, pour over soup and sprinkle shallots and capsicum on top. Serve with croutons.

PAELLA

3 tablespoons oil
2 onions, sliced
1 clove garlic, crushed
1 cup long-grain rice
4 cups tomato juice, boiling
¼ teaspoon turmeric
pinch freshly ground pepper
2 cups cooked, cubed chicken
250 g prawns, shelled and deveined
6 mussels, in the shell, scrubbed and bearded
1 cup frozen peas
½ cup stuffed olives, sliced

Heat oil and saute onion and garlic lightly. Add rice, tomato juice, turmeric and pepper. Cook covered for 20 minutes, stirring occasionally, until rice is tender and liquid is absorbed.

Stir in chicken, prawns, mussels and peas to cook. Heat until prawns turn pink, stirring occasionally.

Stir through olives. Serve hot from pan.

CANNELLONI WITH OLIVES

1 tablespoon oil
2 onions, chopped
350 g minced beef
1½ tablespoons tomato paste
1 teaspoon chopped fresh basil
1 teaspoon sugar
8 stuffed olives
freshly ground pepper, to taste
8 cannelloni tubes, ready to bake
1 tomato, thinly sliced

SAUCE

30 g butter
¼ cup flour
1½ cups milk
¼ cup cream
1 teaspoon prepared mustard
salt and freshly ground pepper to taste
1 cup grated Cheddar cheese

Preheat oven to 190°C (375°F). Heat oil and saute onion until soft. Add minced beef and cook until browned. Stir in tomato paste, basil and sugar. Chop 6 olives and add to beef mixture; season with salt and pepper.

Using piping bag or spoon, fill cannelloni tubes with mixture. Place in shallow ovenproof dish.

To make sauce, melt butter in a saucepan, add flour and cook 1 minute. Remove from heat and add liquid gradually. Return to heat and simmer 2–3 minutes stirring constantly until thickened. Flavour with mustard, salt and pepper. Stir in most of the cheese, keeping some for top.

Pour sauce over cannelloni, sprinkle with remaining cheese and bake 20 minutes. Decorate with sliced olives and tomato. Serve hot, 1 cannelloni per person.

TOMATO AND FETA CHEESE SALAD

1 cos lettuce, well washed
2 tomatoes, cut into quarters
250 g feta cheese, diced
1 white onion, sliced
½ cup black olives
¼ cup Walnut Dressing (see recipe)

Line a salad bowl with the lettuce and top with remaining ingredients. Cover and chill well before serving.

BAKED BREAM AND ORANGE

2 large oranges, peeled and segmented
1 large onion, finely sliced
2 cloves garlic, crushed
40 g butter
2 tablespoons parsley, chopped
freshly ground pepper
1 cup bean sprouts
½ cup slivered almonds, toasted
½ cup red and green capsicum, seeded and chopped
2 whole silver bream (about 1 kg each)
1¼ cups orange juice
Italian parsley, to garnish

Dice half the orange segments. Lightly saute onion and garlic with butter. Add diced orange segments, parsley and seasonings and cook lightly a further 2 minutes. Add bean sprouts, almonds and capsicums.

Trim fish tail and fins using kitchen scissors and remove any scales still attached. Season cavity then stuff each with above orange and onion mixture.

Place fish in large ovenproof dish and cover with orange juice. Top with buttered greaseproof paper. Bake at 180°C (350°F) for approximately 20 minutes or until flesh flakes easily. Arrange remaining orange segments over fish and garnish with parsley.

Serve hot, dividing each fish into 4 equal pieces.

CREME CARAMEL

½ cup water
2¾ cups sugar
1 egg
1 egg yolk
3 tablespoons water
vanilla essence, to taste
700 mL milk
Spun Sugar (see recipe)
300 mL cream, whipped for serving.

Bring ½ cup water and 1 cup sugar to the boil in a heavy-based saucepan. Boil without stirring until mixture is a rich golden caramel colour. Pour caramel into 1 large mould, coating the base and sides, or into 8 individual ramekin dishes. Set aside to cool.

Preheat oven to 180°C (350°F). Combine eggs, 1¾ cups sugar, 3 tablespoons water and vanilla essence. Heat milk, without boiling, and gradually whisk into egg mixture. Strain and pour into mould. Place mould in a baking tin half-filled with water and bake 40–50 minutes, or until set. Individual moulds will only take 20 minutes to cook. Test by inserting a butter knife into the custard. If the knife comes out clean, the custard is set.

Chill thoroughly before turning out onto serving dish. Pour any caramel remaining in the mould around the dish and decorate with Spun Sugar if desired.
Serve with whipped cream.

Creme Caramel

SPUN SUGAR

1 cup caster sugar
pinch cream of tartar
½ cup water

Combine all the ingredients in a small saucepan and heat, gently stirring until the sugar dissolves. Using a wet pastry brush, brush away remaining crystals from the side of the pan as these will cause the syrup to crystallise.

Increase the heat and boil until a rich golden colour. Allow to cool slightly. Working over sheets of baking paper dip two forks into the syrup, join together then draw apart to form fine threads of toffee. Work quickly before the toffee sets and remember that it is very hot. When all the toffee has been used carefully lift the threads from the paper and place a little on top of each cream caramel.
Note: Do not attempt this if the weather is humid as the spun sugar will dissolve within moments of making. Prepare just before serving.

FAMILY CELEBRATION FOR FOUR

Almost every family can testify that once in a while there is cause for celebration. Birthdays, graduation, home comings, engagements or even a sporting victory all deserve their moment of triumph. Serving the following menu is sure to please family members of all ages. To complete the meal, the Black Forest Gateau decorated with chocolate leaves and cherries will delight the guest of honour.

MENU

Avocado and Egg Salad

Chicken Normandy
Sweet Potatoes Duchesse
Broad Beans

Black Forest Gateau

Served with Fume Blanc

PREPARATION TIMETABLE

Prepare ahead and freeze: Black Forest Cake (not topping or filling).
1 day ahead: prepare Sweet Potatoes Duchesse mixture. Store in an airtight container in refrigerator. Prepare filling for Chicken Normandy. Cover and chill in refrigerator. Prepare breadcrumbs and chop cashew nuts. Store in an airtight container.
6 hours ahead: prepare salad ingredients with the exception of sliced avocado. Cover and refrigerate. Make salad dressing. Prepare chicken breasts; enclose filling, dip in flour, egg and crumbs. Place on a tray and refrigerate. Chill Fume Blanc wine.
3 hours ahead: prepare chocolate leaves and curls. Drain cherries and whip cream. Assemble Black Forest Cake, decorate and chill until serving time. Prepare garnishes for other dishes.
1 hour ahead: prepare sauce for Chicken Normandy. Cover with plastic wrap to prevent skin forming and chill until ready to reheat. Pipe sweet potato rosettes onto greased baking tray. Cover lightly with plastic wrap and set aside in refrigerator.
30 minutes ahead: cook broad beans and refresh with cold water. Cover and set aside. Brown prepared chicken breasts and bake in oven.
15 minutes ahead: arrange salad on individual plates. Bake Sweet Potatoes Duchesse. Heat Broad Beans in Tarragon Butter and lemon. Reheat sauce for Chicken Normandy.
Time for dinner: dress individual salads. Strain sauce and pour into sauce boats. Garnish dishes and serve.

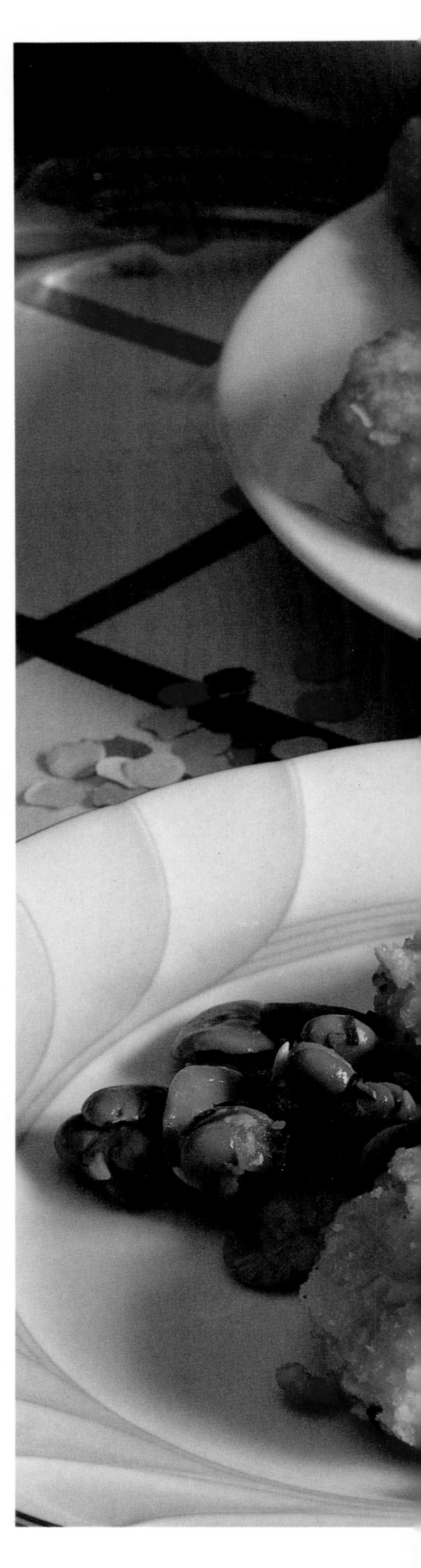

Chicken Normandy and Sweet Potatoes Duchesse

AVOCADO AND EGG SALAD

1 green capsicum (pepper)
1 red capsicum (pepper)
1 cos lettuce
1 large avocado or *2 small, peeled, seeded and sliced*
12 quail eggs, boiled for 2 minutes or *6 hard-boiled eggs*
12 cherry tomatoes
small bunch chives, cut into 3 cm lengths
mustard cress

DRESSING

¼ cup vegetable oil
1 tablespoon vinegar
salt and freshly ground pepper, to taste
1 teaspoon Dijon mustard

Wash capsicums. Slit and remove stalks, seeds and membranes. Blanch capsicums; refresh. Slice lengthways into julienne strips.

Wash and dry lettuce and arrange leaves on 4 individual plates. Fill each with sliced avocado, 3 quail eggs and 3 tomatoes. Garnish salads with chives, capsicums and mustard cress.

Combine dressing ingredients, shake and sprinkle over each salad.

Serve with crusty bread rolls topped with sesame seeds.

SWEET POTATOES DUCHESSE

500 g sweet potatoes, scrubbed
250 g old potatoes, scrubbed
20 g butter
1 whole egg and *1 yolk, beaten*
pinch nutmeg
1 teaspoon grated orange zest
salt and freshly ground pepper, to taste
40 g butter, melted

Boil sweet potatoes and potatoes gently in their skins until cooked. Peel or scrape flesh from skins.

Mash potatoes. Beat in butter and beaten eggs until mixture is smooth.

Mix in nutmeg, orange zest and seasonings. Spoon mixture into a piping bag fitted with a star tube and pipe potato in 5 cm rosettes onto a buttered baking sheet. Brush with melted butter, and bake at 200°C (400°F) for 10–15 minutes until cooked through. Increase oven temperature to 260°C (500°F) to flash bake and brown tops.

CHICKEN NORMANDY

½ cup finely chopped onion
60 g butter
1 large cooking apple, peeled, cored and chopped
1 teaspoon chopped fresh sage or *½ teaspoon dried*
1 teaspoon chopped fresh thyme or *½ teaspoon dried*
salt and freshly ground pepper, to taste
1 teaspoon lemon juice
4 whole chicken breasts, boned, halved and skinned
seasoned flour, for dipping
2 eggs beaten with *1 tablespoon water*
½ cup fine white breadcrumbs combined with *½ cup finely chopped cashew nuts*
¼ cup vegetable oil
4 fresh sage leaves, for garnish

SAUCE

reserved oil from pan
½ cup finely chopped onion
¾ cup dry white wine
¾ cup apple cider
1 cup chicken stock
1 cup thickened cream
1 tablespoon Calvados or *brandy*

Cook onion in foaming butter until softened. Add apple, herbs, salt and pepper. Cover and simmer gently until apple is just tender. Stir in lemon juice. Cool mixture.

Flatten the chicken breasts to 5 mm thick. Place skinned side down. Mound 1 large tablespoon of apple mixture on centre of each and fold over the other half of the breast. Press into a cutlet shape, enclosing filling.

Dip in flour, eggs and crumb and nut mixture. Press firmly onto the flesh. Chill until firm and dry.

Heat oil in a frying pan and brown breasts on both sides. Place in a baking tray. Bake at 160°C (325°F) for 20 minutes. Turn off the oven, cover with aluminium foil and keep warm while preparing sauce. Serve on a platter with sage sprigs.

To make the sauce, pour away excess oil from pan and add onions, wine and cider. Boil mixture until almost evaporated. Add stock and cook until mixture is reduced by half. Add cream and Calvados. Cook until slightly thickened. Strain and pour into a sauce boat.

BROAD BEANS

2 cups shelled broad beans
60 g butter
2 teaspoons lemon juice
2 teaspoons chopped fresh tarragon

Cook the beans gently in boiling salted water until just tender. Refresh under cold water then drain. Reheat in pan with tarragon, butter and lemon juice. Serve hot.

Black Forest Gateau

BLACK FOREST GATEAU

90 g dark chocolate, chopped
1 tablespoon black coffee
4 eggs
¾ cup caster sugar
¾ cup self-raising flour, sifted
1 teaspoon vanilla essence
grated rind 1 lemon
50 g butter, melted

FILLING

3 tablespoons Kirsch or *fruit liqueur*
1 cup sour cherry jam, warmed
1 × 425 g can pitted dark cherries, well drained
600 mL thickened cream, whipped

TOPPING

300 g dark chocolate, chopped
6 red maraschino or *glace cherries, drained*

Grease and line 2 × 23 cm deep cake tins. Preheat oven to 180°C (350°F). Combine chocolate and coffee in double boiler and heat until melted over simmering water.

Beat together eggs and sugar for 10 minutes until light in colour. Gradually fold in the flour, vanilla, lemon rind, melted butter and melted chocolate.

Spoon mixture into the prepared tins and lightly smooth top. Bake in the centre of the oven for approximately 1 hour or until a skewer inserted into the cake comes out clean. Turn out onto a wire rack and cool.

Place the cakes side by side and upside down. Sprinkle with the Kirsch. Spread warmed jam on 1 cake and arrange cherries on top. Sandwich the 2 cakes together with one-third of the whipped cream.

Spread the remainder of the cream over the top and sides of the cake reserving a little for piping.

Melt remaining chocolate in double boiler. Spread half the chocolate thinly on smooth surface such as a marble board and allow to set. Paint the remaining chocolate on lightly oiled ivy leaves and chill until set. Peel chocolate away from ivy.

Using a palette knife, scrape the set chocolate off the marble to make curls. Place on sides of cake. Pipe a border of whipped cream around the top of the cake. Decorate with chocolate leaves and cherries. Chill for 2 hours before serving.

ROMANTIC DINNER FOR TWO

It may be an anniversary, Valentine's Day or a special celebration — whatever the occasion, this menu is designed for romantics. The meal begins with Hearts of Palm Salad, followed by tender lamb and finishing with Raspberry Meringue Hearts. It's a meal to take your time over. Add to the mood with soft lighting and music to match.

MENU

Hearts of Palm Salad

Herbed Rack of Lamb
Pommes Anna
Broccoli with Cherry Tomatoes

Raspberry Meringue Hearts

Served with Cabernet Sauvignon

PREPARATION TIMETABLE

Prepare ahead and freeze: meringue shells (metal trays in level position). Raspberry or strawberry filling (covered container).
1 day ahead: prepare meringue shells and store in an airtight container. Cook broccoli, drain and refresh. Keep in plastic bag in refrigerator. Prepare raspberry or strawberry filling for Meringue Hearts. Store in a covered container in refrigerator
3 hours ahead: prepare salad ingredients and dressing. Prepare garnishes.
1 hour ahead: prepare rack of lamb and herb mixture. Place in a baking pan, cover and refrigerate until cooking time. Prepare Pommes Anna up to cooking stage.
30 minutes ahead: bake Pommes Anna. Bake Herbed Rack of Lamb. Assemble Meringue Hearts on individual plates. Chill in refrigerator. Open red wine and allow to breathe.
15 minutes ahead: arrange salad on individual plates. Complete preparation of Broccoli with Cherry Tomatoes. Keep warm. Prepare pan sauce for Herbed Rack of Lamb.
Time for dinner: pour dressing over Hearts of Palm Salad. Turn out Pommes Anna onto serving plates. Slice and arrange Herbed Rack of Lamb on plates. Garnish dinner and serve.
Dessert: Spoon over sauce and garnish with extra berries.

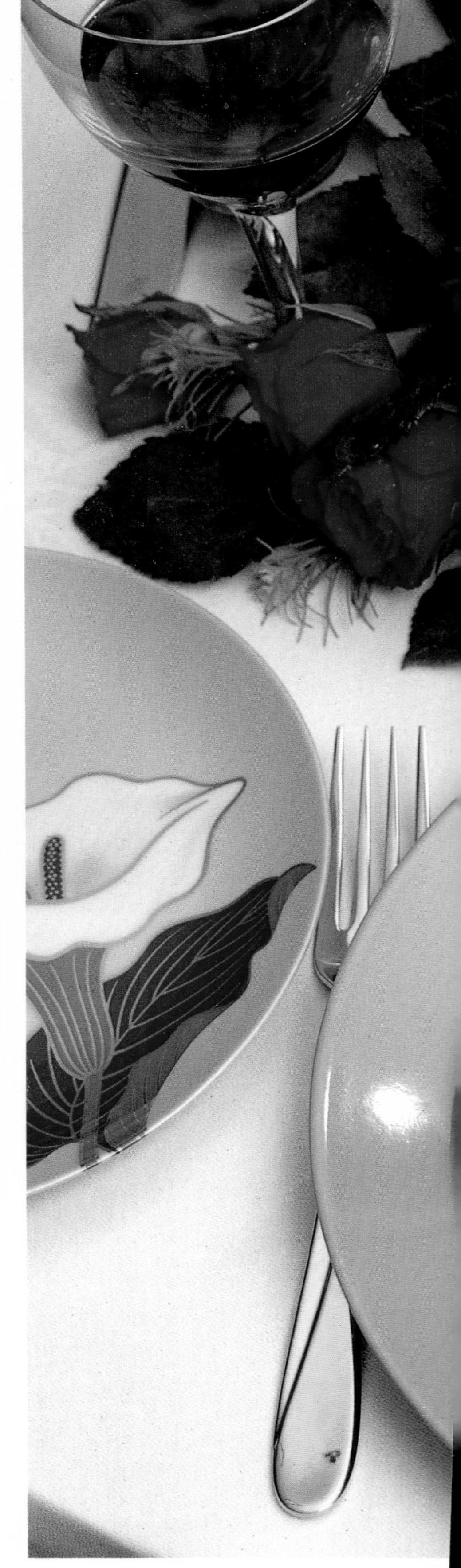

Hearts of Palm Salad

Herbed Rack of Lamb, Pommes Anna and Broccoli with Cherry Tomatoes

HERBED RACK OF LAMB

2 tablespoons chopped parsley
1 tablespoon chopped shallots
1 small clove garlic, crushed
1 teaspoon finely chopped rosemary
½ cup fresh breadcrumbs
40 g butter
salt and freshly ground pepper, to taste
6 rib rack of lamb, trimmed
sprigs fresh watercress, to garnish

Combine parsley, shallots, garlic, rosemary, breadcrumbs and 20 g melted butter in a bowl.

Sprinkle the lamb with salt and pepper. Melt remaining butter in a pan and brown lamb evenly all over.

Cover the lamb with herb mixture and place in a baking dish. Bake at 220°C (425°F) for 15 minutes. Remove and keep warm for 10 minutes.

Slice into individual chops. Arrange 2 chops in heart shape on plates. Serve with pan juices and fresh watercress sprigs for garnish.

POMMES ANNA

250 g potatoes
40 g butter, melted
salt and freshly ground pepper, to taste
grated nutmeg, to garnish

Wash potatoes and pat dry. Slice into very thin even rounds. Dip into melted butter and lay in a buttered mould in overlapping slices. Season layers and fill the mould.

Cover and bake at 200°C (400°F) until crisp and brown on outside and cooked inside. Turn onto serving plates and sprinkle with a little nutmeg.

BROCCOLI WITH CHERRY TOMATOES

200 g broccoli, trimmed and separated into florets
120 g cherry tomatoes
20 g unsalted butter
pinch sugar

Cook broccoli in boiling salted water 3 minutes. Drain and refresh under cold water.

Saute cherry tomatoes in butter in pan for 1 minute. Add sugar. Add broccoli, reheat and serve.

HEARTS OF PALM SALAD

mignonette or soft head lettuce leaves, washed and separated
4 canned baby beetroot
4 canned hearts of palm, split lengthways

DRESSING

1½ tablespoons cream
2 teaspoons lemon juice
½ teaspoon grated horseradish (bottled)
pinch salt
2 teaspoons oil

Arrange prepared lettuce on serving plates. Cut the beetroot into quarters and slice thinly. Drain on paper. Arrange decoratively over hearts of palm.

Whisk the cream, lemon juice, horseradish and salt together in a bowl. Add the oil gradually while continuing to whisk. Spoon dressing over salad.

RASPBERRY MERINGUE HEARTS

MERINGUE

4 egg whites
pinch salt
pinch cream of tartar
1 cup caster sugar

FILLING

1 punnet raspberries or *strawberries*
1½ tablespoons caster sugar
1 teaspoon lemon juice
1 teaspoon liqueur, Curacao or *Framboise, to taste*
½ cup cream, whipped
icing sugar, for dusting

Preheat oven to 110°C (220°F). Prepare well-oiled and lightly floured baking sheets. With your finger, mark 4 heart-shaped outlines, about 9 cm long × 12 cm wide, on each baking sheet.

Whisk egg whites with salt and cream of tartar to a soft foam. Continue whisking, adding 1 cup caster sugar gradually until mixture is firm and stiff.

Fill a piping bag fitted with a 1 cm nozzle and pipe mixture into the heart shapes, working from the guide outlines to the centre.

Bake in prepared oven till set (1½ hours). Do not brown. Cool and store in airtight container.

On the day of the dinner, reserve some berries for serving and macerate remaining fruit for 10 minutes in 1½ tablespoons caster sugar, lemon juice and liqueur for 10 minutes. Drain fruit and reserve liquid. Divide fruit in half. Puree half for sauce and add reserved liquid.

Assemble the hearts on individual dessert plates. Spread or pipe flat side of one meringue with cream, keeping it well inside the edge. Arrange drained berries on top. Top with extra cream. Place second meringue flat side down, on top. Dust with icing sugar.

Serve with sauce and extra berries for garnish.

Note: Meringue Hearts are also delicious served with strawberries.

Raspberry Meringue Hearts

INDEX

- Almond
  - Chocolate Fudge 97
  - Fried Chicken with Spiced Ginger Sauce 31
  - Paste 55
  - Snaps 53
  - Sweetmeats 245
- Aloha Punch 271
- Alphabet Biscuits 94
- Ambrosia 170
- Anchovy
  - Butter 126
  - Cutlets, Fresh 198
  - and Egg Mousse 257
  - and Garlic Stuffed Eggs 257
- Angels on Horseback 262
- Antipasto 17
- Apple
  - Cheese and Olive Savouries 216
  - and Onion Bake 158
  - and Prune Stuffing 34
  - and Red Cabbage Salad with Herbed Yoghurt Dressing 148
  - and Sago Pudding, Baked 170
  - Scones, Tangy 227
  - Spice Cake 231
  - Toffee 97
  - Waldorf Salad 176
- Apricot
  - Bread 231
  - Cheesecake 89
  - and Chilli Sauce 123
  - Citrus Sauce 36
  - and Pawpaw Flan 81
  - Rice Pudding 170
- Artichokes Roman-Style 156
- Asparagus
  - and Bacon Quiche 204
  - and Ham Rolls 104
  - Rolls 225
- Australian Welsh Rarebit 223
- Austrian Cherry Walnut Cake 48
- Avocado
  - Banana and Pawpaw Tropical Superwhip 98
  - Butter 65
  - Chicken
    - Casserole 30
    - Filo 186
  - Cream Filling 238
  - Dip 165
    - Guacamole 249, 280
  - and Egg
    - and Beet Salad 167
    - Salad 288
  - Emerald Smoothie 98
  - Ice Cream 79
    - Split 79
  - and Lettuce Salad with Mustard Seed Dressing 206
  - and Prawn Pate 252
  - Puffs, Creamed 238
  - Sauce 125
  - Seafood Mille-Feuille 192
  - and Sorrel Soup 181
  - with Spinach and Bacon 132
- Bacon
  - and Asparagus Quiche 204
  - and Chicken Pate, Creamy 254
  - and Egg Pie 175
  - and Sausage Plait 72
  - and Spinach
    - Avocado 132
    - Salad 132
  - Wrapped Beef and Apple Burgers 67
- Baked
  - Apple and Sago Pudding 170
  - Bream and Orange 285
  - Mustard Ham 34
  - Oysters 262
  - Snapper 147
  - Vegetable Ring 162
- Banana
  - Apricot Bread 231
  - Avocado and Pawpaw Tropical Superwhip 98
  - Barbecued 137
  - Kebabs, Cocktail 70
  - Plantation Punch 271
- Barbecue
  - Bananas 137
  - Beef
    - Fillet with Horseradish Cream Sauce 118
    - Kebabs 118
    - Whole Fillet 117
  - Chicken 68
  - Duck, Shredded, with Barbecue Sauce 31
  - Fish 111
    - Whole Smoked 111
  - Pork Kebabs 122
  - Sauce 31, 123
    - Digby's Special 67
  - Trout 111
  - Turkey Breast 115
- Barramundi Rossini 266
- Basic
  - Buttercream Icing 83
  - Fancy Cake Mixture 83
  - Frosted Icing 84
  - Pizza Dough 200
- Basil Butter 126
- Batter
  - Beer 26
  - Fried Chicken 75
- Beans
  - Broad 288
  - Chilli Con Carne 280
  - Dip, Hot 280
  - Salad 40
  - Stew, Bolivian 158
  - and Zucchini Salad 131
- Bearnaise Sauce 126
- Bechamel Sauce 276
- Beef
  - and Apple Burgers, Bacon-Wrapped 67
  - and Broccoli with Soy Sauce Dressing 148
  - Burger Supreme 67
  - Carpetbag Steak 118
  - Fillet
    - Barbecued 117
    - Barbecued, with Horseradish Cream Sauce 118
    - with Bearnaise Sauce 117
  - Kebabs, Barbecued 118
  - Minced *See* Minced Beef
    - and Mushrooms, Stir-Fried 32
  - Platter, Sliced, with Green Sauce 32
  - Prime Rib Roast 118
  - Sandwiches 186
  - Sate 118
  - Sausage Pie 220
- Beer Batter 26
- Beetroot
  - Egg and Avocado Salad 167
  - Salad 148
- Beignets, Savoury 259
- Bercy Butter 126
- Berry Muffins 228
- Biscuits
  - Almond Snaps 53
  - Alphabet 94
  - Carob 243
  - Chocolate
    - Chip 94
    - Nut Slice 239
  - Cinnamon 94
  - Citrus Ring 243
  - Coconut
    - Macaroons 240
    - Plum Fingers 235
  - Fruity Coconut Bars 243
  - Hazelnut Shortbread 240
  - Melting Moments 236
  - Monkey Face 243
  - Oaty Date Squares 243
  - Pine Nut Macaroons 213
  - Scotch Shortbread 93
  - Turkish Bonnets 245
  - Walnut Fudgies 94
- Black Forest
  - Crepe Cake 48
  - Gateau 289
- Bloody Mary, Zesty 270
- Boiled Fruit Cake 55
- Bolivian Bean Stew 158
- Brandy Orange Savarin 46
- Bread
  - Apricot Banana 231
  - Damper 129
    - Fruit and Tea 129
  - Date and Orange Raisin 231
  - Fruit and Nut Twist 232
  - Hot
    - Filled Loaves 44
    - Herbed 129
    - Tuna 198
  - Mandelbrodt 225
  - Mango 231
  - Multi-Grain Health 209
  - Parsley Loaf 129
  - Patafla 44
  - Wholemeal Nut 209
  - *See also* Buns
- Bream, Baked, and Orange 285
- Broad Beans 288
- Broccoli
  - and Beef with Soy Sauce Dressing 148
  - and Capsicum Salad 168
  - and Cauliflower Salad 148
  - with Cherry Tomatoes 293
  - with Horseradish 277
- Brown Rice Salad with Tomato Dressing 156
- Buns
  - Caramel Chelsea 232
  - Hot Cross Easter 57
  - Sugar 232
- Bush Baby Salad 77
- Butter
  - Avocado 65
  - Cream
    - Filling 236
    - Icing 277
  - Sauce, Simple
    - Seafood 125
    - Savoury 17
- Butters 126
- Butterfly Cakes, Chocolate 88
- Butterscotch Filling 239
- Cabbage
  - and Apple Salad with Herbed Yoghurt Dressing 148
  - Coleslaw 131
  - Nut Slaw with Tahini Orange Dressing 39
- Cake
  - Apple Spice 231
  - Austrian Cherry Walnut Cake 48
  - Basic Fancy Mixture 83
  - Black Forest
    - Crepe 48
    - Gateau 289
  - Boiled Fruit 55
  - Caraway Seed 228
  - Cassata
    - Sicilian 50
    - Torte 277
  - Chocolate 88
    - Liqueur Roll 50
  - Christmas 177
  - Coffee Cream 228
  - Fudge 213
  - Gingerbread Log Cabin 89
  - Gran's Traditional Christmas 55
  - Lamingtons 234
  - Mango-Filled Roll 87
  - Mocha Mallow 87
  - Nougat Walnut Sponge 48
  - Nursery 86
  - Orange 88
  - Parkin 228
  - Rainbow 86
  - Sweetheart 86
  - Tutti-Frutti Ice-Cream 80
  - Victoria Sandwich 84
- Cakes
  - Cauliflower 84
  - Cherry 84
  - Chocolate Butterfly 88
  - Coffee 84
  - Feather 84
  - Jack-in-the-Box 88
  - Jelly 88
  - Lemon 84
  - Orange 84
  - Patty Parade 87
  - Petits Fours 232
  - Queen 84
- Canapes 17
- Cannelloni with Olives 284
- Capsicum
  - and Broccoli Salad 168
  - Casserole 160
  - and Tomato Salad 148
- Caramel
  - Butterscotch Filling 239
  - Chelsea Bun 232
  - Oranges 50
- Caraway Seed Cake 228
- Carob Cookies 243
- Carpetbag Steak 118
- Carrot Soup, Creamy 166
- Cassata
  - Sicilian 50
  - Torte 277
- Cauliflower and Broccoli Salad 148
- Cauliflower Cakes 84
- Caviar
  - Mousse 254
  - and Mushroom 105
  - Taramasalata 249
- Celery and Potato Salad 40
- Champagne Punch, Citrus 58
- Cheese
  - Apple and Olive Savouries 216
  - Australian Welsh Rarebit 223
  - and Chive Bread 44
  - Filled Pastries 259
  - and Ham Slice 218
  - and Mushroom Savouries 216
  - Pies 72
  - and Prawn Pastries 18
  - Puffs
    - Oyster 18
    - Savoury 261
  - Sausage Rolls 72
  - Scones 227
  - Straws 172
  - Twists 259
- Cheesecake
  - Apricot 89
  - Mocha 46
- Cherry
  - Black Forest Crepe Cake 48
  - Cakes 84
  - and Nut Strudel 46
  - Sauce 36
    - Sour 276
  - Walnut Cake, Austrian 48
- Cherry Tomatoes with Broccoli 293
- Chicken
  - Almond Fried, with Spiced Ginger Sauce 31
  - and Avocado
    - Casserole 30
    - Filo 186
  - and Bacon Pate, Creamy 254
  - Balls, Deep-Fried 186
  - Barbecued 68
  - Batter-fried 75
  - Breasts Rossini 186
  - and Cheese Salad with Italian Dressing 43
  - Curry, Creamy 24
  - Drumsticks, Sesame 75
  - French Roast 147
  - Kebabs 114
  - Legs in a Blanket 75
  - Livers
    - Indian 104
    - Mousse 254
    - and Mushrooms in Bacon 104
  - Mexican 281
  - Mini Clubs 106
  - and Mushroom
    - Kebabs 115
    - Pie 205
  - Normandy 288
  - with Onion and Capsicum 113
  - with Pineapple and Orange 114
  - with Plum and Lychee Sauce 31
  - Salad, Fruited 43
  - Sate 115
  - Stock 166
  - Tandoori 112
  - Tarragon Tempters 113
  - Tomato and Capsicum Casserole 30
  - Vegetable Garden in 30
- Chilled
  - Cucumber and Tomato

    - Soup 182
  - Fruit Punch 58
  - Leek and Potato Soup 167
  - Lemon Souffle 153
- Chilli
  - Butter 126
  - Con Carne 280
  - Meat Filo Delights 18
- Chinese Spring Rolls 200
- Chipolatas 70
- Chocolate
  - Butterfly Cakes 88
  - Cake 88
  - Cases 84
  - Chip Biscuits 94
  - Christmas Bells 56
  - Eggs 57
  - Fudge, Almond 97
  - Icing 88
  - Liqueur Roll 50
  - Meringue Baskets 53
  - Nut Slice 239
- Choux Pastry 259, 261
- Christmas
  - Bells, Chocolate 56
  - Cake 177
    - Gran's Traditional 55
  - Plum Pudding 177
  - Pudding in a Cloth 55
- Cinnamon Biscuits 94
- Citrus
  - Champagne Punch 58
  - Ring Biscuits 243
  - Tomato Salad 135
- Cocktail
  - Banana Kebabs 70
  - Platter 249
- Coconut
  - Bars, Fruity 243
  - Macaroons 240
  - and Mango Delight 270
  - Plum Fingers 234
- Coffee
  - Cakes 84
  - Cream
    - Cake 228
    - Filling for Paris Brest 210
  - Coleslaw 131
- Corn on the Cob, Mexican 281
- Cornish Pasties 175
  - (diabetic), 218
- Cottage Cheese
  - Pancakes 223
  - and Pineapple Dip 142
- Crab Crepes, Party 24
- Cranberry Dressing 42
- Crayfish
  - Curry, Creamy 24
  - Tails 110
- Cream
  - Caramel 285
  - Cheese
    - Canapes 17
    - Filo Delights 18
  - of Spinach Soup 181
- Creamed Avocado Puffs 238
- Creamy
  - Carrot Soup 166
  - Chicken and Bacon Pate 254
  - Crayfish Curry 24
  - Vinaigrette Dressing 151
- Crepes 21
  - Cake, Black Forest 48
  - Party Crab 24
- Crostini with Hot Seafood 266
- Cuban-Style Fish 28
- Cucumber
  - and Grape Mould 257
  - Salad 208
  - and Tomato Soup, Chilled 182
  - and Yoghurt Soup, Herbed 166
- Cumberland Sauce 276
- Curry
  - Creamy Chicken 24
  - Creamy Crayfish 24
  - Creamy Prawn 24
  - Mixed Fruit 164
  - Sauce 123, 196
- Custard Vanilla Squares 239
- Daiquiri, Strawberry 271
- Damper 129
  - Fruit and Tea 129
- Date
  - Halva 245
  - and Orange Raisin Teabread 231
  - Squares, Oaty 243
  - Wholemeal Scones 227
- Deep-Fried Chicken Balls 186
- Digby's Special Sauce 67
- Dijon Mustard Dressing 39
- Dill Butter 126
- Dip
  - Avocado 165
  - Cottage Cheese and Pineapple 142
  - French Onion 173
  - Guacamole 249, 280
  - Hot Bean 280
  - Hot, for Raw Vegetables 251
  - Hummus 249
  - Taramasalata 249
- Dolmades 261
- Dressing 150
  - Coleslaw 131
  - Cranberry 42
  - Creamy Vinaigrette 151
  - Dijon Mustard 39
  - French 151
  - Herbed Yoghurt 150
  - Lemon 156
    - Mayonaise 26
    - Yoghurt 165
  - Monticello 131
  - Mustard Seed 39, 206
  - Russian 65
  - Tahini Orange 39
  - Tomato 156
- Duck
  - Halves in Baskets 115
  - Roast Fruit, with Apricot Citrus Sauce 36
  - Shredded Barbecue, with Barbecue Sauce 31
  - Terrine 252
- Easter Eggs, Chocolate 57
- Eggplant Ratatouille 163
- Eggs
  - and Anchovy Mousse 257
  - and Avocado
    - and Beet Salad 167
    - Salad 288
  - and Bacon Pie 175
  - Boats, Savoury 77
  - Stuffed with Anchovy and Garlic 257
- Emerald Smoothie 98
- Endive and Mushroom Salad 131
- Fancy Cake Mixture, Basic 83
- Farmers's Pie 220
- Feather Cakes 84
- Fennel and Orange Salad 154
- Festive Fruit Tarts 56
- Feta Cheese and Tomato Salad 284
- Fettuccine, Seafood 276
- Fillet of Beef
  - Barbecued
    - with Horseradish Cream Sauce 118
    - Whole 117
  - with Bearnaise Sauce 117
- Fillets
  - of Fish in Sangria Sauce 28
  - of Sole with Zucchini 194
- Filo
  - Avocado Chicken 186
  - Delights 18
- Fish
  - Balls, Mexican, with Avocado Sauce 194
  - Barbecued 111
    - Whole Smoked 111
  - Cuban-Style 28
  - Fillets in Sangria Sauce 28
  - with Herbed Yoghurt Dressing 145
  - Lasagne 194
  - *See also* Anchovy; Barramundi; Bream; Salmon; Seafood; Snapper; Sole; Trout; Tuna
- Flambe Fruit 138
- Flan
  - Apricot and Pawpaw 81
  - Fruit 81, 281
  - Plum 52
- Fondant 57
- Four Seasons Pizza 202
- Frankfurts, Frilly Cheese 72
- French
  - Dressing 151
  - Onion
    - Bread 44
    - Dip 173
  - Roast Chicken 147
  - Terrines 251
- Fresh Anchovy Cutlets 198
- Fried Rice 77
- Frilly Cheese Frankfurts 72
- Fritters, Sweet 53
- Frosted Icing, Basic 84
- Frozen Fruit Popsicles 80
- Fruit
  - Cake, Boiled 55
  - and Chicken Salad 43
  - Cocktail, Piquant 142
  - Coconut Bars 243
  - Cup
    - Mixed 58
    - Mulberry 270
  - Curry, Mixed 164
  - Flambe 138
  - Flan 81, 281
  - Kebabs 137
  - Mince Delight 56
  - and Nut
    - Salad 154
    - Twist 232
  - Platter, Summer 153
  - Popsicles, Frozen 80
  - Punch, Chilled 58
  - Scones 227
  - Tarts, Festive 56
  - and Tea Damper 129
- Fudge
  - Almond Chocolate 97
  - Cake 213
  - Icing 213
- Garlic
  - Butter 126, 206
  - and Herb Bread 44
- Gazpacho 154, 284
- Ginger
  - Sauce, Spiced 31
  - Scallops 145
- Gingerbread Log Cabin 89
- Glace
  - Grapefruit 170
  - Icing 87
- Globe Artichokes Roman-Style 156
- Goose, Roast 36
- Granita, Tomato 142
- Gran's Traditional Christmas Cake 55
- Grape
  - and Cucumber Mould 257
  - Kebabs 80
- Grapefruit, Glace 170
- Green
  - Bean and Zucchini Salad 131
  - Butter 126
  - Salad with Dijon Mustard Dressing 39
  - Sauce 32, 188
- Grilled Trout 111
- Guacamole 249, 280
- Halva, Date 245
- Ham
  - and Asparagus Rolls 104
  - Baked Mustard 34
  - and Blue Cheese Bread 44
  - and Cheese Slice 218
  - Mousse 276
  - and Mushroom
    - Lasagne 202
    - Pasties 218
- Hamburgers 67
  - (diabetic), 173
  - Bacon-Wrapped Beef and Apple 67
  - Beef Supreme 67
  - Minty Lamb 120
  - Sauce 123
- Haricot Bean Salad 40
- Hazelnut Shortbread 240
- Hearts of Palm Salad 293
- Herb
  - Bread, Hot 129
  - Butter 126
  - Rack of Lamb 292
  - Stuffing 34
  - Yoghurt
    - and Cucumber Soup 166
    - Dressing 150
- Hollandaise Sauce 126
- Honeydew Melon
  - and Prosciutto 259
  - Rockmelon and Watermelon Salad 164
- Honeyed
  - Lamb Kebabs 188
  - Prawns 264
- Horseradish
  - Butter 126
  - Cream Sauce 118
- Hot
  - Bean Dip 280
  - Cross Easter Buns 57
  - Dip for Raw Vegetables 251
  - Filled Loaves 43
  - Herbed Bread 129
  - Tuna Bread 198
- Hummus 249
- Ice Cream
  - Avocado 79
    - Split 79
  - Cake, Tutti Frutti 80
  - Mango Whip 98
  - Pineapple Velvet 177
  - Tamarillo 80
  - Zabaglione 210
- Iced Summer Salad 42
- Icing
  - Basic Frosted 84
  - Buttercream 83, 277
  - Chocolate 88
  - Christmas Cake 55
  - Fudge 213
  - Glace 87
  - Mocha 87
  - Mock Cream 83
  - Royal 57, 88
  - Strawberry 88
  - Vanilla 86, 88
- Jack-in-the-Box Cakes 88
- Jamaican Float 271
- Jelly Cakes 88
- Kafta Sandwiches 120
- Kebabs
  - Barbecued
    - Beef 118
    - Pork 122
  - Chicken 114
    - and Mushroom 115
  - Cocktail Banana 70
  - Fruit 137
  - Honeyed Lamb 188
  - King Prawn 109
  - Lamb, Minted 120
    - and Vegetable 147
  - Pineapple Pork 122
  - Seafood 109
  - Turkey Barbecue 115
  - Vegetable 131
  - Weisswurst 70
- King Prawn Kebabs 109
- Lamb
  - Burgers, Minty 120
  - Casserole, Saucy 32
  - Herbed Rack of 292
  - Kafta Sandwiches 120
  - Kebabs
    - Honeyed 188
    - Minted 120
    - with Vegetables 147
  - Noisettes 188
  - Salad, Marinated 43
  - Sate 120
  - Turkish Wedding Soup 181
- Lamingtons 234
- Lasagne 202
  - Fish 194
  - with Ham and Mushrooms 202
- Leek and Potato Soup, Chilled 167
- Lemon
  - Cakes 84
  - Cheese Tartlets 239
  - Dressing 156
  - Mayonnaise 26
  - Souffle, Chilled 153
  - Yoghurt Dressing 165
- Lemonade 98
- Lentil Soup 182
- Lettuce
  - and Avocado Salad with Mustard Seed Dressing 206
  - and Sour Cream Salad 39
- Lime Rice 163
- Lobster Parisian 22
- Log Cabin, Gingerbread 89
- Lychees
  - Cocktail 21

and Scallops in
Bacon 106
Macaroni and Zucchini
Salad 168
Macaroons
Coconut 240
Pine Nut 213
Mandelbrodt 225
Mango
Bread 231
and Coconut
Delight 270
Filled Roll 87
Ice Cream Whip 98
Seafood Sauce 26
Marinated Lamb Salad 43
Marshmallow Mocha
Cake 87
Mayonnaise, Lemon 26
Meat Platter 188
Meatballs
Boats 75
Spiced 104
Melba Toast 209
Melon
Dessert 80
and Prosciutto 259
Salad 164
Melting Moments 236
Meringue
Baskets 53
Hearts, Raspberry 293
Pecan Nut 53
Mexican
Chicken 281
Corn on the Cob 281
Fish Balls with Avocado
Sauce 194
Rice and Sausages 280
Mince Pies 56
Minced Beef
Cannelloni with
Olives 284
Chilli Con Carne 280
Cornish Pasties 175
Hamburgers *See*
Hamburgers
Meatballs
Boats 75
Spiced 104
Mini Clubs of
Chicken 106
Mini Pizza 73
Minted Lamb
Kebabs 120
Burgers 120
Mixed Fruit
Cup 58
Curry 164
Mocha
Cheesecake 46
Icing 87
Mallow Cake 87
Mock Cream 83, 88
Monkey Face Biscuits 243
Monticello Dressing 131
Mousse
Anchovy and Egg 257
Caviar 254
Chicken Liver 254
Ham 276
Roquefort 254
Tomato 251
Muffins, Berry 228
Mulberry Fruit Cup 270
Multi-Grain Health
Bread 209
Mushrooms
and Caviar 105
and Cheese Savouries
216
and Chicken
Kebabs 115
Livers in Bacon 104
Pie 205
and Endive Salad 131
and Ham
Lasagne 202
Pasties 218
Quiche 204
with Garlic and
Parsley 160
Mussels
Bread 44
and Rice Salad with
Prawns 40
and Snow Peas 145
Steamed 142
Mustard
Dressing, Dijon 39
Ham, Baked 34
Seed Dressing 39, 206
Noodle and Tuna Bake
75
Nougat Walnut Sponge
48
Nursery Cake 86
Nut Bread,
Wholemeal 209
Oaty
Date Squares 243
Scones 227
Onion
and Apple Bake 158
Dip, French 173
and Tomato Salad 135
Open-faced
Sandwiches 65
Orange
Bombs 80
Cake 88
Cakes 84
Caramelised 50
and Date Raisin
Teabread 231
and Fennel Salad 154
Savarin, Brandy 46
Sorbet 153
Oregano Butter 126
Oysters
Angels on
Horseback 262
Baked 262
Cheese Puffs 18
Rockefeller 262
Smoked, Canapes 17
Stuffing 34
Pacific Puffs 265
Paella 26, 284
Pancakes
Cottage Cheese 223
Potato 223
Paradise Pineapple 271
Paris Brest with Coffee
Cream Filling 210
Parisian Lobster 22
Parkin 228
Parsley
Lemon Butter 126
Loaf 129
Salad (Tabouli) 135
Party
Cocktail Trifle 50
Crab Crepes 24
Punch 58
Passiona Punch 271
Passionfruit Punch 98,
Pasta *See* Cannelloni;
Fettuccine; Lasagne;
Macaroni; Noodles
Pasties
Cornish 175 (diabetic),
218
Ham and Mushroom
218
Pastries
Cheese-Filled 259
Prawn and Cheese 18
Seafood Avocado Mille-
Feuille 192
Pastry, Choux 259, 261
Patafla 44
Pate
Creamy Chicken and
Bacon 254
Prawn and
Avocado 252
See also Terrine
Patty Cake Parade 87
Pawpaw
and Apricot Flan 81
Avocado and Banana
Tropical Superwhip
98
with Prawns 21
Peaches in Spumante
52
Peanut
and Orange Scones 227
Sauce 123
Pears in White Wine 213
Peasant Salad 208
Pecan Nut Meringues 53
Peppercorn Butter 126
Petits Fours 232
Pie
Chicken and
Mushroom 205
Egg and Bacon 175
Farmer's 220
Say Cheese 72
Tomato 221
Vegetarian 206
Pikelets 93
Pine Nut Macaroons 213
Pineapple
and Cottage Cheese Dip
142
Nectar 270
Paradise 271
and Pork
Kebabs 122
Hotpot 31
Sorbet 138
Velvet Ice Cream 177
Watermelon Punch 58
Pinwheels 62
Piquant Fruit Cocktail
142
Pissaladiere 225
Pizza
Dough, Basic 200
Four Seasons 202
with Ham and Olives
202
Margherita 200
Mini 73
Napolitana 200
Plain Scones 225
Plantation Punch 271
Plum
and Chilli Sauce 123
Flan 52
Pudding, Christmas
177
Pommes Anna 292
Popcorn
Balls 97
Rainbow 97
Popsicles, Frozen Fruit 80
Pork
and Pineapple
Hotpot 31
Kebabs 122
Kebabs, Barbecued 122
Roast with Cherry Sauce
36
Sate 122
Sausages *See* Sausages
and Veal Terrine 251
See also Bacon; Ham
Potatoes
and Celery Salad 40
and Leek Soup, Chilled
167
Pancake 223
Pommes Anna 292
Salad 176
Poultry *See* Chicken;
Duck; Goose; Turkey
Prawns
and Avocado Pate 252
and Cheese Pastries 18
with Creamy Sate Sauce
109
Curry, Creamy 24
Honeyed 264
Kebabs 109
Pacific Puffs 265
with Pawpaws 21
Piggybacks 265
and Rice Salad with
Mussels 40
Rissoles 194
Prime Rib Roast 118
Profiteroles with Coffee
Cream Filling 210
Prosciutto and Melon 259
Prune and Apple Stuffing
34
Puftaloons 245
Pumpkin
Scones 177
Soup 166
Punch
Aloha 271
Chilled Fruit 58
Citrus Champagne 58
Party 58
Passiona 271
Passionfruit 98
Plantation 271
Sangria 281
Watermelon Pineapple
58
Pyramid Sandwiches
65
Queen Cakes 84
Quiche
Bacon and
Asparagus 204
Mushroom 204
Smoked Salmon 22
Quince Paste 245
Rack of Lamb, Herbed
292
Rainbow
Cake 86
Popcorn 97
Raspberry
Meringue Hearts 293
Soup 182
Ratatouille 163
Red Cabbage
and Apple Salad with
Herbed Yoghurt
Dressing 148
Nut Slaw with Tahini
Orange Dressing 39
Red Currant Sauce 125,
276
Red Lentil Soup 182
Rhubarb Fool 170
Ribbon Sandwiches 62
Rice
Fried 77
Lime 163
Mexican Spicy, and
Sausages 280
Pudding, Apricot 170
Salad 176
with Prawns and
Mussels 40
Savoury 135
with Tomato
Dressing 156
Roast
Beef Sandwiches 186
Chicken, French 147
Fruit Duck with Apricot
Citrus Sauce 36
Goose 36
Pork with Cherry
Sauce 36
Prime Rib 118
Turkey 34
Rockmelon
and Prosciutto 259
Honeydew Melon and
Watermelon Salad
164
Stuffed with Cheese 21
and Watermelon Dessert
80
Roquefort Mousse 254
Rosemary Butter 126
Royal Icing 57, 88
Russian Dressing 65
Sago and Apple Pudding,
Baked 170
Salad
Avocado
and Egg 288
and Lettuce, with
Mustard Seed
Dressing 206
Beetroot 148
Broccoli and
Capsicum 168
Bush Baby 77
Cauliflower and
Broccoli 148
Chicken and Cheese,
with Italian Dressing
43
Coleslaw 131
Dressing *See* Dressing
Egg, Avocado and
Beet 167
Fennel and Orange 154
Fruit
and Chicken 43
and Nut 154
Green, with Dijon
Mustard Dressing 39
Greens with Tomato
Dressing 154
Haricot Bean 40
Hearts of Palm 293
Iced Summer 42
Lettuce and Sour
Cream 39
Macaroni and
Zucchini 168
Marinated Lamb 43
Melon 164
Mushroom and Endive
131
Peasant 208
Potato 176
and Celery 40
Red Cabbage
and Apple, with
Herbed Yoghurt
Dressing 148
Nut Slaw with Tahini
Orange
Dressing 39
Rice, 176
Brown, with Tomato
Dressing 156
with Prawn and
Mussels 40
Savoury 135
Spinach
and Bacon 132
and Bacon with
Avocado 132
and Edam 40
Springtime 132
Tabouli 135
Tartlets,
Wholemeal 223

Tomato
and Capsicum 148
Citrus 135
and Feta Cheese 284
Tuna Olive, with Garlic
Toast 206
Turkey and Roquefort,
with Cranberry
Dressing 42
Waldorf 176
Watermelon 77
Zucchini and Green Bean
Salad 131
Salmon, Smoked, Quiche
22
Sandwiches
Fillings for 63
Open-faced 65
Pinwheels 62
Pyramid 65
Ribbon 62
Roast Beef 186
Traffic Lights 62
Sangria Punch 281
Sardine Canapes,
Spicy 17
Sate
Beef 118
Chicken 115
Lamb 120
Pork 122
Sauce 123
Sauce
Apricot
and Chilli 123
Citrus 36
Avocado 125
Barbecue 31, 123
Bearnaise 126
Bechamel 276
Cherry 36
Cumberland 276
Curry 123, 196
Digby's Special 67
Green 32, 188
Hamburger 123
Hollandaise 126
Horseradish Cream 118
Mango Seafood 26
Peanut 123
Plum and Chilli 123
Red Currant 125
Sate 123
Simple Seafood
Butter 125
Sour Cherry 276
Spiced Ginger 31
Spiked Seafood 125
Sweet and Sour 125
Tropical 125
Saucy Lamb Casserole 32
Sausages
and Bacon Plait 72
Barbecued 68
in Blankets 70
and Buns 68
Chipolatas 70
Frilly Cheese
Frankfurts 72
Pie 220
Rolls 173
Cheesy 72
and Spicy Mexican
Rice 280
Stuffed 70
Weisswurst Kebabs 70
Savarin, Brandy Orange
46
Savoury
Beignets 259
Butters 17
Cheese Puffs 261
Egg Boats 77
Rice Salad 135
Say Cheese Pies 72
Scallops
Gingered 145
and Lychees in
Bacon 106
Scones
Date Wholemeal 227
Plain 225
Pumpkin 177
Variations on 227
Scotch Shortbread 93
Seafood
Avocado Mille-Feuille
192
Butter Sauce, Simple
125
Fettuccine 276
Filo Delights 18
Hot, with Crostini 266
Kebabs 109
Paella 26, 284
Platter with Two Spicy
Sauces 26
Sauce
Mango 26
Spiked 125
Stuffed Snapper with
Curry Sauce 196
See also Crab; Crayfish;
Fish; Lobster;
Mussels; Oysters;
Prawns; Scallops;
Squid
Sesame Drumsticks 75
Shortbread
Hazelnut 240
Scotch 93
Shredded Barbecue Duck
with Barbecue sauce 31
Sicilian Cassata 50
Simple Seafood Butter
Sauce 125
Sliced Beef Platter with
Green Sauce 32
Smoked
Fish, Barbecued Whole
111
Oyster Canapes 17
Salmon Quiche 22
Smoothie, Emerald 98
Snapper
Baked 147
Stuffed with Seafood
with Curry Sauce
196
Sole Fillets with
Zucchini 194
Sorbet
Orange 153
Pineapple 138
Sorrel and Avocado
Soup 181
Souffle, Chilled Lemon
153
Soup
Chilled
Cucumber and
Tomato 182
Leek and Potato 167
Cream of Spinach 181
Creamy Carrot 166
Gazpacho 154, 284
Herbed Yoghurt and
Cucumber 166
Pumpkin 166
Raspberry 182
Red Lentil 182
Sorrel and
Avocado 181
Turkish Wedding 181
Sour Cherry Sauce 276
Spanish Pie 206
Spiced
Beef Meatballs 104
Ginger Sauce 31
Spicy
Mexican Rice and
Sausages 280
Sardine Canapes 17
Spiked Seafood Sauce 125
Spinach
and Bacon
with Avocado 132
Salad 132
and Edam Salad 40
Cheese Filo Delights 18
Rolls 160
Soup 181
Turnovers 216
Sponge, Nougat Walnut
48
Spring Rolls, Chinese 200
Springtime Salad 132
Spun Sugar 285
Squid, Stuffed Baked 196
Steak, Carpetbag 118
Steamed Mussels 142
Stir-Fried Beef and
Mushrooms 32
Stock, Chicken 16
Strawberry
Daiquiri 271
Icing 88
Meringue Hearts 293
in Red Wine 210
Snow 153
Soda Whizz 98
Strudel, Cherry and Nut
46
Stuffed
Baked Squid 196
Sausages 70
Stuffing
Apple and Prune 34
Herb 34
Oyster 34
for Veal Pot-Roast 191
Sugar
Buns 232
Spun 285
Summer
Fruit Platter 153
Roll 21
Sundowner 270
Sweet
Fritters 53
Potatoes Duchesse 288
and Sour Sauce 125
Sweetheart Cake 86
Tabouli 135
Tacos 173
Tahini Orange
Dressing 39
Tamarillo Ice Cream 80
Tandoori Chicken 112
Tangy Apple Scones 227
Tarama Caviar 249
Taramasalata 249
Tarragon Tempters 113
Tartlets
Lemon Cheese 239
Wholemeal Salad 223
Tarts, Festive Fruit 56
Terrine
Duck 252
French 251
Toffee Apples 97
Tomato
and Capsicum Salad
148
Cherry, with Broccoli
293
Citrus Salad 135
and Cucumber Soup,
Chilled 182
Dressing 156
and Feta Cheese Salad
284
Granita 142
Mousse 251
and Onion Salad 135
Pie 221
Soup (Gazpacho) 154,
284
Traffic Lights 62
Trifle, Party Cocktail 50
Tropical
Sauce 125
Superwhip 98
Trout
Barbecued 111
Grilled 111
Tuna
and Noodle Bake 75
and Veal 191
Bread 63
Bread, Hot 198
Casserole 176
Olive Salad with Garlic
Toast 206
Turkey
Barbecue Kebabs 115
Breast 277
Barbecued 115
Roast 34
and Roquefort Salad
with Cranberry
Dressing 42
Turkish
Bonnets 245
Wedding Soup 181
Tutti Frutti Ice Cream
Cake 80
Vanilla
Icing 86, 88
Squares, Custard 239
Veal
and Pork Terrine 251
Pot-Roast with Stuffing
191
Steaks Francais 191
with Tuna Sauce 191
Vegetable
Garden in a Chicken 30
Kebabs 131
Ring, Baked 162
Vegetarian Pie 206
Victoria Sandwich 84
Vinaigrette Dressing,
Creamy 151
Vine Leaves, Stuffed
(Dolmades) 261
Waldorf Salad 176
Walnut
Fudgies 94
Nougat Sponge 48
Watermelon
and Honeydew Melon
Salad 164
and Rockmelon
Dessert 80
Pineapple Punch 58
Salad 77
Weisswurst Kebabs 70
Welsh Rarebit,
Australian 223
Wheatmeal Scones 227
Wholemeal
Nut Bread 209
Salad Tartlets 223
Yoghurt
and Cucumber Soup,
Herbed 166
Dressing, Herbed 150
and Lemon Dressing
165
Zabaglione 210
Ice Cream 210
Zesty Bloody Mary 270
Zucchini
and Green Bean Salad
131
and Macaroni Salad
168
Ratatouille 163